Day by Day with Saint Francis

Day by Day with Saint Francis
365 Meditations

Gianluigi Pasquale, OFM Cap.
(editor)

New City Press
Hyde Park, New York

Published in the United States by New City Press
202 Comforter Blvd., Hyde Park, NY 12538
www.newcitypress.com
© 2011 New City London (English edition)

First published in Italy
as *365 giorni con San Francesco*
by Edizioni San Paolo s.r.l.
© Edizioni San Paolo s.r.l. 2008

English translations taken from Francis of Assisi: Early Documents published by
New City Press, 202 Comforter Blvd., Hyde Park, New York 12538
(The Saint, The Founder, The Prophet © 1999, 2000, 2001 Franciscan Institute of
St. Bonaventure University, St. Bonaventure, NY, USA)

Cover design by Durva Correia

Library of Congress Cataloging-in-Publication-Data
Francis, of Assisi, Saint, 1182-1226.
  [365 giorni con San Francesco. English]
  Day by day with Saint Francis : 365 meditations / edited by Gianluigi Pasquale.
     p. cm.
  Includes bibliographical references.
  ISBN 978-1-56548-394-1 (pbk. : alk. paper)
  1. Devotional calendars—Catholic Church. 2. Catholic Church—Prayers and
devotions. 3. Francis, of Assisi, Saint, 1182-1226—Meditations.
  I. Pasquale, Gianluigi. II. Title.
  BX2179.F64E5 2011b
  242'.2—dc23   2011027219

Printed in the United States of America

Contents

Foreword 7

January 11

February 41

March 69

April 97

May 127

June 157

July 189

August 221

September 251

October 279

November 309

December 339

Foreword

Francis Gave Space to Christ

In two thousand years of Christianity, among all the people who have lived, only one man has touched history in the exceptional way Francis of Assisi has. Looking at this person who lived in poverty and was utterly in love with Jesus Christ, Christian believers, followers of other religions and even those who declare they have no faith, find they have, in some way, something in common with him, something that stirs their sympathy; and this happens entirely naturally. Centuries ago, in 1209, when he was just twenty-eight years old, this young man from the Umbrian region of Italy who was to have such an effect upon Christian witness, went to his "Lord Father." He sought permission to "live according to the form of the holy Gospel," that is, permission to live exactly as Jesus Christ had done: poor, obedient, celibate. And in 1209, for a number of years already, the Franciscan ideal had been shining like a brilliant dawn that bit by bit dispelled the shadows troubling the thirteenth century Church. The brotherhood had spread over the whole region of Umbria. Towns and villages had seen its rough-clad laughing members appearing all over the place. They sang at the tops of their voices or played jokes to get people to come and hear the Good News. These happy-go-lucky witnesses were called by Francis: "God's jesters," as if the Lord was at play among the people. They begged their bread and offered in exchange their labor in bringing in the harvest, sweeping, washing and, if they knew how, making things of wood. They never accepted any money and would take shelter where they could, sometimes with the priest, or under the eves of a building, in a granary or a haystack, and often beneath the stars.

People became used to them, as even today we can easily become used to a Franciscan friar whom we meet, perhaps, during the course of our daily life. Whether they were welcomed or not, they preached with the fervor of beginners and their faith had profound effects. They were the prophets of a new world where disgust with riches and passion for the Gospel transformed life and brought everyone happiness. The new friars walked down the streets two by two, one behind the other — just as Francis had foreseen one day when in a prophetic vision he has heard their footsteps. On a personal note, it was not difficult for me to think of this vision when in summer 2007 I found myself in "San Francisco," USA, and I recalled how in 1769 brother Juniper Serra left to go on his journey to Upper California from the bay of San Diego. He was to found the first of the famous missions of California, Loreto, the capital of Upper and Lower California, which was followed by other missions in many towns with "Franciscan" names: San Diego, Los Angeles, San Francisco, Sacramento, and so on.

But, those beginnings of Franciscanism, all those centuries ago, with its appearance of gentle anarchy was bound to develop into an Order. Each year Francis saw the number of his friars double. They came from all the corners of the earth, and some of them were destined to play an important role in one of the greatest Christian adventures. Even more sensitive to the appeal of mysticism than their male counterparts, women sought at San Damiano that inner peace which was threatened by the disorder of a world given to violence. The light of Francis spread, in this way, to the first convents of the Poor Clares with their powerful attraction to the contemplative life of Christ. A hymn of joy rose to heaven also from all those followers, men and women who wore no habit but who wished to live the spirit of Francis in ordinary life: they were the future "Franciscan Tertiaries" and still today they are the widest spread lay movement in the Catholic Church. Those beginnings were destined never to be repeated so completely in the future. Lightning does not strike in the same place twice. Let's see why.

On that Spring day of 1209, the exact date of which escapes even the most learned historians, Pope Innocent III was pacing up and down in the so-called Mirror Gallery in the Lateran, which at that time was the symbol of the Church's catholicity. As a result of the kind of irony history seems to delight in, the very day that Francis wished to present himself to the pope it would have been impossible to find in the whole of Italy, from Sicily to the north, a busier or more worried man than this one who called himself the Prince of all the earth. Now, one of the ideas causing most trouble beneath the pope's pointed and gold-encrusted triple tiara was about how to sort out once and for all the dissolute state of the Church, calling in the whole of Europe for a crusade of renunciation and poverty. From a distance he saw Francis and his eleven companions who wished to obtain permission from him to live according to their Gospel "proposal for a way of life" inspired by God, but he had Francis sent away, banishing from his presence the very man sent by providence who more than any other could have turned his hope into reality. As is well-known, later on the pope, as red faced but decked in gold like the setting sun, recalled a dream that had come to him a little before and that had left him uneasy. He had seen himself lying asleep on his bed, the triple tiara on his head, the Lateran basilica leaning dangerously to one side, when suddenly a little earth-colored monk, looking like a beggar, supported it with his shoulder and stopped it from collapsing. "But of course," the pope said to himself, "that monk was Francis of Assisi!" How could he refuse to listen to him? The same challenge faces us today through what he wrote, the tales and the biographies that tell of the "Poverello" in his earth-colored robe: that is, we could see a new dawn reversing the decline all around us in his coming among us again.

In gathering this collection of thoughts for each day from what Francis himself wrote and from other Franciscan sources I have had the heart of someone who eight centuries on is his follower but above all of someone aware that Francis, besides being the patron saint of Italy is the Italian saint, who has totally fascinated me as he has very many other people who today follow him putting on the habit or wearing around their necks the Tau cross typical of Franciscan laypeople. Indeed, if more or less eight hundred years ago the Poverello went to his "Lord Pope" to ask for permission to live as Jesus did, it was twenty-five years ago, in the summer of 1983, that at the age of sixteen I chanced to meet for the first time a very humble Capuchin friar, Fr Sisto Zarpellon, who at this moment is the spiritual father of the College of San Lorenzo da Brindisi in Rome. I will never forget that vividly lit summer when I saw coming into our village church of Lerino (VI) that friar, barefoot, white-bearded, dressed in a rough habit: he was the very image of a Capuchin, that is, a Franciscan! "But," I thought to myself, "didn't all the Capuchins disappear after Friar Christopher from The Betrothed, Manzoni's classic that I'd only just studied." Yet that son of Francis was there before me in flesh and blood, bringing Assisi to my very own home. And I was dumbstruck, shaken to the core. Especially because, with enthusiasm and yet with a gentle voice, during the homily in church he spoke to us of his vocation and his desire to be another Francis, which, for him, had begun during World War II. But what really convinced me was when, at the end of the homily, he knelt in silent respect before the tabernacle to entrust to Jesus who knows what secrets. Then, and only then, I understood that that Franciscan with a dazzling smile and eyes shining with optimism was, just like the Poverello, in love with Jesus and I felt myself immediately called to follow them both, and from that moment I felt a happiness never to be equalled — the joy of existence, which we all desire, even if we never say it.

After eight hundred years there is profound similarity between the people of Francis's time and the people we meet along our streets: they have a hunger for something "more," a unease in the heart that the emptiness of pleasure cannot fill. For this reason I am sure that this collection of thoughts from and about Francis offers us a comforting companion for each day, freeing us of the fear that tomorrow will only bring trouble. Francis, who the pope even called "another Christ" because "he gave space to him,"[1] understood quite clearly that living the Gospel in poverty of spirit is the most wonderful and the simplest adventure a person can embark upon in order to be happy, in the conviction that tomorrow Jesus awaits us. Recently also Benedict XVI invited us to look towards that historical figure of faith who translated the beatitude of the poor in spirit "into human existence in the most intense manner: Francis of Assisi."[2] But already half a century ago, in 1959, Joseph Ratzinger wrote that "in these latter times of Church will have imposed upon it the way of living of Francis of Assisi who as a 'simpleton' and an 'idiot' knew more of God than all the learned people of his time — because he loved him more than they did."[3] These latter times, for us, whether we are Franciscans or not, will make our lives a true "Canticle of the Creatures." For the secret of the Franciscan life is this: that even the tears of pain are transformed, out of love for Jesus Christ, into tears of joy.

Gianluigi Pasquale O.F.M. Cap.

---

1. Pius XI, encyclical *Rite Expiatis*, 30 April 1926.
2. Benedict XVI, *Gesù di Nazaret*, Rizzoli, Milan 2007, 102.
3. Joseph Ratzinger, *San Bonaventura. La teologia della storia*, Porziuncola, Assisi 2008, 209–10.

January

1 JANUARY

All-powerful, most holy, Almighty and supreme God, Holy and just Father, Lord King of heaven and earth we thank You for Yourself for through Your holy will and through Your only Son with the Holy Spirit You have created everything spiritual and corporal and, after making us in Your own image and likeness, You placed us in paradise.

Through our own fault we fell.

We thank You for as through Your Son You created us, so through Your holy love with which You loved us You brought about His birth as true God and true man by the glorious, ever-virgin, most blessed, holy Mary and You willed to redeem us captives through His cross and blood and death.

We thank You for Your Son Himself will come again in the glory of His majesty to send into the eternal fire the wicked ones who have not done penance and have not known You and to say to all those who have known You, adored You and served You in penance: "Come, you blessed of my Father, receive the kingdom prepared for you from the beginning of the world." [Mt 25:43]

Because all of us, wretches and sinners, are not worthy to pronounce Your name, we humbly ask our Lord Jesus Christ, Your beloved Son, in Whom You were well pleased, together with the Holy Spirit, the Paraclete, to give You thanks, for everything as it pleases You and Him, Who always satisfies You in everything, through Whom You have done so much for us. Alleluia!

The Earlier Rule (The Rule without a Papal Seal), XXIII, 1–5
The Saint, 81–3

2 JANUARY

Because of Your love, we humbly beg the glorious Mother, the most blessed, ever-virgin Mary, Blessed Michael, Gabriel, and Raphael, all the choirs of the blessed seraphim, cherubim, thrones, dominations, principalities, powers, virtues, angels, archangels, Blessed John the Baptist, John the Evangelist, Peter, Paul, the blessed patriarchs and prophets, the innocents, apostles, evangelists, disciples, the martyrs, confessors and virgins, the blessed Elijah and Henoch, all the saints who were, who will be, and who are to give You thanks for these things, as it pleases You, God true and supreme, eternal and living, with Your most beloved Son, our Lord Jesus Christ, and the Holy Spirit, the Paraclete, world without end. Amen. Alleluia!

All of us lesser brothers, useless servants, humbly ask and beg those who wish to serve the Lord God within the holy Catholic and Apostolic Church and all the following orders: priests, deacons, subdeacons, acolytes, exorcists, lectors, porters, and all clerics, all religious men and women, all penitents and youths, the poor and the needy, kings and princes, workers and farmers, servants and masters, all virgins, continent and married women, all lay people, men and women, all children, adolescents, young and old, the healthy and the sick, all the small and the great, all peoples, races, tribes, and tongues, all nations and all peoples everywhere on earth, who are and who will be to persevere in the true faith and in penance for otherwise no one will be saved.

The Earlier Rule (The Rule without a Papal Seal), XXIII, 6–7
The Saint, 83–4

3 JANUARY

With our whole heart, our whole soul, our whole mind, with our whole strength and fortitude with our whole understanding, with all our powers with every effort, every affection, every feeling, every desire and wish, let us all love the Lord God Who has given and gives to each one of us our whole body, our whole soul and our whole life, Who has created, redeemed and will save us by His mercy alone, Who did and does everything good for us, miserable and wretched, rotten and foul, ungrateful and evil ones.

Therefore, let us desire nothing else, let us want nothing else, let nothing else please us and cause us delight except our Creator, Redeemer and Savior, the only true God, Who is the fullness of good, all good, every good, the true and supreme good, Who alone is good, merciful, gentle, delightful, and sweet, Who alone is holy, just, true, holy, and upright, Who alone is kind, innocent, clean, from Whom, through Whom and in Whom is all pardon, all grace, all glory of all penitents and just ones, of all the blessed rejoicing together in heaven.

Therefore, let nothing hinder us, nothing separate us, nothing come between us.

Wherever we are, in every place, at every hour, at every time of the day, every day and continually, let all of us truly and humbly believe, hold in our heart and love, honor, adore, serve, praise and bless, glorify and exalt, magnify and give thanks to the Most High and Supreme Eternal God Trinity and Unity, Father, Son and Holy Spirit, Creator of all, Savior of all Who believe and hope in Him, and love Him, Who, without beginning and end, is unchangeable, invisible, indescribable, ineffable, incomprehensible, unfathomable, blessed, praiseworthy, glorious, exalted, sublime, most high, gentle, lovable, delightful, and totally desirable above all else for ever. Amen.

The Earlier Rule (The Rule without a Papal Seal), XXIII, 8–11
The Saint, 84–6

4 JANUARY

In all of his preaching, before he presented the word of God to the assembly, he prayed for peace saying, "May the Lord give you peace." [2 Thes 3:16] He always proclaimed this to men and women, to those he met and to those who met him. Accordingly, many who hated peace along with salvation, with the Lord's help wholeheartedly embraced peace. They became themselves children of peace, now rivals for eternal salvation.

Among these there was a man from Assisi with a holy and simple character, who was the first to follow devoutly the man of God.

After him, brother Bernard, embracing the delegation of peace, eagerly ran after the holy man of God to gain the kingdom of heaven. He had often received the blessed father as a guest, had observed and tested his life and conduct. Refreshed by the fragrance of his holiness, he conceived fear and gave birth to the spirit of salvation. He used to see him praying all night long, sleeping rarely, praising God and the glorious Virgin, His mother. He was amazed and said, "This man truly is from God." So he hurried to sell all he had and distributed it to the poor, not to his relatives. Grasping the title of a more perfect way, he fulfilled the counsel of the holy gospel: "If you wish to be perfect, go and sell all you own, and give to the poor, and you will have treasure in heaven; then come, follow me." [Mt 19: 21] When he had done this, he joined the holy man, Francis, in the same life and habit, and was always with him, until the brothers increased in number and he, with the obedience of his devoted father, was sent to other regions.

His conversion to God stood out as a model for those being converted in the way he sold his possessions and distributed them to the poor. The holy man Francis rejoiced with very great joy over the arrival and conversion of such a man, because the Lord seemed to be caring for him, giving him a needed companion and a faithful friend.

Thomas of Celano, The Life of Saint Francis, First Book, X, 24–25
The Saint, 203–4

5 JANUARY

Therefore as the truth of the man of God's simple teaching and life became known to many, some men began to be moved to penance and, abandoning all things, joined him in habit and life. The first among these was Bernard, a venerable man, who was made a sharer in the divine vocation and merited to be the firstborn son of the blessed Father, both in priority of time and in the gift of holiness.

For this man, as he was planning to reject the world perfectly after his example, once he had ascertained for himself the holiness of Christ's servant, sought his advice on how to carry this out. On hearing this, God's servant was filled with the consolation of the Holy Spirit over the conception of his first child. "This requires counsel that is from God," he said.

When morning had broken they went into the church of Saint Nicholas, and, after they had prepared with a prayer, Francis, a worshiper of the Trinity, opened the book of the Gospels three times asking God to confirm Bernard's plan with a threefold testimony. At the first opening of the book this text appeared: If you will be perfect, go, sell all that you have, and give to the poor [Mt 19:21]. At the second: Take nothing on your journey [Lk 9:3]. And at the third: If anyone wishes to come after me, let him deny himself and take up his cross and follow me [Mt 16:24]. "This is our life and rule," the holy man said, "and that of all who wish to join our company. Go, then, if you wish to be perfect [Mt 19:21], and carry out what you have heard."

Bonaventure, The Major Legend of Saint Francis, III, 3
The Founder, 543–4

6 JANUARY

Among the gifts of charisms which Francis obtained from the generous Giver, he merited, as a special privilege, to grow in the riches of simplicity through his love of the highest poverty. The holy man, realizing that she was a close friend of the Son of God, yet was nowadays an outcast throughout almost the whole world, was eager to espouse her in an everlasting love. For her sake, he not only left his father and mother, but also scattered everything he could have.

No one coveted gold as he coveted poverty; no one was as careful of guarding a treasure as he was of this pearl of the Gospel. In this especially would his sight be offended: if he saw in the brothers anything which did not accord completely with poverty.

Truly, from the beginning of his religious life until his death, his wealth was a tunic, a cord, and underwear, with these he was content. He frequently brought to mind with tears the poverty of Jesus Christ and his mother, claiming that she was the queen of the virtues because she shone so remarkably in the King of Kings and in the Queen, his mother.

For when the brothers were seeking at a gathering about which of the virtues makes one a greater friend of Christ, he replied, as if opening the secret of his heart: "You know, brothers, that poverty is the special way to salvation, as the stimulus of humility and the root of perfection, whose fruit is many, but hidden. For this is the hidden treasure of the Gospel field; to buy it, everything must be sold, and, in comparison, everything that cannot be sold must be spurned."

Bonaventure, The Major Legend of Saint Francis, VI, 1
The Founder, 577–8

7 JANUARY

I speak to you, as best I can, about the state of your soul. You must consider as grace all that impedes you from loving the Lord God and whoever has become an impediment to you, whether brothers or others, even if they lay hands on you. And may you want it to be this way and not otherwise. And let this be for you the true obedience of the Lord God and my true obedience, for I know with certitude that it is true obedience. And love those who do those things to you and do not wish anything different from them, unless it is something the Lord God shall have given you. And love them in this and do not wish that they be better Christians. And let this be more than a hermitage for you.

And if you have done this, I wish to know in this way if you love the Lord and me, His servant and Yours: that there is not any brother in the world who has sinned — however much he could have sinned — who, after he has looked into your eyes, would ever depart without your mercy, if he is looking for mercy. And if he were not looking for mercy, you would ask him if he wants mercy. And if he would sin a thousand times before your eyes, love him more than me so that may draw him to the Lord; and always be merciful with brothers such you as these.

A Letter to a Minister, 2–11
The Saint, 97–8

8 JANUARY

He himself originally planted the Order of Lesser Brothers and on the occasion of its founding gave it this name. For when it was written in the Rule, "Let them be lesser ...," at the uttering of this statement, at that same moment he said, "I want this fraternity to be called the Order of Lesser Brothers."

They were truly lesser who, by being subject to all, always sought the position of contempt, performing duties which they foresaw would be the occasion of some affront. In this way they might merit to be grounded on the solid rock of true humility and to have the well-designed spiritual structure of all the virtues arise in them.

Yes, the noble building of charity rises upon the foundation of perseverance; and in it living stones, gathered from every part of the world, have been built into a dwelling place of the Holy Spirit. What a great flame of charity burned in the new disciples of Christ! What great love of devout company flourished in them! When they all gathered somewhere or met each other on the road (which frequently happened), in that place a shoot of spiritual love sprang up, scattering over all love the seeds of real delight.

What more can I say? There were chaste embraces, delightful affection, a holy kiss, sweet conversation, modest laughter, joyful looks, a clear eye, a supple spirit, a peaceable tongue, a mild answer, a single purpose, prompt obedience, and untiring hands.

Thomas of Celano, The Life of Saint Francis, First Book, XV, 38
The Saint, 217–18

9 JANUARY

Another time, blessed Francis said: "The religion and life of the Lesser Brothers is a little flock, which the Son of God in this very last hour has asked of His heavenly Father, saying: 'Father, I want you to make and give me a new and humble people in this very last hour, who would be unlike all others who preceded them by their humility and poverty, and be content to have me alone.' And the Father said to His beloved Son: 'My Son, Your request has been fulfilled.' "

This is why blessed Francis would say: "Therefore, the Lord has willed that they be called Lesser Brothers, because they are the people whom the Son of God asked of the Father. They are the ones of whom the Son of God speaks in the Gospel: Do not be afraid, little flock, for it has pleased your Father to give you the kingdom [Lk 12:32]; and again: What you did for one of these, the least of my brothers, you did it for me. [Mk 25:40] For, although the Lord may be understood to be speaking of all the spiritually poor, he was nevertheless predicting the religion of the Lesser Brothers that was to come in His Church."

Therefore, as it was revealed to blessed Francis that it was to be called the Religion of the Lesser Brothers, he had it so written in the first Rule, when he brought it before the Lord Pope Innocent III, and he approved and granted it, and later announced it to all in the Council. Likewise, the Lord also revealed to him the greeting that the brothers should use, as he had written in his Testament: "The Lord revealed a greeting to me that we should say 'May the Lord give you peace.' "

At the beginning of the religion, when blessed Francis would go with a brother who was one of the first twelve brothers, that brother would greet men and women along the way as well as those in their field, saying: "May the Lord give you peace."

And because people had never before heard such a greeting from any religious, they were greatly amazed. Indeed, some would say almost indignantly: "What does this greeting of yours mean?" As a result that brother began to be quite embarrassed. Then he said to blessed Francis "Let me use another greeting."

Blessed Francis told him: "Let them talk, for they do not grasp what is of God. But do not be embarrassed, for one day the nobles and princes of this world will show respect to you and the other brothers because of a greeting of this sort." And blessed Francis said: "Isn't it great that the Lord wanted to have a little people among all those who preceded them who would be content to have Him alone, the Most High and most glorious?"

The Assisi Compilation, 101
The Founder, 204–5

10 JANUARY

Since they looked down on all earthly things and never loved themselves selfishly, they poured out all their loving affection in common, hiring themselves out for wages to provide for their brothers' needs. They gathered together out of desire and were delighted to stay together; but they found being apart a burden, parting bitter, and separation hard.

But these obedient soldiers never dared to put anything before the orders of obedience: before the word of obedience was uttered, they prepared themselves to carry out the order. They almost ran headlong to carry out what they were asked with no thought of contradicting it, knowing nothing about distinguishing precepts.

As followers of most holy poverty, since they had nothing, they loved nothing; so they feared losing nothing. They were satisfied with a single tunic, often patched both inside and out. Nothing about it was refined, rather it appeared lowly and rough so that in it they seemed completely crucified to the world. They wore crude trousers with a cord for a belt. They held firmly to the holy intention of remaining this way and having nothing more. So they were safe wherever they went. Disturbed by no fears, distracted by no cares, they awaited the next day without any worry. Though frequently on hazardous journeys, they were not anxious about where they might stay the next day. Often they needed a place to stay in extreme cold, and a baker's oven would receive them; or they would hide for the night humbly in caves or crypts.

During the day those who knew how worked with their own hands, staying in the houses of lepers or in other suitable places, serving everyone humbly and devoutly. They did not want to take any job that might give rise to scandal; but rather always doing what was holy and just, honest and useful, they inspired all they dealt with to follow their example of humility and patience.

Thomas of Celano, The Life of Saint Francis, First Book, XV, 39
The Saint, 218

11 JANUARY

The virtue of patience so enveloped them that they sought to be where they would suffer persecution of their bodies rather than where their holiness would be known and praised, lifting them up with worldly favor. Often mocked, objects of insult, stripped naked, beaten, bound, jailed, and not defending themselves with anyone's protection, they endured all of these abuses so bravely that from their mouths came only the sound of praise and thanksgiving.

They never or hardly ever stopped praying and praising God. Instead, in ongoing discussion, they recalled what they had done. They gave thanks to God for the good done and, with groans and tears, paid for what they neglected or did carelessly. They would have thought themselves abandoned by God if they did not experience in their ordinary prayers that they were constantly visited by the spirit of devotion. For when they felt like dozing during prayer, they would prop themselves up with a stick, so that sleep would not overtake them. Some anchored themselves with cords, so furtive sleep would not disturb prayer. Some bound themselves with irons; and others shut themselves in wooden cells. Whenever their moderation was upset, as normally happens, by too much food or drink, or if they went over the line of necessity because of weariness from travel, they punished themselves severely with many days of fasting. They strove to restrain the burning of the flesh by such harsh treatment that they did not hesitate to strip themselves on freezing ice, and to cover themselves in blood from gashing their bodies with sharp thorns.

Thomas of Celano, The Life of Saint Francis, First Book, XV, 40
The Saint, 219

12 JANUARY

They so spurned earthly things that they barely accepted the most basic necessities of life; and, as they were usually far from bodily comfort, they did not fear hardship. In all these things, they sought peace and meekness with all. Always doing what was modest and peaceful, they scrupulously avoided all scandal. For they hardly spoke even when necessary; nor did anything harmful or useless come out of their mouth, so that in all their life and action nothing immodest or unbecoming could be found. Their every act was disciplined, their bearing modest. With eyes fixed on the ground and their minds set on heaven, all their senses were so subdued that they scarcely allowed themselves to hear or see anything except what their holy purpose demanded.

Among them there was no envy, no malice, no rancor, no mocking, no suspicion, no bitterness. Instead, there was great harmony, constant calm, thanksgiving, and songs of praise. These are the lessons by which the devoted father instructed his new sons not so much in words and speech but in deed and truth.

Thomas of Celano, The Life of Saint Francis, First Book, XV, 41
The Saint, 219–20

13 JANUARY

All my brothers: let us pay attention to what the Lord says: Love your enemies and do good to those who hate you [Mt 5:44] for our Lord Jesus Christ, Whose footprints we must follow, called His betrayer a friend and willingly offered Himself to His executioners.

Our friends, therefore, are all those who unjustly inflict upon us distress and anguish, shame and injury, sorrow and punishment, martyrdom and death. We must love them greatly for we shall possess eternal life because of what they bring us.

And let us hate our body with its vices and sins, because by living according to the flesh, the devil wishes to take away from us the love of Jesus Christ and eternal life and to lose himself in hell with everyone else. Because, by our own fault, we are disgusting, miserable and opposed to good, yet prompt and inclined to evil, for, as the Lord says in the Gospel: From the heart proceed and come evil thoughts, adultery, fornication, murder, theft, greed, malice, deceit, licentiousness, envy, false witness, blasphemy, foolishness. All these evils come from within, from a person's heart, and these are what defile a person [Mt 15:19–20; Mk 7:21–23].

Now that we have left the world, however, we have nothing else to do but to follow the will of the Lord and to please Him.

The Earlier Rule (The Rule without a Papal Seal), XXII, 1–9
The Saint, 79

14 JANUARY

Let us be careful that we are not earth along the wayside, or that which is rocky or full of thorns, in keeping with what the Lord says in the Gospel: The word of God is a seed [Lk 8:11].

What fell along the wayside and was trampled under foot, however, are those who hear the word [Lk 8:5] and do not understand it. The devil comes immediately and snatches what was planted in their hearts and takes the word from their hearts that they may not believe and be saved [Mt 13:19; Mk 4:15; Lk 8:12].

What fell on rocky ground, however, are those who, as soon as they hear the word, receive it at once with joy. But when tribulation and persecution come because of the word, they immediately fall away [Mt 13:20–21; Mk 4:16–17; Lk 4:13]. These have no roots in them; they last only for a time, because they believe only for a time and fall away in time of trial.

What fell among thorns, however, are those who hear the word of God and the anxiety and worries of this world, the lure of riches, and other inordinate desires intrude and choke the word and they remain without fruit [Mt 13:22; Mk 4:18–19; Lk 8:14].

But what was sown in good soil are those who hear the word with a good and excellent heart, understand and preserve it and bear fruit in patience [Mt 13:23; Mk 4:19; Lk 8:15].

Therefore, as the Lord says, brothers, let us let the dead bury their own dead [Mt 8:22]. And let us beware of the malice and craftiness of Satan, who does not want anyone to turn his mind and heart to God. And prowling around he wants to ensnare a person's heart under the guise of some reward or assistance, to choke out the word and precepts of the Lord from our memory, and, desiring a person's heart, [he wants] to blind it through worldly affairs and concerns and to live there, as the Lord says: When an unclean spirit goes out of a person, it roams through arid and waterless regions seeking rest; and not finding any, it says: "I will return to my home from which I came." And coming upon it, it finds it empty, swept, clean and tidied. And it goes off and brings seven other spirits more wicked than itself, who move in and dwell there, and the last state of that person is worse than the first [Mt 12:43–45; Lk 11:24–26].

Therefore, all my brothers, let us be very much on our guard that, under the guise of some reward or assistance, we do not lose or take our mind away from God. But, in the holy love which is God, I beg all my brothers, both the ministers and the others, after overcoming every impediment and putting aside every care and anxiety, to serve, love, honor and adore the Lord God with a clean heart and a pure mind in whatever way they are best able to do so, for that is what He wants above all else.

The Earlier Rule (The Rule without a Papal Seal), XXII, 10–26
The Saint, 79–80

15 JANUARY

Let us always make a home and a dwelling place there for Him Who is the Lord God Almighty, Father, Son and Holy Spirit, Who says: Be vigilant at all times and pray that you have the strength to escape the tribulations that are imminent and to stand before the Son of Man [Lk 21:36; Mk 11–25]. When you stand to pray say: Our Father in heaven [Lk 11:2; Mt 6:9]. And let us adore Him with a pure heart, because it is necessary to pray always and not lose heart; for the Father seeks such [Lk 18:1; Jn 4:23] people who adore Him. God is Spirit and those who adore Him must adore Him in Spirit and truth [Lk 4:24]. Let us have recourse to Him as to the Shepherd and Guardian of our souls [1 Pt 2:25], Who says: "I am the Good Shepherd Who feeds My sheep and I lay down My life for my sheep." [1 Jn 10:14–15]

All of you are brothers. Do not call anyone on earth your father; you have but one Father in heaven. Do not call yourselves teachers; you have but one Teacher [Mt 23:8–10] in heaven. If you remain in me and my words remain in you, ask for whatever you want and it will be done for you [Jn 15:7]. Wherever two or three are gathered together in my name, there am I in the midst of them [Mt 18:20]. Behold I am with you until the end of the world [Mt 23:20]. The words I have spoken to you are spirit and life [Jn 6:63]. I am the Way, the Truth, and the Life [Jn 14:6].

Let us, therefore, hold onto the words, the life, the teaching and the Holy Gospel of Him Who humbled Himself to beg His Father for us and to make His name known saying: Father, glorify Your name [Jn 12:28a] and glorify Your Son that Your Son may glorify You [Jn 17b].

Father, I have made Your name known to those whom You have given me [Jn 17:6]. The words You gave to me I have given to them, and they have accepted them and truly have known that I came from You and they have believed that You sent me. I pray for them, not for the world, but for those You have given me, because they are Yours and everything of mine is Yours [Jn 17:8–10]. Holy Father, keep in Your name those You have given me that they may be one as We are [Jn 17:11b]. I say this while in the world that they may have joy completely. I gave them Your word, and the world hated them, because they do not belong to the world as I do not belong to the world. I do not ask you to take them out of the world but that you keep them from the evil one. Glorify them in truth. Your word is truth [Jn 17:13b–17].

As You sent me into the world, so I sent them into the world. And I sanctify myself for them that they also may be sanctified in truth. I ask not only for them but also for those who will believe in me through them [Jn 17:18–20], that they may be brought to perfection as one, and the world may know that You have sent me and loved them as You loved me [Jn 17:23]. I shall make known to them Your name, that the love with which You loved me may be in them and I in them [Jn 17:26]. Father, I wish that those whom You have given me may be where I am that they may see Your glory [Jn 17:24] in Your kingdom [Mt 29:21].

The Earlier Rule (The Rule without a Papal Seal), XXII, 27–55
The Saint, 80–1

16 JANUARY

Blessed Francis gathered with the others in a place called Rivo Torto near the city of Assisi. In this place there was an abandoned hut. Under its cover lived these despisers of great and beautiful houses, protecting themselves from the torrents of rain. As the saint said, "It is easier to get to heaven from a hut than from a palace." All his sons and brothers were living in that same place with the blessed Father, with great labor, and lacking everything. Often they were deprived of the comfort of bread, content with turnips they begged in their need here and there on the plain of Assisi. The place in which they were staying was so narrow that they could barely sit or sleep in it.

Yet there was no complaining about this, no grumbling; but with peaceful heart, the soul filled with joy preserved the virtue of patience.

Saint Francis used to engage carefully in a daily, or rather, constant examination of himself and his followers. Allowing nothing dangerous to remain in them, he drove from their hearts any negligence. Unbending in his discipline, he was watchful of his guard at every hour. For if, as happens, any temptation of the flesh struck him, he would immerse himself in a ditch filled in winter with ice, remaining in it until every seduction of the flesh went away. The others avidly followed his example of mortifying the flesh.

He taught them to mortify not only vices and to check the promptings of the flesh, but also to check the external senses, through which death enters the soul.

Thomas of Celano, The Life of Saint Francis, First Book, XVI, 42–43
The Saint, 220–1

17 JANUARY

Although the evangelist Francis preached to the simple, in simple, concrete terms, since he knew that virtue is more necessary than words, still, when he was among spiritual people with greater abilities he gave birth to life-giving and profound words. With few words he would suggest what was inexpressible, and, weaving movement with fiery gestures, he carried away all his hearers toward the things of heaven. He did not use the keys of distinctions, for he did not preach about things he had not himself discovered. Christ, true Power and Wisdom, made his voice a voice of power.

A physician, a learned and eloquent man, once said: "I remember the sermons of other preachers word for word, only what the saint, Francis, says eludes me. Even if I memorize some of his words, they don't seem to me like those that originally poured from his lips."

Thomas of Celano, The Remembrance of the Desire of a Soul,
Second Book, LXXIII, 107
The Founder, 318

18 JANUARY

One day, while he was praying enthusiastically to the Lord, he received this response: "Francis, everything you loved carnally and desired to have, you must despise and hate, if you wish to know my will. Because once you begin doing this, what before seemed delightful and sweet will be unbearable and bitter; and what before made you shudder will offer you great sweetness and enormous delight."

He was overjoyed at this and was comforted by the Lord. One day he was riding his horse near Assisi, when he met a leper. And, even though he usually shuddered at lepers, he made himself dismount, and gave him a coin, kissing his hand as he did so. After he accepted a kiss of peace from him, Francis remounted and continued on his way. He then began to consider himself less and less, until, by God's grace, he came to complete victory over himself.

After a few days, he moved to a hospice of lepers, taking with him a large sum of money. Calling them all together, as he kissed the hand of each, he gave them alms. When he left there, what before had been bitter, that is, to see and touch lepers, was turned into sweetness. For, as he said, the sight of lepers was so bitter to him, that he refused not only to look at them, but even to approach their dwellings. If he happened to come near their houses or to see them, even though he was moved by piety to give them alms through an intermediary, he always turned away his face and held his nose. With the help of God's grace, he became such a servant and friend of the lepers, that, as he testified in his Testament, he stayed among them and served them with humility.

Changed into good after his visit to the lepers, he would take a companion, whom he loved very much, to secluded places, telling him that he had found a great and precious treasure. The man was not a little overjoyed, and gladly went with him whenever he was summoned. Francis often led him to a cave near Assisi, and, while he went alone inside, he left his companion outside, eager for the treasure. Inspired by a new and extraordinary spirit, he would pray to his Father in secret, wanting no one to know what was happening within except God alone, whom he consulted about acquiring heavenly treasure.

The Legend of the Three Companions, IV, 11–12
The Founder, 74–5

19 JANUARY

The same [Brother Leonard] related in the same place that one day at Saint Mary's, blessed Francis called Brother Leo and said: "Brother Leo, write." He responded: "Look, I'm ready!" "Write," he said, "what true joy is."

"A messenger arrives and says that all the Masters of Paris have entered the Order. Write: this isn't true joy! Or, that all the prelates, archbishops and bishops beyond the mountains, as well as the King of France and the King of England [have entered the Order]. Write: this isn't true joy! Again, that my brothers have gone to the non-believers and converted all of them to the faith; again, that I have so much grace from God that I heal the sick and perform many miracles. I tell you true joy doesn't consist in any of these things."

"Then what is true joy?"

"I return from Perugia and arrive here in the dead of night. It's winter time, muddy, and so cold that icicles have formed on the edges of my habit and keep striking my legs and blood flows from such wounds. Freezing, covered with mud and ice, I come to the gate and, after I've knocked and called for some time, a brother comes and asks: "Who are you?" "Brother Francis," I answer. "Go away!" he says. "This is not a decent hour to be wandering about! You may not come in!" When I insist, he replies: "Go away! You are simple and stupid! Don't come back to us again! There are many of us here like you — we don't need you!" I stand again at the door and say: "For the love of God, take me in tonight!" And he replies: "I will not! Go to the Crosiers' place and ask there!"

"I tell you this: If I had patience and did not become upset, true joy, as well as true virtue and the salvation of my soul, would consist in this."

True and Perfect Joy (from The Undated Writings)
The Saint, 166–7

20 JANUARY

We who were with blessed Francis bear witness that, sick or well, he displayed such charity and piety, not only to his brothers, but also toward the poor, whether healthy or sick. Thus, he deprived himself of the necessities of his body that the brothers procured for him with great devotion and solicitude. At first coaxing us not to worry, with great inner and outer joy, he would then offer to others things he had denied his own body, even though they were extremely necessary for him.

And that is why the general minister and his guardian ordered him not to give his tunic to any brother without their permission. Because the brothers, out of the devotion they had for him, would occasionally ask him for his tunic, and he would immediately give it to them. Or he himself, if he saw a sickly or poorly clad brother, would at times cut his habit in half, giving one part to him and keeping the other for himself, for he wanted to have and to wear only one tunic.

The Assisi Compilation, 89
The Founder, 193

21 JANUARY

From a reflection on the primary source of all things, filled with even more abundant piety, he would call creatures, no matter how small, by the name of "brother" or "sister", because he knew they shared with him the same beginning. However, he embraced more affectionately and sweetly those which display the pious meekness of Christ in a natural likeness and portray him in the symbols of Scripture. He often paid to ransom lambs that were being led to their death, remembering that most gentle Lamb who willed to be led to slaughter to pay the ransom of sinners.

One night when the servant of God was a guest at the monastery of San Verecondo in the diocese of Gubbio, a little sheep gave birth to a baby lamb. There was a very cruel sow there, which did not spare the life of the innocent, but killed it with her ravenous bite. When the pious father heard this, he was moved to remarkable compassion and, remembering the Lamb without stain, lamented for the dead baby lamb, saying in front of everyone: "Alas, brother lamb, innocent animal, always displaying Christ to people! Cursed be the pitiless one who killed you, and neither man nor beast shall eat of her!" It is amazing to tell! Immediately the vicious sow began to get sick and, after paying the bodily punishment for three days, finally suffered an avenging death. She was thrown into the monastery's ditch and, lying there for a long time, dried up like a board, and did not become food for any hungry creature.

Therefore, let human impiety pay attention to how great a punishment might at last be inflicted on it, if such animal cruelty is punished with so horrible a death. Let also the devotion of the faithful weigh how the piety in God's servant was of such marvelous power and of such abundant sweetness that even the nature of animals acknowledged it in their own way.

>Bonaventure, The Major Legend of Saint Francis, VIII, 6
>*The Founder,* 590–1

22 JANUARY

On another occasion he was travelling through the Marches and the same brother [Paul] was gladly accompanying him when he came across a man on his way to market. The man was carrying over his shoulder two little lambs bound and ready for sale. When blessed Francis heard the bleating lambs, his innermost heart was touched and, drawing near, he touched them as a mother does with a crying child, showing his compassion. "Why are you torturing my brother lambs," he said to the man, "binding and hanging them this way?" "I am carrying them to market to sell them, since I need the money," he replied. The holy man asked: "What will happen to them?" "Those who buy them will kill them and eat them," he responded. At that, the holy man said: "No, this must not happen! Here, take my cloak as payment and give me the lambs." The man readily gave him the little lambs and took the cloak since it was much more valuable. The cloak was one the holy man had borrowed from a friend on the same day to keep out the cold. The holy man of God, having taken the lambs, now was wondering what he should do with them. Asking for advice from the brother who was with him, he gave them back to that man, ordering him never to sell them or allow any harm to come to them, but instead to preserve, nourish, and guide them carefully.

>Thomas of Celano, The Life of Saint Francis, First Book, XXVIII, 79
>*The Saint,* 249–50

31

23 JANUARY

O Our Father [Mt 6:9] most holy: Our Creator, Redeemer, Consoler, and Saviour:

Who are in heaven [Mt 6:9]: In the angels and the saints, enlightening them to know, for You, Lord, are light [1 Jn 1:5] inflaming them to love, for You, Lord, are love dwelling in them and filling them with happiness for You, Lord, are Supreme Good, the Eternal Good from Whom all good comes without Whom there is no good.

Holy be Your Name [Mt 6:9]: May knowledge of You become clearer in us that we may know the breadth of Your blessings, the length of Your promises, the height of Your majesty, the depth of Your judgments [Eph 3:18].

Your kingdom come [Mt 6:10]: That You may rule in us through Your grace and enable us to come to Your kingdom [Lk 23:42] where there is clear vision of You, perfect love of You, blessed companionship with You, eternal enjoyment of You.

Your will be done on earth as in heaven [Mt 6:10]: That we may love You with our whole heart [Dt 6:5] by always thinking of You, with our whole soul by always desiring You, with our whole mind by always directing all our intentions to You, and by seeking Your glory in everything, with all our whole strength by exerting all our energies [Lk 10:27] and affections of body and soul in the service of Your love and of nothing else; and we may love our neighbor as ourselves by drawing them all to Your love with our whole strength, by rejoicing in the good of others as in our own, by suffering with others at their misfortunes, and by giving offence to no one [1 Cor 6:3].

Give us this day [Mt 6:11]: in remembrance, understanding, and reverence of that love which [our Lord Jesus Christ] had for us and of those things that He said and did and suffered for us.

Our daily Bread [Mt 6:11]: Your own beloved Son, our Lord Jesus Christ.

Forgive us our trespasses [Mt 6:12]: through Your ineffable mercy through the power of the passion of Your beloved Son and through the merits and intercession of the ever blessed Virgin and all Your elect.

As we forgive those who trespass against us [Mt 6:12]: And what we do not completely forgive, make us, Lord, forgive completely that we may truly love our enemies because of You and we may fervently intercede for them before You, returning no one evil for evil [1 Thes 5:15] and we may strive to help everyone in You.

And lead us not into temptation [Mt 6:13]: hidden or obvious, sudden or persistent.

But deliver us from evil [Mt 6:13]: past, present, and to come.

Glory to the Father, and to the Son, and to the Holy Spirit. As it was in the beginning, is now, and will be forever. Amen.

A Prayer Inspired y the Our Father (Expositio in Pater Noster)
The Saint, 158–60

24 JANUARY

As the teachings of the gospel had declined seriously in practice — not just in some cases but in general everywhere — this man [Francis] was sent from God so that everywhere, throughout the whole world, after the example of the Apostles, he might bear witness to the truth. And so it was, with the Christ leading, that his teaching showed clearly that all the wisdom of the world was foolish, and quickly, he turned all toward the true wisdom of God through the foolishness of his preaching.

In these last times, a new Evangelist, like one of the rivers of Paradise, has poured out the streams of the gospel in a holy flood over the whole world. He preached the way of the Son of God and the teaching of truth in his deeds. In him and through him an unexpected joy and a holy newness came into the world. A shoot of the ancient religion suddenly renewed the old and decrepit. A new spirit was placed in the hearts of the elect and a holy anointing has been poured out in their midst. This holy servant of Christ, like one of the lights of heaven, shone from above with a new rite and new signs. The ancient miracles have been renewed through him. In the desert of this world a fruitful vine has been planted in a new Order but in an ancient way, bearing flowers, sweet with the fragrance of holy virtues and stretching out everywhere branches of holy religion.

Although like us, subject to suffering, he was not satisfied with observing the ordinary precepts. Rather, overflowing with burning charity, he set out on the way of full perfection, reached out for the peak of perfect holiness, and saw the goal of all perfection. That is why every order, sex, and age finds in him a clear pattern of the teaching of salvation and an outstanding example of holy deeds. If people intend to put their hand to difficult things and strive to seek the higher gifts of a more excellent way, let them look into the mirror of his life, and learn all perfection. There are some who tend to lower, more level paths, fearing to walk the steep route and climb to the summit of the mountain: they too shall find in him suitable reminders. Finally, those who seek signs and miracles, let them ask his holiness, and they will receive what they request.

Yes, his glorious life reveals in even brighter light the perfection of earlier saints; the passion of Jesus Christ proves this, and His cross shows it clearly. For the venerable father was in fact marked in five parts of his body with the marks of the passion and the cross, as if he had hung on the cross with the Son of God. This is a great sacrament, and evidence of the grandeur of a special love. But there is hidden here some secret; here is concealed some awesome mystery, one we believe is known to God alone, though it was partly revealed by the Saint to one person.

Thomas of Celano, The Life of Saint Francis, Second Book, I, 89–90
The Saint, 259–61

25 JANUARY

In Celano at winter time Saint Francis was wearing a piece of folded cloth as a cloak, which a man from Tivoli, a friend of the brothers, had lent him. While he was at the palace of the bishop of the Marsi, an old woman came up to him begging for alms. He quickly unfastened the cloth from his neck, and, although it belonged to someone else, he gave it to the poor old woman, saying: "Go and make yourself a tunic; you really need it." The old woman laughed; she was stunned — I don't know if it was out of fear or joy — and took the piece of cloth from his hands. She ran off quickly, so that delay might not bring the danger of having to give it back, and cut it with scissors. But when she saw that the cut cloth would not be enough for a tunic, she returned to the saint, knowing his earlier kindness, and showed him that the material was not enough. The saint turned his eyes on his companion, who had just the same cloth covering his back. "Brother," he said, "do you hear what this old woman is saying? For the love of God, let us bear with the cold! Give the poor woman the cloth so she can finish her tunic." He gave his, the companion offered his as well, and both were left naked so the old woman could be clothed.

Thomas of Celano, The Remembrance of the Desire of a Soul,
Second Book, LIII, 86
The Founder, 304

26 JANUARY

In the brothers' hermitage at Sarteano that evil one who always envies the progress of God's children dared to attempt something against the saint. Seeing that the holy man was becoming even holier, and not overlooking today's profit because of yesterday's, as the saint gave himself one night to prayer in his cell, the evil one called him three times: "Francis! Francis! Francis!" And he replied saying: "What do you want?" The reply was: "There is no sinner in the world whom the Lord will not forgive if he is converted. But if anyone kills himself by hard penance, for all eternity he will find no mercy." At once by a revelation, the saint recognized the enemy's cunning, how he was trying to call him back to being lukewarm. What then? The enemy did not give up. He tried a new line of attack. Seeing that he had not been able to hide this snare, he prepared a different one, namely, an urge of the flesh. But to no use, since the one who detected a clever trick of the spirit could not be fooled by the flesh. The devil sent into him a violent temptation to lust, but as soon as the blessed father felt it, he took off his clothes and lashed himself furiously with the cord, saying: "Come on, Brother Ass, that's the way you should stay under the whip! The tunic belongs to religion: no stealing allowed! If you want to leave, leave!"

However, when he saw that the temptation did not leave even after the discipline, though he painted welts all over his limbs black and blue, he opened the cell, went out to the garden, and threw himself naked into the deep snow. Taking snow by the handful he packed it together into balls and made seven piles. Showing them to himself, he began to address his body: "Here, this large one is your wife, and those four over there are your two sons and your two daughters; the other two are your servant and your maid who are needed to serve them. So hurry," he said, "get all of them some clothes, because they're freezing to death! But if complicated care of them is annoying, then take care to serve one Master!" At that the devil went away in confusion, and the saint returned to his cell praising God.

A certain spiritual brother was giving himself to prayer at that time, and he saw it all in the bright moonlight. When the saint later learned that the brother had seen him that night, he was very disturbed, and ordered him not to reveal it to anyone as long as he lived in the world.

Thomas of Celano, The Remembrance of the Desire of a Soul,
Second Book, LXXXII,116–17
The Founder, 324–5

27 JANUARY

To all my reverend and dearly beloved brothers ... Brother Francis, a worthless and weak man, your very little servant sends his greetings in Him Who has redeemed and washed us in His most precious blood. When you hear His name, the name of that Son of the Most High, our Lord Jesus Christ, Who is blessed forever, adore His name with fear and reverence, prostrate on the ground!

Listen, sons of the Lord and my brothers, pay attention to my words. Incline the ear of your heart and obey the voice of the Son of God. Observe His commands with your whole heart and fulfill His counsels with a perfect mind. Give praise to Him because He is good; exalt Him by your deeds; for this reason He has sent you into the whole world: that you may bear witness to His voice in word and deed and bring everyone to know that there is no one who is all-powerful except Him. Persevere in discipline and holy obedience and, with a good and firm purpose, fulfill what you have promised Him. The Lord God offers Himself to us as to His children.

Kissing your feet, therefore, and with all that love of which I am capable, I implore all of you brothers to show all possible reverence and honor to the most holy Body and Blood of our Lord Jesus Christ in Whom that which is in heaven and on earth has been brought to peace and reconciled to almighty God.

A Letter to the Entire Order, 2–13
The Saint, 116–17

28 JANUARY

I also beg in the Lord all my brothers who are priests, or who will be, or who wish to be priests of the Most High that whenever they wish to celebrate Mass, being pure, they offer the true Sacrifice of the most holy Body and Blood of our Lord Jesus Christ with purity and reverence, with a holy and unblemished intention, not for any worldly reason or out of fear or love of anyone, as if they were pleasing people. But let all their will, as much as grace helps, be directed to God, desiring, thereby, to please only the Most High Lord Himself because He alone acts there as He pleases, for He Himself says: Do this in memory of me [Lk 22:19]. If anyone acts differently, he becomes Judas the traitor and guilty of the Body and Blood of the Lord.

My priest brothers, remember what is written in the law of Moses: whoever committed a transgression against even externals died without mercy by a decree of the Lord. How much greater and more severe will the punishment be of the one who tramples on the Son of God, and who treats the Blood of the Covenant in which he was sanctified as unclean and who insults the Spirit of grace? For a person looks down upon, defiles and tramples upon the Lamb of God when, as the Apostle says, not distinguishing and discerning the holy bread of Christ from other foods or actions, he either unworthily or, even if he is worthy, eats It in vain and unworthily since the Lord says through the prophet: The person is cursed who does the work of the Lord deceitfully. He will, in truth, condemn priests who do not wish to take this to heart, saying: I will curse your blessings [Mal 2:2].

A Letter to the Entire Order, 14–15
The Saint, 117

29 JANUARY

Listen, my brothers: If the Blessed Virgin is so honored, as is becoming, because she carried Him in her most holy womb; if the Baptist trembled and did not dare to touch the holy head of God; if the tomb in which He lay for some time is held in veneration, how holy, just and fitting must be he who touches with his hands, receives in his heart and mouth, and offers to others to be received the One Who is not about to die but Who is to conquer and be glorified, upon Whom the angels longed to gaze.

See your dignity, [my] priest brothers, and be holy because He is holy. As the Lord God has honored you above all others because of this ministry, for your part love, revere and honor Him above all others. It is a great misery and a miserable weakness that when you have Him present in this way, you are concerned with anything else in the whole world!

Let everyone be struck with fear, let the whole world tremble, and let the heavens exult when Christ, the Son of the living God, is present on the altar in the hands of a priest! O wonderful loftiness and stupendous dignity! O sublime humility! O humble sublimity! The Lord of the universe, God and the Son of God, so humbles Himself that for our salvation He hides Himself under an ordinary piece of bread! Brothers, look at the humility of God, and pour out your hearts before Him! Humble yourselves that you may be exalted by Him! Hold back nothing of yourselves for yourselves, that He Who gives Himself totally to you may receive you totally!

A Letter to the Entire Order, 21–9
The Saint, 118

30 JANUARY

Once when he was at Colle in the county of Perugia Saint Francis met a poor man whom he had known before in the world. He asked him: "Brother, how are you doing?" The man malevolently began to heap curses on his lord, who had taken away everything he had. "Thanks to my lord, may the Almighty Lord curse him, I'm very badly off!" Blessed Francis felt more pity for the man's soul, rooted in mortal hatred, than for his body. He said to him: "Brother, forgive your lord for the love of God, so you may set your soul free, and it may be that he will return to you what he has taken. Otherwise you will lose not only your property but also your soul." He replied: "I can't entirely forgive him unless he first gives back what he took." Blessed Francis had a mantle on his back, and said to him: "Here, I'll give you this cloak, and beg you to forgive your lord for the love of the Lord God." The man's mood sweetened, and, moved by this kindness, he took the gift and forgave the wrongs.

Thomas of Celano, The Remembrance of the Desire of a Soul,
Second Book, LVI, 89
The Founder, 305

31 JANUARY

The father of the poor, the poor Francis, conforming himself to the poor in all things, was distressed to see anyone poorer than himself, not out of any desire for empty glory, but from a feeling of simple compassion. Though he was content with a ragged and rough tunic, he often wished to divide it with some poor person. This richest poor man, moved by a great feeling of pity, in order to help the poor in some way, used to approach the rich people of this world during the coldest times of the year, asking them to loan him their cloaks or furs. As they responded even more gladly than the blessed father asked, he used to say to them, "I shall accept this from you only on the condition that you never expect to have it returned." The first poor man who happened to meet him, he would then clothe with whatever he had received, exulting and rejoicing.

He was deeply troubled whenever he saw one of the poor insulted or heard a curse hurled at any creature. It happened that a certain brother insulted a poor man begging alms, saying: "Are you sure that you are not really rich and just pretending to be poor?" When Saint Francis, the father of the poor, heard this, he was deeply hurt and he severely rebuked the brother who had said these things. Then he ordered the brother to strip naked in front of the poor man and to kiss his feet, to beg his forgiveness. He used to say: "Anyone who curses the poor insults Christ whose noble banner the poor carry, since Christ made himself poor for us in this world." That is also why, when he met poor people burdened with wood or other heavy loads, he would offer his own weak shoulders to help them.

Thomas of Celano, The Life of Saint Francis, First Book, XXVIII, 76
The Saint, 247–8

February

1 FEBRUARY

Francis, the servant of God, was small in stature, humble in attitude, and lesser by profession. While living in the world he chose a little portion of the world for himself and his followers, since he could not serve Christ unless he had something of this world. Since ancient times, prophetically, this place was called "the Little Portion," since it was the lot ceded to those who wished to hold nothing of this world. In this place there was a church built for the Virgin Mother, who by her unique humility deserved, after her Son, to be the head of all the saints. It is here the Order of Lesser Ones had its beginning. As their numbers increased, there "a noble structure arose upon their solid foundation." The saint loved this place more than any other. He commanded his brothers to venerate it with special reverence. He wanted it, like a mirror of the Order, always preserved in humility and highest poverty, and therefore kept its ownership in the hands of others, keeping for himself and his brothers only the use of it.

There the most rigid discipline was kept in all things: as much in silence and in labor as in other religious observances. The entrance there was not open except to specially selected brothers, gathered from every region, whom the saint wanted to be truly devoted to God and perfect in every respect. Similarly, entrance was completely forbidden to any secular person. He did not want the brothers dwelling there — always kept below a certain number — to have their ears itching for worldly news and, interrupting their contemplation of heavenly things, to be dragged down to dealing with lower things by the talk of gossips. No one was allowed to speak idle words there, nor to repeat those spoken by others. And, if anyone happened to do this, punishment taught him to avoid further harm and not to repeat this in the future. Day and night, without interruption, those living in the place were engaged in the praises of God and, scented with a wonderful fragrance, they led the life of angels. This was only right! According to the stories of the old neighbors, that church used to be called by another name, "Saint Mary of the Angels." As the blessed Father used to say, God revealed to him, that among all other churches built in her honor throughout the world, the blessed Virgin cherished that church with special affection. For that reason the saint also loved it more than all others.

> Thomas of Celano, The Remembrance of the Desire of a Soul,
> First Book, XII, 18–19
> *The Founder,* 256–8

※

2 FEBRUARY

Holy of holies,
that truly place of places,
worthily held worthy
of the greatest of graces.

Blessed nickname,
more blessed name,
chosen with such a surname
as an omen of its fame.

An angelic power
habitually hymns do shower
here to dazzle the light,
here to dispel the night.

After lying in ruins was all,
Francis undid its downfall,
one plus a pair
that father repaired.

This the father chose
when in sack his members clothed;
here the body he opposed
and to his mind did dispose.

In this temple's confines
the wondrous life of the father shines;
thus was born the Lessers' Order
and here a crowd of men was quartered.

The bride of God, Clare,
here first shed her hair,
the world's pomp refused,
and her Christ pursued.

Thus a sacred mother
to ladies and to brothers
gives forth a brilliant birth
for whom she brings Christ on earth.

Here has been narrowly cast
an aging world's broad path
while virtue has been extended
in a people befriended.

A rule was kindled,
holy poverty enkindled,
glory was appalled,
in its midst the cross recalled.

If anywhere preoccupied
and at any time sorely tried,
here was Francis soothed
and his mind renewed.

Here was touted
the truth that might be doubted,
moreover it was given
whatever the father himself had bidden.

A Mirror of Perfection, IV, 84
The Prophet, 330–3

3 FEBRUARY

Thus did Francis dissolve mentally and bodily into the engraving of the wounds of his Beloved in the vision, and the lover was transformed into the Loved One. Fire has resilience, and while consuming earthly material, always reaches for the highest objects; characteristically it thrusts upwards. And so, the fire of divine love consuming the heart of Francis and, enkindling his flesh by burning a pattern into it, lifted him up to its own heights. Fulfilled in him then was what he used to pray would befall him: ... [there follows a Prayer of Love, Absorbeat.]

Ubertino di Casale, The Tree of the Crucified Life of Jesus, V, IV, 436b48
The Prophet, 190

ॐ

4 FEBRUARY

Absorbeat

I beg you, Lord, let the glowing and honey-sweet force of Your love draw my mind away from all things that are under heaven, that I may die for love of the love of You, who thought it a worthy thing to die for love of the love of me.

Ubertino di Casale, The Tree of the Crucified Life of Jesus, V, IV, 436b48
The Prophet, 190–1

ॐ

5 FEBRUARY

Perhaps it would be useful and worthwhile to touch briefly on the special devotions of Saint Francis. Although this man was devout in all things, since he enjoyed the anointing of the Spirit, there were special things that moved him with special affection.

Among other expressions used in common speech, he could not hear "the love of God" without a change in himself. As soon as he heard "the love of God" he was excited, moved, and on fire, as if these words from the outside were a pick strumming the strings of his heart on the inside.

He used to say that it was a noble extravagance to offer such a treasure for alms, and that those who considered it less valuable than money were complete fools. As for himself, he kept until his death the resolution he made while still entangled in the things of this world: he would never refuse any poor person who asked something "for the love of God."

Once a poor man begged something of him "for the love of God," and since he had nothing, he secretly picked up scissors and hurried to cut his small tunic in two. And he would have done just that, except that he was caught by the brothers and they had the poor man supplied with a different compensation.

He said: "The love of him who loved us greatly is greatly to be loved!"

Thomas of Celano, The Remembrance of the Desire of a Soul,
Second Book, CXLVIII, 196
The Founder, 373

6 FEBRUARY

While he embraced spiritual joy, he carefully avoided the false kind, knowing that what perfects should fervently be loved, but what corrupts should be carefully avoided. He strove to uproot empty boasting as it sprouted, not allowing anything that would displease the eyes of his Lord to survive even for a moment. Many times it happened, as he was being highly praised, he felt pain and grief, instantly turning the feeling into sadness.

One winter his holy little body was covered with only a single tunic. It was mended with cheap patches. His guardian, who was also his companion, acquired a piece of fox fur and brought it to him, saying: "Father, you're suffering illness in your spleen and stomach; so I'm begging your charity in the Lord to allow this skin to be sewn inside your tunic. And if you don't want the whole skin, at least take some of it to cover your stomach." The blessed Francis answered him: "If you want me to put up with this under my tunic, have another piece of the same size sewn on the outside, telling people that a piece of fur is hidden underneath." The brother heard, but did not agree; he insisted, but got nowhere. At last his guardian gave in, and one piece was sewn on top of the other, so that Francis should not appear differently on the outside than he was on the inside.

Oh, the same in word and life! The same outside and inside! The same as subject and as prelate! You, who would always boast in the Lord, loved nothing of outward glory, nothing of personal glory! But, please I do not wish to offend those covered in furs, if I say: "skin for skin!" [Jb 2:4] After all, we know those stripped of innocence needed tunics made of skins! [Gn 3:21]

Thomas of Celano, The Remembrance of the Desire of a Soul,
Second Book, XCIII, 130
The Founder, 372–3

ಸ

7 FEBRUARY

Blessed is the person who supports his neighbor in his weakness as he would want to be supported were he in a similar situation.

Blessed is the servant who returns every good to the Lord God because whoever holds onto something for himself hides the money of his Lord God within himself, and what he thinks he has will be taken away from him.

Blessed is the servant who does not consider himself any better when he is praised and exalted by people than when he is considered worthless, simple, and looked down upon, for what a person is before God, that he is and no more.

Woe to that religious who has been placed in a high position by others and [who] does not want to come down by his own will.

Blessed is that servant who is not placed in a high position by his own will and always desires to be under the feet of others.

Blessed is that religious who has no pleasure and delight except in the most holy words and deeds of the Lord and, with these, leads people to the love of God with gladness and joy.

Woe to that religious who delights in idle and empty words and leads people to laughter with them.

Blessed is the servant who, when he speaks, does not disclose everything about himself under the guise of a reward and is not quick to speak, but who is wisely cautious about what he says and how he responds.

Woe to that religious who does not hold in his heart the good things the Lord reveals to him and does not reveal them by his behavior, but, under the guise of a reward, wishes instead to reveal them with his words. He receives his reward and his listeners carry away little fruit.

The Admonitions, XVIII–XXI
The Saint, 134–5

8 FEBRUARY

Blessed is the servant who endures discipline, accusation, and reprimand from another as patiently as he would from himself.

Blessed is the servant who, after being reprimanded, agrees courteously, submits respectfully, admits humbly, and makes amends willingly.

Blessed is the servant who is not quick to excuse himself, and endures with humility, shame, and reprimand for a sin, when he did not commit the fault.

Blessed is the servant who has been found as humble among his subjects as he was among his masters.

Blessed is the servant who always remains under the rod of correction.

Faithful and prudent is the servant who does not delay in punishing himself for all his offences, inwardly through contrition and outwardly through confession and penance for what he did.

Blessed is the servant who loves his brother as much when he is sick and cannot repay him as when he is well and can repay him.

Blessed is the servant who loves and respects his brother as much when he is far away from him as when he is with him, and who would not say anything behind his back that he would not say with charity in his presence.

Blessed is the servant who has faith in the clergy who live uprightly according to the rite of the Roman Church.

Woe to those who look down upon them; for even though they be sinners, no one should judge them because the Lord alone reserves judgment on them to Himself. For just as their ministry is greater in its concerns for the most holy Body and

Blood of our Lord Jesus Christ, which they receive and they alone administer to others, so those who sin against them commit more of a sin than [if they had sinned] against all other persons in this world.

The Admonitions, XXII–XVI
The Saint, 135–6

9 FEBRUARY

Francis, ever growing in likeness to Jesus, realized that while he was at home in the body he was exiled from the Lord, that he had become, through the charity of Christ Jesus, altogether unaffected by external things and earthly desires. This made him strive, by means of unremitting prayer, to keep his spirit ever in the presence of God. Prayer was a solace to this contemplative who, going the rounds of the mansions above, had already become a fellow citizen of the angels, gazing upon their secrets. With burning desire he was seeking his Beloved, from whom the only partition separating him was his flesh. Prayer was likewise a safeguard to this man of action who, rather than rely on his own efforts in everything he undertook, would ask in persevering prayer to be guided by the blessed Jesus. By every possible means he would urge his brothers to be earnest in prayer.

He was so constant himself in giving time to prayer that, whether walking, sitting down, working or resting, indoors or outside, he seemed to be always praying. It was as though he had dedicated to holy prayer, not only heart and body, but every piece of his activity and time.

Ubertino da Casale, The Tree of the Crucified Life of Jesus, V, III, 18, 34
The Prophet, 180–1

10 FEBRUARY

Many a time he was held in ecstatic contemplation to the extent that, caught up above himself and perceiving something beyond human experience, he was completely unaware of what was going on around him. He would seek out places of solitude and make his way to abandoned churches at night to pray, because the effect of solitude is to focus the human spirit on interior things, and intimate union with the Bridegroom is achieved far away from the gazing multitude. Although in solitude he was to undergo dreadful attacks from demons, that physically fought him hand to hand as they tried to impede his concentration on prayer, victory was his and, getting the better of them, he was on his own again and in a state of peace.

In solitude he would fill the groves with sighs. There were times when brothers discovered him and could hear him interceding aloud that sinners might obtain God's clemency, and bemoaning the Lord's passion at the top of his voice, as though it were happening in front of him. At night he was seen praying with hands stretched out in the form of a cross, his entire body raised up from the ground and surrounded by a little shining cloud. The extraordinary brilliance around his body was there to testify to the marvelous illumination within his soul. In that solitude the secrets of divine wisdom were opened up to him, and it was there he learned what he wrote in the Rule and placed in the most holy Testament, and what he commanded the brothers to observe. For it is also most patently true that an unwearied dedication to prayer and a habitual exercise of the virtues had led the man of God to such serenity of soul that, although he had no expert knowledge of the sacred writings acquired from scholarship, his mind could probe the depths of Scripture with remarkable discernment, and in the brilliant rays of a light not of this world. In solitude, too, he obtained from God a vivid spirit of prophecy, by which in his own time he predicted many future happenings which came to pass exactly as he had said they would, and of which many corroborations are given in the Legend.

It was also while in solitude he received the most vivid and lucid revelation concerning the progression of the Order and the path Christ wished the brothers themselves to take, that is, the path the saint himself unfolded to them by word and demonstrated by example. Nonetheless, he was shown simultaneously the disastrous path the brothers would in fact take; something he tried in everyway to impede while he lived, and banned in his most holy Testament when lying on his deathbed, about to cross the threshold to Jesus in glory. To no avail, however, as far as the deviant were concerned, for their conceited, foolhardy prudence of the flesh and dogged rancor had prevailed. It was otherwise with his true sons, even though few of these survive, who in the light of all he said and of his most holy Testament carry on in the footprints of Jesus Christ, even while enduring much harassment from the unspiritual sons.

Ubertino da Casale, The Tree of the Crucified Life of Jesus,
V, III, 34, 50, 433a14
The Prophet, 181–2

11 FEBRUARY

Yes, that most holy father, like another Abraham, had two sons, one by the slave girl and one by the freewoman. The son of the slave girl came to be born in the way of the flesh, and it is all too evident that his steps for the most part have been guided by the prudence of human nature. But the son of the freewoman came to be born through a promise; sure that Christ did not lie to his servant Francis, and sure that the same faithful servant, Francis, lied not in what he wrote in the Rule and the most holy Testament. Those who are like this son, therefore, are sure of their way through the depths of that same Rule and through the observance of what is written in it, and do not at all suspect it contains anything impossible or unobservable. However, just as at that time, the child born in the way of the flesh persecuted the son born through the Spirit, so now. It is as true now as of old that there is an Ishmael abroad, and he is a bowman shooting arrows at the sons who are true to the Rule, arrows in the shape of oppressions, censures, preposterous decrees, harsh pronouncements. But what is it that Scripture says? "Drive away that slave girl and her son; the slave girl's son is not to share the inheritance with the son of the freewoman." For to Abraham it was said: "Isaac is the one through whom your name will be carried on. But the slave girl's son I shall also make into a great nation, for he too is your child." [Gn 21:10–13]

We are asking, with great groaning of heart, for the expulsion of this slave girl's son, an illegitimate one as far as the Rule's observance is concerned. Not that we are asking that he be deprived of his paternal inheritance, should he be minded to walk the road of the Rule, but that he give up his deviant way of acting, his assuming a name under false pretenses, and his persecuting the legitimate heir.

Ubertino da Casale, The Tree of the Crucified Life of Jesus, V, III, 28, 47
The Prophet, 182–3

12 FEBRUARY

Most High,
glorious God,
enlighten the darkness of my heart
and give me
true faith,
certain hope,
and perfect charity,
sense and knowledge,
Lord,
that I may carry out
Your holy and true command.

The Prayer before the Crucifix
The Saint, 40

13 FEBRUARY

When the father [of Francis] saw that he could not recall him from the journey he had begun ... he led the son to the bishop of the city to make him renounce into the bishop's hands all rights of inheritance and return everything that he had. Not only did he not refuse this, but he hastened joyfully and eagerly to do what was demanded.

When he was in front of the bishop, he neither delayed nor hesitated, but immediately took off and threw down all his clothes and returned them to his father. He did not even keep his trousers on, and he was completely stripped bare before everyone. The bishop, observing his frame of mind and admiring his fervor and determination, got up and, gathering him in his own arms, covered him with the mantle he was wearing. He clearly understood that this was prompted by God and he knew that the action of the man of God, which he had personally observed, contained a mystery. After this he became his helper. Cherishing and comforting him, he embraced him in the depths of charity.

Look! Now he wrestles naked with the naked. After putting aside all that is of the world, he is mindful only of divine justice. Now he is eager to despise his own life, by setting aside all concern for it. Thus there might be peace for him, a poor man on a hemmed-in path, and only the wall of the flesh would separate him from the vision of God.

Thomas of Celano, The Life of Saint Francis, First Book, VI, 14–15
The Saint, 193–4

14 FEBRUARY

He who once enjoyed wearing scarlet robes now traveled about half-clothed. Once while he was singing praises to the Lord in French in a certain forest, thieves suddenly attacked him. When they savagely demanded who he was, the man of God answered confidently and forcefully: "I am the herald of the great King! What is it to you?" They beat him and threw him into a ditch filled with deep snow, saying: "Lie there, you stupid herald of God!" After they left, he rolled about to and fro, shook the snow off himself and jumped out of the ditch. Exhilarated with great joy, he began in a loud voice to make the woods resound with praises to the Creator of all.

Eventually he arrived at a cloister of monks, where he spent several days covered with only a cheap shirt, serving as a scullery boy in the kitchen. He wanted to be fed at least some soup. No mercy was shown him and he was not even able to get some old clothes. Not moved by anger but forced by necessity, he moved on to the city of Gubbio, where he obtained a cheap tunic from an old friend. Shortly afterward, when the fame of the man of God had grown far and wide and his name was spread among the people, the prior of that monastery, when he recalled the event and understood what had been done to the man of God, came to him and, out of reverence for the Savior, begged forgiveness for himself and his monks.

Thomas of Celano, The Life of Saint Francis, First Book, VII, 16
The Saint, 194–5

15 FEBRUARY

Then the holy lover of profound humility moved to the lepers and stayed with them. For God's sake he served all of them with great love. He washed all the filth from them, and even cleaned out the pus of their sores, just as he said in his Testament: "When I was in sin, it seemed too bitter for me to see lepers, and the Lord led me among them and I showed mercy to them." For he used to say that the sight of lepers was so bitter to him that in the days of his vanity when he saw their houses even two miles away, he would cover his nose with his hands.

When he started thinking of holy and useful matters with the grace and strength of the Most High, while still in the clothes of the world, he met a leper one day. Made stronger than himself, he came up and kissed him. He then began to consider himself less and less, until by the mercy of the Redeemer, he came to complete victory over himself.

While staying in the world and following its ways, he was also a helper of the poor. He extended a hand of mercy to those who had nothing and he poured out compassion for the afflicted. One day, contrary to his custom (since he was very polite), he rebuked a poor person seeking alms from him, and he was immediately led to penance. He began to say to himself that to refuse what was asked by someone begging in the name of such a great King would be both a shame and a disgrace. And so he fixed this in his heart: to the best of his ability, never to deny anything to anyone begging from him for God's sake. This he did and with such care that he offered himself completely, in every way, first practicing before teaching the gospel counsel: "Give to the one who begs from you, and do not turn away from the one who wants to borrow from you." [Mt 5:42]

Thomas of Celano, The Life of Saint Francis, First Book, VII, 17
The Saint, 195–6

16 FEBRUARY

With his heart already completely changed — soon his body was also to be changed — he was walking one day by the church of San Damiano, which was abandoned by everyone and almost in ruins. Led by the Spirit he went in to pray and knelt down devoutly before the crucifix. He was shaken by unusual experiences and discovered that he was different from when he had entered. As soon as he had this feeling, there occurred something unheard of in previous ages: with the lips of the painting, the image of Christ crucified spoke to him. "Francis," it said, calling him by name, "go rebuild My house; as you see, it is all being destroyed." Francis was more than a little stunned, trembling, and stuttering like a man out of his senses. He prepared himself to obey and pulled himself together to carry out the command. He felt this mysterious change in himself, but he could not describe it. So it is better for us to remain silent about it too. From that time on, compassion for the Crucified was impressed into his holy soul. And we honestly believe the wounds of the sacred Passion were impressed deep in his heart, though not yet on his flesh.

> Thomas of Celano, The Remembrance of the Desire of a Soul,
> First Book, VI, 10
> *The Founder,* 249

---

17 FEBRUARY

What an admirable thing, unheard of in earlier ages! Who would not be amazed at this? Who ever heard of anything like it? Who could ever doubt that Francis, as he returned to his homeland, already appeared crucified? Christ spoke to him from the wood of the cross in a new and unheard of miracle, even when to all appearances, he had not yet completely forsaken the world. From that very hour his soul melted as the Beloved spoke to him. A little while afterward his heart's love showed in the wounds of his body.

From then on, he could not hold back his tears, even weeping loudly over the Passion of Christ, as if it were constantly before his eyes. He filled the roads with his sobbing, and, as he remembered the wounds of Christ, he would take no comfort. Once, upon meeting a close friend, he explained the reason for this sorrow, moving him also to bitter tears.

He does not forget to care for that holy image nor hesitate to carry out the command. He gives the priest money to buy a lamp and some oil, lest the sacred image lack, even for a moment, the honor of light. He then runs quickly to fulfill the rest, working tirelessly to rebuild that church. Although the divine word spoken to him was really about that Church which Christ acquired with His own blood, he did not immediately reach that level, but moved gradually from flesh to spirit.

> Thomas of Celano, The Remembrance of the Desire of a Soul,
> First Book, VI, 11
> *The Founder,* 249–50

18 FEBRUARY

Meanwhile, the holy man of God, having changed his habit and rebuilt that church, moved to another place near the city of Assisi, where he began to rebuild a certain church that had fallen into ruin and was almost destroyed. After a good beginning he did not stop until he had brought all to completion.

From there he moved to another place, which is called the "Portiuncula," where there stood a church of the Blessed Virgin Mother of God built in ancient times. At that time it was deserted and no one was taking care of it. When the holy man of God saw it so ruined, he was moved by piety because he had a warm devotion to the Mother of all good and he began to stay there continually. The restoration of that church took place in the third year of his conversion. At this time he wore a sort of hermit's habit with a leather belt. He carried a staff in his hand and wore shoes.

One day the gospel was being read in that church about how the Lord sent out his disciples to preach. The holy man of God, who was attending there, in order to understand better the words of the gospel, humbly begged the priest after celebrating the solemnities of the Mass to explain the gospel to him. The priest explained it all to him thoroughly line by line. When he heard that Christ's disciples should not possess gold or silver or money, or carry on their journey a wallet or a sack, nor bread nor a staff, nor to have shoes nor two tunics [Mt 10:9–10], but that they should preach the kingdom of God and penance [Lk 9:2; Mk 6:12], the holy man, Francis, immediately exulted in the spirit of God. "This is what I want," he said, "this is what I seek, this is what I desire with all my heart." The holy father, overflowing with joy, hastened to implement the words of salvation, and did not delay before he devoutly began to put into effect what he heard. Immediately, he took off the shoes from his feet, put down the staff from his hands, and, satisfied with one tunic, exchanged his leather belt for a cord. After this, he made for himself a tunic showing the image of the cross, so that in it he would drive off every fantasy of the demons. He made it very rough, so that in it he might crucify the flesh with its vices and sins. He made it very poor and plain, a thing that the world would never covet. As for the other things he heard, he set about doing them with great care and reverence. For he was no deaf hearer of the gospel; rather he committed everything he heard to his excellent memory and was careful to carry it out to the letter.

> Thomas of Celano, The Life of Saint Francis, First Book, IX, 21–222
> *The Saint*, 201–2

19 FEBRUARY

But, now that he was set upon works of piety, his father in the flesh began to persecute him. Judging it madness to be a servant of Christ, he would lash out at him with curses wherever he went. The servant of God then called a lowly, rather simple man to help him. Substituting him for his father, he asked him for a blessing whenever his father cursed him. He turned into deeds the words of *the prophet,* revealing the meaning of that verse: Let them curse; you give your blessing. [Ps 109:28]

The man of God gave back to his father the money he wanted to spend for work on the church. He did this on the advice of the bishop of the town, a very devout man, because it was wrong to spend ill-gotten gain for sacred purposes. Within earshot of many who had gathered about, he declared: "From now on I will say freely: "Our Father who art in heaven," and not "My father, Pietro di Bernardone." Look, not only do I return his money; I give him back all my clothes. I will go to the Lord naked."

Oh how free is the heart of a man for whom Christ is already enough!

The man of God was found to be wearing a hair shirt under his clothes, rejoicing in the reality of virtue rather than in its appearance.

His brother in the flesh, just like his father, hounded him with poisoned words. One winter's morning, when he saw Francis praying, covered with pitiful rags and shivering with cold, that wicked man said to a neighbor: "Tell Francis that now he should be able to sell you a penny's worth of sweat!" When the man of God heard this, he was very happy, and answered with a smile: "Actually, I'll sell it at a higher price to my Lord!"

Nothing could have been closer to the truth! He not only received a hundredfold in this life, but even a thousand times more, and in the world to come eternal life [Mt 16:29] not only for himself, but also for many others.

Thomas of Celano, The Remembrance of the Desire of a Soul,
First Book, VII, 12
The Founder, 251–2

20 FEBRUARY

He struggled to turn his earlier, luxurious way of life in a different direction, and to lead his unruly body back to its natural goodness....

Once he began serving the common Lord of all, he loved doing what was common, and avoided singularity in everything, which reeks of every vice.

He continued the sweaty work of repairing that church as Christ had commanded him, and from being over-delicate he changed into a rough and work-worn man. The priest who had that church saw him worn out with constant labor and, moved to piety, began to serve him each day some of his own food, although nothing very tasty, since he was poor. Francis appreciated the priest's concern and welcomed his kindness, but said to himself: "You won't find a priest like this everywhere, always bringing you food! This is not the life for someone professing poverty; you'd better not get used to this, or you'll slowly return to what you've rejected, and you'll drift back to your easy ways! Get up, stop being lazy, and beg scraps from door to door!"

He went through Assisi begging leftovers from door to door. When he saw his bowl filled with all kinds of scraps, he was at first struck with revulsion; but he remembered God and, overcoming himself, ate it with spiritual relish. Love softens all, and changes the bitter to sweet.

Thomas of Celano, The Remembrance of the Desire of a Soul,
First Book, VIII–IX, 13–14
The Founder, 252–3

21 FEBRUARY

We must first consider how the glorious Sir Saint Francis was conformed to the blessed Christ in all the acts of his life; as Christ at the beginning of His preaching chose twelve apostles to despise all worldly things, and to follow Him in poverty and in the other virtues; in the same way Saint Francis chose at the beginning of the foundation of the Order twelve companions who possessed highest poverty. And just as one of the twelve Apostles, the one called Judas Iscariot, became an apostate from the apostolate, betraying Christ, and hanging himself by the neck [Mt 27:5], so one of the twelve companions of Saint Francis, who was named Brother John of Cappella, became an apostate and finally hung himself by the neck. And to the chosen this is a great example and cause for humility and fear, considering that no one is certain of persevering to the end in the grace of God. And as those holy Apostles were admirable to the whole world for their holiness and humility, and full of the Holy Spirit, so these holy companions of Saint Francis were men of such holiness, that from the time of the Apostles the world did not have such admirable and holy men. For one of them was caught up to the third heaven like Saint Paul [2 Cor 12:2], and this was Brother Giles. One of them, that is Brother Philip the Tall, was touched on the lips by the Angel with the fiery coal like Isaiah the prophet [Is 6:6–7]. One of them, and that was Brother Sylvester, spoke with God as one friend with another, as Moses did [Ex 33:11]. One through subtlety of intelligence soared to the light of divine wisdom like an eagle, that is, John the Evangelist [Hb 1:8], and this was the very humble Brother Bernard, who explained the depths of Holy Scripture. One of them was sanctified by God and canonized in heaven while still living in the world, and that was Brother Rufino, a gentleman of Assisi. Thus all were marked by a singular sign of holiness, as described in what follows.

The Little Flowers of Saint Francis, 1
The Prophet, 566–7

22 FEBRUARY

At the beginning of the religion, Saint Francis had gathered in a place with his brothers to speak of Christ. In fervor of spirit he commanded one of them in the name of God to open his mouth and speak of God as the Holy Spirit inspired him. As the brother fulfilled the command, speaking wonderfully of God, Saint Francis imposed silence on him, and commanded a similar thing of another brother. As he obeyed and spoke subtly of God, Saint Francis similarly imposed silence on him; and commanded the third one to speak of God. He similarly began to speak so profoundly of the secret things of God that Saint Francis knew for certain that he, like the other two, spoke by the Holy Spirit. And this was shown by an example and a clear sign, since while they were speaking, the blessed Christ appeared in their midst in the appearance and form of a very handsome young man, who blessed them all, filling them with such grace and sweetness that all were rapt out of themselves, lying as if dead, feeling nothing of this world. Then, as they returned to themselves, Saint Francis said to them, "My dearest brothers, give thanks to God who has willed to reveal the treasures of divine wisdom through the mouths of the simple, since God is the one who opens the mouth of the mute, and makes the tongues of the simple speak very wisely."

The Little Flowers of Saint Francis, 14
The Prophet, 589

23 FEBRUARY

Brother Francis, your little and looked-down-upon servant in the Lord God, wishes health and peace to all mayors and consuls, magistrates and governors throughout the world and to all others to whom these words may come.

Reflect and see that the day of death is approaching. With all possible respect, therefore, I beg you not to forget the Lord because of this world's cares and preoccupations and not to turn away from His commandments, for all those who leave Him in oblivion and turn away from His commandments are cursed and will be left in oblivion by Him.

When the day of death does come, everything they think they have shall be taken from them. The wiser and more powerful they may have been in this world, the greater will be the punishment they will endure in hell.

Therefore I strongly advise you, my Lords, to put aside all care and preoccupation and receive the most holy Body and Blood of our Lord Jesus Christ with fervor in holy remembrance of Him. May you foster such honor to the Lord among the people entrusted to you that every evening an announcement may be made by a messenger or some other sign that praise and thanksgiving may be given by all people to the all-powerful Lord God. If you do not do this, know that, on the day of judgment, you must render an account before the Lord Your God, Jesus Christ.

Let those who keep this writing with them and observe it know that they will be blessed by the Lord God.

A Letter to the Rulers of the Peoples
The Saint, 58–9

24 FEBRUARY

Once Saint Francis was alongside the Lake of Perugia on the day of Carnival, at the house of a man devoted to him, where he was lodged for the night. He was inspired by God to go to make that Lent on an island in the lake. So Saint Francis asked this devout man that, for love of Christ, he carry him with his little boat to an island of the lake where no one lived, and that he do this on the night of the Day of the Ashes, so that no one would notice. And this man, out of love — from the great devotion he had for Saint Francis — promptly fulfilled his request and carried him to that island. And Saint Francis took nothing with him except two small loaves of bread. Arriving at the island, as his friend was departing to return home, Saint Francis asked him kindly not to reveal to anyone that he was there, and that he should not come for him until Holy Thursday. And so that man departed, and Saint Francis remained alone.

Since there was no dwelling in which he could take shelter, he went into some very thick brush that was formed like a little den or a little hut by many bushes and saplings. And in this place he put himself in prayer and contemplation of heavenly things. And there he stayed the whole of Lent without eating or drinking, except for half of one of those little loaves, as his devoted friend found on Holy Thursday when he returned for him; for of the two loaves he found one whole one and a half; the other half, it is supposed, Saint Francis ate, out of reverence for the fast of the blessed Christ, who fasted for forty days and forty nights without taking any material food. And thus, with that half of a loaf he drove away from himself vainglory, and after the example of Christ he fasted forty days and forty nights.

The Little Flowers of Saint Francis, 7
The Prophet, 578–9

25 FEBRUARY

All those who love the Lord with their whole heart, with their whole soul and mind, with their whole strength and love their neighbors as themselves, who hate their bodies with their vices and sins, who receive the Body and Blood of our Lord Jesus Christ, and who produce worthy fruits of penance. O how happy and blessed are these men and women while they do such things and persevere in doing them, because the Spirit of the Lord will rest upon them and make Its home and dwelling place among them, and they are children of the heavenly Father Whose works they do, and they are spouses, brothers, and mothers of our Lord Jesus Christ [Mt 12:50].

We are spouses when the faithful soul is joined by the Holy Spirit to our Lord Jesus Christ. We are brothers to Him when we do the will of the Father who is in heaven. We are mothers when we carry Him in our heart and body through a divine love and a pure and sincere conscience and give birth to Him through a holy activity which must shine as an example before others.

O how glorious it is to have a holy and great Father in heaven! O how holy, consoling to have such a beautiful and wonderful Spouse! O how holy and how loving, gratifying, humbling, peace-giving, sweet, worthy of love, and, above all things, desirable: to have such a Brother and such a Son, our Lord Jesus Christ, Who laid down His life for His sheep and prayed to His Father, saying:

Holy Father, in your name, save those whom you have given me in the world; they were yours and you gave them to me [Jn 17:11; Jn 6]. The words that you gave to me I have given to them, and they accepted them and have believed in truth that I have come from you and they have known that you have sent me [Jn 17:8].

I pray for them and not for the world [Jn 17:9]. Bless and sanctify them [Jn 17:17]; I sanctify myself for them [Jn 17:19]. I pray not only for them, but for those who will believe in me through their word that they might be [Jn 17:20; Jn 17:23] sanctified in being one as we are [Jn 17:11].

I wish, Father, that where I am, they also may be with me that they may see my glory in your kingdom [Jn 17:24; Mt 20:21]. Amen.

Earlier Exhortation to the Brothers and Sisters of Penance
(The First Version of the Letter to the Faithful), I, 1–19
The Saint, 41-2

26 FEBRUARY

All those men and women who are not living in penance, who do not receive the Body and Blood of our Lord Jesus Christ, who practice vice and sin and walk after the evil concupiscence and the evil desires of their flesh, who do not observe what they have promised to the Lord, and who in their body serve the world through the desires of the flesh, the concerns of the world and the cares of this life: They are held captive by the devil, whose children they are, and whose works they do. They are blind because they do not see the true light, our Lord Jesus Christ. They do not possess spiritual wisdom because they do not have the Son of God, the true wisdom of the Father. It is said of them: Their wisdom has been swallowed up [Ps 107:27] and Cursed are those who turn away from your commands [Ps 119:21]. They see and acknowledge, know and do evil, and knowingly lose their souls.

See, you blind ones, deceived by your enemies: the flesh, the world, and the devil, because it is sweet for the body to sin and it is bitter to serve God, for every vice and sin flow and proceed from the human heart as the Lord says in the Gospel [Mt 15:19; Mk 7:21]. And you have nothing in this world or in that to come. And you think that you will possess this world's vanities for a long time, but you are deceived because a day and an hour will come of which you give no thought, which you do not know, and of which you are unaware when the body becomes weak, death approaches, and it dies a bitter death. And no matter where, when, or how a person dies in the guilt of sin without penance and satisfaction, if he can perform an act of satisfaction and does not do so, the devil snatches his soul from its body with such anguish and distress that no one can know [what it is like] except the one receiving it.

And every talent, ability, knowledge, and wisdom they think they have will be taken away from them [Lk 8:18; Mk 4:25]. And they leave their wealth to their relatives and friends who take and divide it and afterwards say: "May his soul be cursed because he could have given us more and acquired more than what he distributed to us." Worms eat his body and so body and soul perish in this brief world and they will go to hell where they will be tortured forever.

In the love which is God we beg all those whom these words reach to receive those fragrant words of our Lord Jesus Christ written above with divine love and kindness. And let whoever does not know how to read have them read to them frequently. Because they are spirit and life, they should preserve them together with a holy activity to the end.

Earlier Exhortation to the Brothers and Sisters of Penance
(The First Version of the Letter to the Faithful), II, 1–21
The Saint, 43–4

27 FEBRUARY

The most high Father made known from heaven through His holy angel Gabriel this Word of the Father — so worthy, so holy and glorious — in the womb of the holy and glorious Virgin Mary, from whose womb He received the flesh of our humanity and frailty. Though He was rich, He wished, together with the most Blessed Virgin, His mother, to choose poverty in the world beyond all else [2 Cor 8:9].

And as His Passion was near, He celebrated the Passover with His disciples and, taking bread, gave thanks, blessed and broke it, saying: Take and eat: This is My Body [Mt 26:27]. And taking the cup He said: This is My Blood of the New Covenant which will be poured out for you and for many for the forgiveness of sins [Mt 26:28]. Then He prayed to His Father, saying: Father, if it can be done, let this cup pass from me [Lk 22:42]. And His sweat became as drops of blood falling on the ground [Lk 22:42]. Nevertheless, He placed His will in the will of His Father, saying: Father, let Your will be done; not as I will, but as You will [Mt 26:39, 42]. His Father's will was such that His blessed and glorious Son, Whom He gave to us and Who was born for us, should offer Himself through His own blood as a sacrifice and oblation on the altar of the cross: not for Himself through Whom all things were made, but for our sins, leaving us an example that we might follow His footprints.

And He wishes all of us to be saved through Him and receive Him with our heart pure and our body chaste. But, even though His yoke is easy and His burden light, there are few who wish to receive Him and be saved through Him.

Later Admonition and Exhortation to the Brothers and Sisters of Penance
(Second Version of the Letter to the Faithful), 4–15
The Saint, 46

28 FEBRUARY

But how happy and blessed are those who love God and do as the Lord Himself says in the Gospel: You shall love the Lord your God with all your heart and all your mind, and your neighbor as yourself [Mt 22:37, 39]. Let us love God, therefore, and adore Him with a pure heart and a pure mind, because He Who seeks this above all things has said: True adorers adore the Father in Spirit and Truth [Jn 4:23]. For all who adore Him must adore Him in the Spirit of truth. And day and night let us direct praises and prayers to Him, saying: Our Father, Who art in heaven . . . for we should pray always and not become weary.

We must, of course, confess all our sins to a priest and receive the Body and Blood of our Lord Jesus Christ from him. Whoever does not eat His flesh and drink His blood cannot enter the kingdom of God. But let him eat and drink worthily because anyone who receives unworthily, not distinguishing, that is, not discerning, the Body of the Lord, eats and drinks judgment on himself.

In addition, let us produce worthy fruits of penance.

And let us love our neighbors as ourselves. And if anyone does not want to love them as himself, let him at least not do them any harm, but let him do good.

Later Admonition and Exhortation to the Brothers and Sisters of Penance
(Second Version of the Letter to the Faithful), 18–26
The Saint, 46–7

March

1 MARCH

Let whoever has received the power of judging others pass judgment with mercy, as they would wish to receive mercy from the Lord. For judgment will be without mercy for those who have not shown mercy.

Let us, therefore, have charity and humility and give alms because it washes the stains of our sins from our souls. For, although people lose everything they leave behind in this world, they, nevertheless, carry with them the rewards of charity and the alms they have given for which they will receive a reward and a fitting repayment from the Lord.

We must also fast and abstain from vices and sins and from an excess of food and drink and be Catholics.

We must also frequently visit churches and venerate and revere the clergy not so much for themselves, if they are sinners, but because of their office and administration of the most holy Body and Blood of Christ which they sacrifice upon the altar, receive and administer to others. And let all of us know for certain that no one can be saved except through the holy words and Blood of our Lord Jesus Christ which the clergy pronounce, proclaim and minister. And they alone must minister and not others. Religious, however, who have left the world, are bound to do more and greater things, but not to overlook these.

Later Admonition and Exhortation to the Brothers and Sisters of Penance
(Second Version of the Letter to the Faithful), 28–36
The Saint, 47–8

2 MARCH

We must love our enemies and do good to those who hate us.

We must observe the commands and counsels of our Lord Jesus Christ. We must also deny ourselves and place our bodies under the yoke of servitude and holy obedience as each one has promised to the Lord. And let no one be bound to obey another in anything in which a crime or sin would be committed. Instead, let the one to whom obedience has been entrusted and who is considered the greater be the lesser and the servant of the other brothers. And let him have and show mercy to each of his brothers as he would want them to do to him were he in a similar position. Let him not become angry at the fault of a brother but, with all patience and humility, let him admonish and support him.

We must not be wise and prudent according to the flesh, but, instead, we must be simple, humble and pure. And let us hold our bodies in scorn and contempt because, through our own fault, we are all wretched and corrupt, disgusting and worms, as the Lord says through the prophet: I am a worm and not a man, the scorn of men and the outcast of the people [Ps 22:7].

We must never desire to be above others, but, instead, we must be servants and subject to every human creature for God's sake.

Later Admonition and Exhortation to the Brothers and Sisters of Penance
(Second Version of the Letter to the Faithful), 38–47
The Saint, 48

3 MARCH

One time in the very beginning, that is, at the time when blessed Francis began to have brothers, he was staying with them at Rivo Torto. One night, around midnight, when they were all asleep in heir beds, one of the brothers cried out, saying: "I'm dying! I'm dying!" Startled and frightened all the brothers woke up.

Getting up, blessed Francis said: "Brothers, get up and light a lamp." After the lamp was lit, blessed Francis said: "Who was it who said, 'I'm dying?'"

"I'm the one," the brother answered.

"What's the matter, brother?" blessed Francis said to him. "Why are you dying?"

"I'm dying of hunger," he answered.

So that that brother would not be ashamed to eat alone, blessed Francis, a man of great charity and discernment, immediately had the table set and they all ate together with him. This brother, as well as the others, were newly converted to the Lord and afflicted their bodies excessively. After the meal, blessed Francis said to the other brothers: "My brothers, I say that each of you must consider his own constitution, because, although one of you may be sustained with less food than another, I still do not want one who needs more food to try imitating him in this. Rather, considering his constitution, he should provide his body with what it needs. Just as we must beware of overindulgence in eating, which harms body and soul, so we must beware of excessive abstinence even more, because the Lord desires mercy and not sacrifice [Hos 6:6; Mt 9:13; 14:7]."

The Assisi Compilation, 50
The Founder, 149

4 MARCH

The first brothers and those who came after them for a long time mortified their bodies excessively, not only by abstinence in food and drink, but also in vigils, cold, and manual labour. Next to their skin, those who could get them wore iron rings and breastplates and the roughest hair shirts, which they were even better able to get. Considering that the brothers could get sick because of this, and in a short time some were already ailing, the holy father therefore commanded in one of the chapters that no brother wear anything next to the skin except the tunic.

We who were with him bear witness to this fact about him: from the time he began to have brothers, and also during his whole lifetime, he was discerning with the brothers, provided that in the matter of food and other things, they did not deviate at any time from the norm of the poverty and decency of our religion, which the early brothers observed. Nevertheless, even before he had brothers, from the beginning of his conversion and during his whole lifetime, he was severe with his own body, even though from the time of his youth he was a man of a frail and weak constitution, and when he was in the world he could not live without comforts.

One time, perceiving that the brothers had exceeded the norm of poverty and decency in food and in things, he said in a sermon he gave, speaking to a few brothers, who stood for all the brothers: "Don't the brothers think that my body needs special food? But because I must be the model and example for all the brothers, I want to use and be content with poor food and things, not fine ones."

The Assisi Compilation, 50
The Founder, 150

5 MARCH

One night, after praying for a long time, he gradually grew drowsy and fell asleep. Then his holy soul was brought into the sanctuary of God, and, among other things, he saw in a dream a lady who looked like this: Her head seemed to be of gold, her breast and arms of silver, her belly was crystal, and her lower parts of iron. She was tall in stature, slim and harmonious in form. But that very beautiful lady was covered by a filthy mantle. When the blessed Father got up the next morning he told this vision to the holy man, Brother Pacifico, but without explaining what it meant.

Many have interpreted it as they please, but I do not think it out of place to keep to the interpretation of Pacifico, which the Holy Spirit suggested to him as he was hearing it. "This very beautiful lady," he said, "is the beautiful soul of Saint Francis. Her golden head is his contemplation and wisdom about things of eternity; her silver breast and arms are the words of the Lord meditated in the heart and carried out in deeds. The hardness of the crystal is his sobriety, its sparkle is his chastity, and iron is his steadfast perseverance. Finally, consider the filthy mantle as the little and despised body covering his precious soul."

However, many others who also have the Spirit of God understand this Lady, as the father's bride, Poverty. "The reward of glory made her golden," they say, "the praise of fame made her silver; profession made her crystal, because she was internally and externally the same, without a money-pouch; and perseverance until the end made her iron. But the opinion of carnal men has woven a filthy garment for this exceptional lady."

Many also apply this vision to the Order, following the successive periods of Daniel. But it is evident that the vision is principally about the father, since to avoid vanity he absolutely refused to interpret it. Surely if it had touched on the Order, he would not have passed over it in total silence.

Thomas of Celano, The Remembrance of the Desire of a Soul,
Second Book, L, 82
The Founder, 301

6 MARCH

Although this blessed man was not educated in scholarly disciplines, still he learned from God wisdom from above and, enlightened by the splendors of eternal light, he understood Scripture deeply. His genius, pure and unstained, penetrated hidden mysteries. Where the knowledge of teachers is outside, the passion of the lover entered. He sometimes read the Sacred Books, and whatever he once put into his mind, he wrote indelibly in his heart. His memory took the place of books, because, if he heard something once, it was not wasted, as his heart would mull it over with constant devotion. He said this was the fruitful way to read and learn, rather than to wander through a thousand treatises. He considered a true philosopher the person who never set anything ahead of the desire for eternal life. He affirmed that it was easy to move from self-knowledge to knowledge of God for someone who searches Scripture intently with humility and not with presumption. He often untangled the ambiguities of questions. Unskilled in words, he spoke splendidly with understanding and power.

Thomas of Celano, The Remembrance of the Desire of a Soul,
Second Book, LXVIII, 102
The Founder, 314–15

7 MARCH

When he went to the hermitage of La Verna to observe a forty-day fast in honor of the Archangel Michael, birds of different kinds flew around his cell, with melodious singing and joyful movements, as if rejoicing at his arrival. They seemed to be inviting and enticing the devoted father to stay. When he saw this, he said to his companion: "I see, brother, that it is God's will that we stay here for some time, for our sisters the birds seem so delighted at our presence."

When he extended his stay there, a falcon nesting there bound itself to him in a great covenant of friendship with him. For at the hour of the night when the holy man usually rose for the divine office, it anticipated him with its noise and song. This pleased God's servant very much because such great concern for him shook out of him all sluggish laziness. But when Christ's servant was more than usually burdened with illness, the falcon would spare him and would not announce such early vigils. As if instructed by God, at about dawn it would ring the bell of its voice with a light touch.

In the joy of the different kinds of birds and in the song of the falcon, there certainly seems to have been a divine premonition of when this praiser and worshiper of God would be lifted up on the wings of contemplation and then would be exalted with a seraphic vision.

Bonaventure, The Major Legend of Saint Francis, VIII, 10
The Founder, 593–4

8 MARCH

In those days, the man of God was travelling to "Le Celle" of Cortona. A noble woman from a village called Volusiano heard of this and hurried to see him. Exhausted from the long journey since she was very refined and delicate, she finally reached the saint. Our holy father was moved with compassion on seeing her exhausted and gasping for breath. "What pleases you, my lady?" he asked. "Father, please bless me," she said. The saint asked: "Are you married or single?" She replied: "Father, I have a husband, a very cruel man, an antagonist to my service of Jesus Christ. He stops me from putting into action the good will the Lord has inspired in me; and this is my greatest sorrow. So I beg you, holy man, pray for him, that divine mercy will humble his heart." The father was amazed at virility in a female, an ageing spirit in a child. Moved by piety, he said to her: "Go, blessed daughter, and, regarding your husband, know that you will soon have consolation." And he added: "You may tell him for God and for me, that now is the time of salvation, and later it will be the time for justice."

After receiving his blessing, the lady returned home, found her husband and relayed the message. Suddenly the Holy Spirit came upon him, and he was changed from the old to the new man, prompting him to reply very meekly: "My lady, let us serve the Lord and save our souls in our own house." And his wife replied: "It seems to me that continence should be placed in the soul as its foundation, and the other virtues built upon it." "This," he said, "pleases me as it pleases you." They lived a celibate life for many years until, on the same day, both departed happily — one as a morning holocaust, and the other as an evening sacrifice.

What a fortunate woman! She softened her lord for the sake of life! In her was fulfilled that text from the Apostle: The unbelieving husband will be saved by his believing wife [1 Cor 7:14].

>Thomas of Celano, The Remembrance of the Desire of a Soul,
>Second Book, IX, 38
>*The Founder*, 271–2

9 MARCH

Listen, little poor ones called by the Lord,
who have come together from many parts and provinces.
Live always in truth,
that you may die in obedience.

Do not look at the life without,
for that of the Spirit is better.
I beg you out of great love,
to use with discernment
the alms the Lord gives you.
Those weighed down by sickness
and the others wearied because of them,
all of you: bear it in peace.
For you will sell this fatigue at a very high price
and each one will be crowned queen
in heaven with the Virgin Mary.

> The Canticle of Exhortation for the Ladies of San Damiano
> *The Saint*, 115

10 MARCH

The Lord said to Adam: Eat of every tree; you may not eat, however, of the tree of the knowledge of good and evil [Gn 2:16–17].

He was able to eat of every tree of paradise, because he did not sin as long as he did not go against obedience. For that person eats of the tree of the knowledge of good who makes his will his own and, in this way, exalts himself over the good things the Lord says and does in him. And so, through the suggestion of the devil and the transgression of the command, it became the apple of the knowledge of evil. Therefore it is fitting that he suffer the punishment.

> The Admonitions, II
> *The Saint*, 129

11 MARCH

The Lord says in the Gospel: Whoever does not renounce all that he possesses cannot be my disciple [Lk 14:33]; and: Whoever wishes to save his life must lose it [Lk 9:24].

That person who offers himself totally to obedience in the hands of his prelate leaves all that he possesses and loses his body. And whatever he does and says which he knows is not contrary to his will is true obedience, provided that what he does is good.

And should a subject see that some things might be better and more useful for his soul than what a prelate commands, let him willingly offer such things to God as a sacrifice; and, instead, let him earnestly strive to fulfill the prelate's wishes. For this is loving obedience because it pleases God and neighbor.

If the prelate, however, commands something contrary to his conscience, even though he may not obey him, let him not, however, abandon him. And if he then suffers persecution from others, let him love them all the more for the sake of God. For whoever chooses to suffer persecution rather than wish to be separated from his brothers truly remains in perfect obedience because he lays down his life for his brothers. In fact, there are many religious who, under the pretext of seeing things better than those which the prelate commands, look back, and return to the vomit of their own will. These people are murderers and, because of their bad example, cause many to lose their souls.

The Admonitions, III
The Saint, 130

12 MARCH

Let all my blessed brothers, both clerics and lay, confess their sins to priests of our religion. If they cannot, let them confess to other discerning and Catholic priests, knowing with certainty that, when they have received penance and absolution from any Catholic priest, they are without doubt absolved from their sins, provided they have humbly and faithfully fulfilled the penance imposed on them.

If they have not been able to find a priest, however, let them confess to their brother, as the Apostle James says: Confess your sins to one another [Jas 5:16]. Nevertheless, because of this, let them not fail to have recourse to a priest because the power of binding and loosing is granted only to priests [Mt 18:18].

Contrite and having confessed in this way, let them receive the Body and Blood of our Lord Jesus Christ with great humility and respect remembering what the Lord says: Whoever eats my flesh and drinks my blood has eternal life [Jn 6:54] and Do this in memory of me [Lk 22:19].

The Earlier Rule (The Rule without a Papal Seal), XX, 1–5
The Saint, 77–8

13 MARCH

Consider, O human being, in what great excellence the Lord God has placed you, for He created and formed you to the image of His beloved Son according to the body and to His likeness according to the Spirit.

And all creatures under heaven serve, know, and obey their Creator, each according to its own nature, better than you. And even the demons did not crucify Him, but you, together with them, have crucified Him and are still crucifying Him by delighting in vices and sins.

In what, then, can you boast? Even if you were so skilful and wise that you possessed all knowledge, knew how to interpret every kind of language, and to scrutinize heavenly matters with skill: you could not boast in these things. For, even though someone may have received from the Lord a special knowledge of the highest wisdom, one demon knew about heavenly matters and now knows more about those of earth than all human beings.

In the same way, even if you were more handsome and richer than everyone else, and even if you worked miracles so that you put demons to flight: all these things are contrary to you; nothing belongs to you; you can boast in none of these things.

But we can boast in our weaknesses [and] in carrying each day the holy cross of our Lord Jesus Christ.

The Admonitions, V
The Saint, 131

14 MARCH

The holy man would often repeat this: "As far as the brothers will withdraw from poverty, that far the world will withdraw from them; they will seek," he said, "but will not find. But if they would only embrace my Lady Poverty, the world would nourish them, for they are given to the world for its salvation." He would also say: "There is an exchange between the brothers and the world: they owe the world good example, and the world owes them the supply of necessities of life. When they break faith and withdraw their good example, the world withdraws its helping hand, a just judgment."

Concerned about poverty, the man of God feared large numbers: they give the appearance, if not the reality, of wealth. Because of this he used to say: "Oh, if it were possible, I wish the world would only rarely get to see Lesser Brothers, and should be surprised at their small number!" Joined by an unbreakable bond to Lady Poverty, he expected her dowry in the future, not in the present. He also sang with warmer feeling and livelier joy the psalms that praise poverty, such as, "The patience of the poor will not perish in the end" [Ps 9:18] and, "Let the poor see this and rejoice [Ps 69:32]."

Thomas of Celano, The Remembrance of the Desire of a Soul,
Second Book, XL, 70
The Founder, 294

15 MARCH

As the holy father advanced in virtue and merit of life his large crop of children increased everywhere in number and grace. With an amazing abundance of fruit, their branches extended to the farthest ends of the earth.

But he often worried about those new plants, how they could be cared for and helped to grow, tied together in a bond of unity. He saw that many people howled like wolves at that little flock. Those grown old in wickedness would take every opportunity to hurt it just because it was new. He could foresee that even his sons might do things opposed to holy peace and unity. He feared that some might turn into rebels, as often happens among the chosen, puffed up by their self-importance, ready for battle and prone to scandals.

Mulling over these things, the man of God saw this vision. As he slept one night, he saw a small black hen, similar to a common dove, with feathered legs and feet. She had countless chicks, and they kept running around her frantically, but she could not gather all of them under her wings. The man of God woke up, remembering his concerns, interpreted his own vision. "I am the hen," he said, "small in size and dark by nature, whose innocence of life should serve dove-like simplicity, which is as rare in this world as it is swift in flight to heaven. The chicks are the brothers, multiplied in number and grace. The strength of Francis is not enough to defend them from human plotting and contradicting tongues.

"Therefore, I will go and entrust them to the holy Roman Church. The evil-minded will be struck down by the rod of her power. The sons of God will enjoy complete freedom, which will help to increase eternal salvation everywhere. From now on, let the children acknowledge their mother's sweet favor, and always follow her holy footprints with special devotion. With her protection, nothing evil will happen to the Order, and no son of Belial will trample the vineyard of the Lord unpunished. She, that holy one, will emulate the glory of our poverty and will prevent the praises of humility from being obscured by clouds of pride. She will preserve intact among us the bonds of charity and peace, striking dissidents with harsh punishments. In her sight the sacred observance of the purity of the Gospel will constantly flourish and she will not allow the sweet fragrance of their life to vanish even for an hour."

This was the saint's full intent in embracing this submission; this is precious proof of the man of God's foreknowledge of the need for this protection in the future.

Thomas of Celano, The Remembrance of the Desire of a Soul,
Second Book, XVI, 23–4
The Founder, 260–1

16 MARCH

Although he tried his best to hide the treasure found in the field, he could not prevent at least some from seeing the stigmata in his hands and feet, although he always kept his hands covered and from that time on always wore shoes.

A number of the brothers saw them while he was still alive. Although they were men of outstanding holiness and so completely trustworthy, nevertheless to remove all doubt they confirmed under oath, touching the most sacred Gospels, that this was so and that they had seen it.

Also some of the cardinals saw them because of their close friendship with the holy man; and they inserted praises of the sacred stigmata in the hymns, antiphons, and sequences which they composed in his honor, and thus by their words and writings gave testimony to the truth.

Even the Supreme Pontiff Lord Alexander, in a sermon preached to the people at which many of the brothers and I myself were present, affirmed that he had seen the sacred stigmata with his own eyes while the saint was still alive.

More than fifty brothers with the virgin Clare, who was most devoted to God, and her sisters, as well as innumerable laymen, saw them after his death. Many of them kissed the stigmata out of devotion and touched them with their own hands to strengthen their testimony, as we will describe in the proper place.

But the wound in his side he so cautiously concealed that as long as he was alive no one could see it except by stealth. One brother who used to zealously take care of him induced him with a pious care to take off his tunic to shake it out. Watching closely, he saw the wound, and he even quickly touched it with three of his fingers determining the size of the wound by both sight and touch.

Bonaventure, The Major Legend of Saint Francis, XIII, 8
The Founder, 636

17 MARCH

At one time while blessed Francis was staying at Saint Mary of the Portiuncula, and there were still only a few brothers, blessed Francis sometimes used to go through the villages and churches in the area around the city of Assisi, proclaiming and preaching to the people that they should do penance. And he would carry a broom to sweep the churches.

For blessed Francis was very sad when he entered some church and saw that it was not clean. Therefore, after preaching to the people, at the end of the sermon he would always have all the priests who were present assembled in some remote place so he could not be overheard by secular people. He would preach to them about the salvation of souls and, in particular, that they should exercise care and concern in keeping churches clean, as well as altars and everything that pertained to the celebration of the divine mysteries.

One day blessed Francis went to a church in a village of the city of Assisi and began to sweep it. Immediately talk about this spread through that village, especially because those people enjoyed seeing and hearing him.

A man named John heard it, a man of amazing simplicity, who was ploughing in a field of his near the church, and he immediately went to him. Finding him sweeping the church, he said to him: "Brother, give me the broom because I want to help you." Taking the broom from him, he swept the rest.

When they sat down, he said to blessed Francis: "Brother, it's a long time now that I've wanted to serve God, especially after I heard talk about you and your brothers, but I did not know how to come to you. Now that it pleased God that I see you, I want to do whatever pleases you."

Considering his fervor, blessed Francis rejoiced in the Lord, especially because he then had few brothers, and because it seemed to him that, on account of his pure simplicity, he would make a good religious. So he said to him: "Brother, if you wish to belong to our life and company, you must rid yourself of all your things that you can get without scandal, and give them to the poor according to the counsel of the holy Gospel, because my brothers who were able to do so have done this."

The Assisi Compilation, 60–1
The Founder, 162–3

18 MARCH

There was a brother who, to all appearances, led a life of extraordinary holiness, but who stood out for his singular ways. He spent all his time in prayer, and kept such strict silence that he used to make his confession by gestures instead of words. He took in the words of Scripture with such great fervor that on hearing them he gave signs of feeling great sweetness. What more shall I say? Everyone considered him holy three times over.

It happened that the blessed father came to that place to see and hear this holy brother. While everyone was commending and praising the man, our father replied: "Brothers, stop! Don't sing me the praises of his devilish illusions. You should know the truth. This is diabolical temptation, deception and fraud. I am sure about this. And the fact that he won't go to confession proves it."

The brothers took this very hard, especially the saint's vicar. "How can this be true?" they asked. "How can lies and such deception be disguised under all these signs of perfection?" "Tell him to go to confession twice or even once a week," the father said. "If he doesn't do it, you will know what I said is true."

The vicar took the brother aside. He first chatted pleasantly with him, finally telling him to go to confession. He spat back, put his finger to his mouth, and shook his head, showing he would never make his confession. The brothers were speechless, fearing the scandal of a false saint. A few days later he left religion on his own, turned back to the world and returned to his vomit. Finally, after doing even worse things, he was deprived of both repentance and life.

Beware of singularity: it is nothing but a beautiful abyss. Experience shows that many who seem so unique rise up to the heavens, and then fall into the depths. Realize the power of a good confession. It is both a cause and sign of holiness.

Thomas of Celano, The Remembrance of the Desire of a Soul,
Second Book, II, 28
The Founder, 264–5

19 MARCH

He thought he committed a serious offence if he was disturbed by empty imaginings while he was at prayer. When such a thing would happen, he did not fail to confess it and immediately make amends. He had made such a habit of this carefulness that he was rarely bothered by this kind of "flies."

One Lent he had been making a small cup, so as not to waste any spare time. But one day as he was devoutly saying terce, his eyes casually fell on the cup and he began to look at it, and he felt his inner self was being hindered in its devotion. He grieved that the cry of his heart to the divine ears had been interrupted, and when terce ended he said, so the brothers could hear: "Alas, that such a trifle had such power over me as to bend my soul to itself! I will sacrifice it to the Lord, whose sacrifice it had interrupted!" Saying this he grabbed the cup and burned it in the fire. "Let us be ashamed," he said, "to be seized by petty distractions when we are speaking with the Great King at the time of prayer."

Thomas of Celano, The Remembrance of the Desire of a Soul,
Second Book, LXIII, 97
The Founder, 311

20 MARCH

Day by day the blessed father Francis was being filled with the consolation and the grace of the Holy Spirit, and, with all vigilance and concern, he was forming his new sons with new instruction, teaching them to walk with steady steps the way of holy poverty and blessed simplicity.

One day he was marveling at the Lord's mercy in the kindness shown to him. He wished that the Lord would show him the course of life for him and his brothers, and he went to a place of prayer, as he so often did. He remained there a long time with fear and trembling before the Ruler of the whole earth. He recalled in the bitterness of his soul the years he spent badly, frequently repeating this phrase: "Lord, be merciful to me, a sinner [Lk 18:13]." Gradually, an indescribable joy and tremendous sweetness began to well up deep in his heart.

He began to lose himself; his feelings were pressed together; and that darkness disappeared which fear of sin had gathered in his heart. Certainty of the forgiveness of all his sins poured in, and the assurance of being revived in grace was given to him. Then he was caught up above himself and totally engulfed in light, and, with his inmost soul opened wide, he clearly saw the future. As that sweetness and light withdrew, renewed in spirit, he now seemed to be changed into another man.

> Thomas of Celano, The Life of Saint Francis, First Book, XI, 26
> *The Saint*, 205

21 MARCH

He returned and said to the brothers with joy: "Be strong, dear brothers, and rejoice in the Lord. Do not be sad, because you seem so few, and do not let my simplicity or yours discourage you. The Lord has shown me that God will make us grow into a great multitude, and will spread us to the ends of the earth. I must also tell you what I saw about your future, though it would please me more to remain silent, if charity did not compel me to tell you. I saw a great multitude of people coming to us, wishing to live with us in the habit of a holy way of life and in the rule of blessed religion. Listen! The sound of them is still in my ears, their coming and going according to the command of holy obedience. I seemed to see highways filled with this multitude gathering in this region from nearly every nation. Frenchmen are coming, Spaniards are hurrying, Germans and Englishmen are running, and a huge crowd speaking other languages is rapidly approaching."

When the brothers heard this, they were filled with wholesome joy, either because of the grace which the Lord God had conferred on His holy one, or because they eagerly thirsted for the profit of their neighbors, whom they wanted to increase in number daily in order to be saved.

And the holy man said to them: "So that we may give thanks faithfully and devotedly to the Lord our God for all His gifts and that you may know how our present and future brothers should live, understand this truth about the course of things to come. In the beginning of our way of life together we will find fruit that is very sweet and pleasant. A little later fruit that is less pleasant and sweet will be offered. Finally, fruit full of bitterness will be served, which we will not be able to eat. Although displaying some outward beauty and fragrance, it will be too sour for anyone to eat. As I told you, the Lord certainly will make us grow into a great nation. But in the end it will turn out as follows: it is like a man who tosses his nets into the sea or a lake and catches a great number of fish. When he has loaded them all into his boat, he is reluctant to carry them all because of their great number. So he would pick out for his baskets the larger ones and those he likes, but the others he would throw out."

Thomas of Celano, The Life of Saint Francis, First Book, XI, 27–8
The Saint, 205–6

22 MARCH

At that same time, another good man entered their religion, and they increased their number to eight. Then the blessed Francis called them all to himself and told them many things about the kingdom of God, contempt of the world, denial of their own will, and subjection of the body. He separated them into four groups of two each.

"Go, my dear brothers," he said to them, "two by two through different parts of the world, announcing peace to the people and penance for the remission of sins. Be patient in trials, confident that the Lord will fulfill His plan and promise. Respond humbly to those who question you. Bless those who persecute you [Rom 12:14]. Give thanks to those who harm you and bring false charges against you, for because of these things an eternal kingdom is prepared [Mt 25:34] for us."

Accepting the command of holy obedience with much joy and gladness, they humbly prostrated themselves on the ground before Saint Francis. Embracing them, he spoke sweetly and devotedly to each one: "Cast your care upon the Lord, and he will sustain you [Ps 55:22]." He used to say this phrase whenever he transferred brothers by obedience.

Thomas of Celano, The Life of Saint Francis, First Book, XII, 29
The Saint, 207

23 MARCH

Heading to the hermitage of Greccio, blessed Francis was crossing the lake of Rieti in a small boat. A fisherman offered him a little water-bird so he might rejoice in the Lord over it. The blessed Father received it gladly, and with open hands, gently invited it to fly away freely. But the bird did not want to leave: instead it settled down in his hands as in a nest, and the saint, his eyes lifted up, remained in prayer. Returning to himself as if after a long stay in another place, he sweetly told the little bird to return to its original freedom. And so the bird, having received permission with a blessing, flew away expressing its joy with the movement of its body.

> Thomas of Celano, The Remembrance of the Desire of a Soul,
> Second Book, CXXVI, 167
> *The Founder,* 355

※

24 MARCH

When blessed Francis, fleeing, as was his custom, from the sight of human company, came to stay in a certain hermitage place, a falcon nesting there bound itself to him in a great covenant of friendship. At night-time with its calling and noise, it anticipated the hour when the saint would usually rise for the divine praises. The holy one of God was very grateful for this because the falcon's great concern for him shook him out of any sleeping-in. But when the saint was burdened more than usual by some illness, the falcon would spare him, and would not announce such early vigils. As if instructed by God, it would ring the bell of its voice with a light touch about dawn.

It is no wonder that other creatures revere the greatest lover of the Creator.

> Thomas of Celano, The Remembrance of the Desire of a Soul,
> Second Book, CXXVII, 168
> *The Founder,* 355–6

※

25 MARCH

A nobleman from the area of Siena sent a pheasant to blessed Francis while he was sick. He received it gladly, not with the desire to eat it, but because it was his custom to rejoice in such creatures out of love for their Creator. He said to the pheasant: "Praised be our Creator, Brother Pheasant!" And to the brothers he said: "Let's make a test now to see if Brother Pheasant wants to remain with us, or if he'd rather return to his usual places, which are more fit for him." At the saint's command a brother carried the pheasant away and put him down in a vineyard far away. Immediately the pheasant returned at a brisk pace to the father's cell.

The saint ordered it to be carried out again, and even further away, but with great stubbornness it returned to the door of the cell, and as if forcing its way, it entered under the tunics of the brothers who were in the doorway. And so the saint commanded that it should be lovingly cared for, caressing and stroking it with gentle words. A doctor who was very devoted to the holy one of God saw this, and asked the brothers to give it to him, not because he wanted to eat it, but wanting rather to care for it out of reverence for the saint. What else? The doctor took it home with him, but when separated from the saint it seemed hurt, and while away from his presence it absolutely refused to eat. The doctor was amazed, and at once carried the pheasant back to the saint, telling him in order all that happened. As soon as it was placed on the ground, and saw its father, it threw off its sadness and began to eat with joy.

Thomas of Celano, The Remembrance of the Desire of a Soul,
Second Book, CXXIX, 170
The Founder, 356–7

26 MARCH

A cricket lived in a fig tree by the cell of the holy one of God at the Portiuncula, and it would sing frequently with its usual sweetness. Once the blessed father stretched out his hand to it and gently called it to him: "My Sister Cricket, come to me!" And the cricket, as if it had reason, immediately climbed onto his hand. He said to it: "Sing, my sister cricket, and with joyful song praise the Lord your Creator!" The cricket, obeying without delay, began to chirp, and did not stop singing until the man of God, mixing his own songs with its praise, told it to return to its usual place. There it remained constantly for eight days, as if tied to the spot. Whenever the saint would come down from the cell he would always touch it with his hands and command it to sing, and it was always eager to obey his commands. And the saint said to his companions: "Let us give permission to our sister cricket to leave, who has up to now made us so happy with her praises, so that our flesh may not boast vainly in any way." And as soon as it had received permission, the cricket went away and never appeared there again. On seeing all this, the brothers were quite amazed.

Thomas of Celano, The Remembrance of the Desire of a Soul,
Second Book, CXXX, 170
The Founder, 357

27 MARCH

He zealously and carefully safeguarded Lady Holy Poverty. In order to avoid the superfluous, he would not even permit a small plate to remain in the house if, without it, he could avoid dire need. He said it was impossible to satisfy necessity without bowing to pleasure. He rarely or hardly ever ate cooked foods, but if he did, he would sprinkle them with ashes or dampen the flavor of spices with cold water. Often, when he was wandering through the world to preach the gospel of God, he was called to a dinner given by great princes who venerated him with much fondness. He would taste some meat in order to observe the holy gospel [Lk 10:7–8]. The rest, which he appeared to eat, he put in his lap, raising his hand to his mouth so that no one could know what he was doing. What shall I say about drinking wine, when he would not allow himself to drink even enough water when he was burning with thirst?

Now as to his bed: wherever he received hospitality, he refused to use a straw mattress or blankets. The naked ground received his naked body, with only a thin tunic between them. Sometimes when he would refresh his small body with sleep, he would often sleep sitting up, not lying down, using a stone or a piece of wood as a pillow.

As normally happens, sometimes the craving to eat something came upon him, but afterwards he would barely allow himself to eat it. Once, because he was ill, he ate a little bit of chicken. When his physical strength returned, he entered the city of Assisi. When he reached the city gate, he commanded the brother who was with him to tie a cord around his neck and drag him through the whole city as if he were a thief, loudly crying out: "Look! See this glutton who grew fat on the flesh of chickens that he ate without your knowledge." Many people ran to see this grand spectacle and, groaning and weeping, they said: "Woe to us! We are wretches and our whole life is steeped in blood! With excess and drunkenness we feed our hearts and bodies to overflowing!" They were touched in their hearts and were moved to a better way of life by such an example.

He often did things in this way both to despise himself fully and to invite others to everlasting honors. Toward himself he had become like a broken vessel, burdened by no fear or concern for his body. He would zealously expose himself to insults so that he would not be forced by self-love to lust for anything temporal. A true scorner of himself, he taught others to despise themselves by word and example. To what end? He was honored by all and merited high marks from everyone. He alone considered himself vile and was the only one to despise himself fervently.

Thomas of Celano, The Life of Saint Francis, First Book, XVI, 51–53
The Saint, 227–8

28 MARCH

Another time when he was walking with a brother through the marshes of Venice, he came upon a large flock of birds singing among the reeds. When he saw them, he said to his companion: "Our Sister Birds are praising their Creator; so we should go in among them and chant the Lord's praises and the canonical hours." When they had entered among them, the birds did not move from the place; and on account of the noise the birds were making, they could not hear each other saying the hours. The saint turned to the birds and said: "Sister Birds, stop singing until we have done our duty of praising God!" At once they were silent and remained in silence as long as it took the brothers to say the hours at length and to finish their praises. Then the holy man of God gave them permission to sing again. When the man of God gave them permission, they immediately resumed singing in their usual way.

Bonaventure, The Major Legend of Saint Francis, VIII, 9
The Founder, 592–3

29 MARCH

Often honored by others, he suffered great sorrow. Shunning human praise, he had someone, as an antidote, revile him. He would call one of the brothers to him, saying, "I command you under obedience to insult me harshly and speak the truth against their lies." When the brother, though unwilling, called him a boor and a useless hired-hand, he would smile and clap loudly, saying: "May the Lord bless you, for you are really telling the truth; that is what the son of Pietro Bernardone needs to hear." Speaking in this fashion, he called to mind the humble origins of his birth.

In order to show himself contemptible and to give others an example of true confession, when he did something wrong he was not ashamed to confess it in his preaching before all the people. In fact, if he had perhaps thought ill of someone or for some reason let slip a harsh word, he would go with all humility to the person of whom he had said or thought something wrong and, confessing his sin, would ask forgiveness. His conscience, a witness of total innocence, guarding itself with all care, would not let him rest until it gently healed the wound of his heart. In every type of praiseworthy deed he wished to be outstanding, but to go unnoticed. In every way he fled praise to avoid all vanity.

Woe to us who have now lost you, O worthy father, model of all kindness and humility! Since we did not strive to know you when we had you, we have lost you by a just judgment!

Thomas of Celano, The Life of Saint Francis, First Book, XIX, 53–4
The Saint, 228–9

30 MARCH

The great grace that God showed many times to the evangelical poor who abandoned the world for love of Christ was shown in Brother Bernard of Quintavalle who, after he had taken the habit of Saint Francis, was very frequently rapt in God through contemplation of heavenly things. Among other times, once he was in church to hear Mass, and while his whole spirit was suspended in God, he became so absorbed and rapt in contemplation that, when the Body of Christ was being elevated he noticed nothing, nor did he kneel, nor did he pull back his capuche as the others did who were there. But without blinking his eyes, with a fixed stare, he remained out of his senses from morning until None. Returning to himself after None, he went through the place crying out in admiration: "Oh brothers! Oh brothers! Oh brothers! There is no one in this region so great or so noble for whom, if he were promised a very beautiful palace full of gold, it would not be easy to carry a sack full of manure in order to gain so noble a treasure."

Brother Bernard was so lifted up in spirit to this heavenly treasure, promised to lovers of God, that continually for fifteen years he always went about with his spirit and his face lifted toward heaven. And during that time he never relieved his hunger at table, though he ate a little of what was placed before him, because he said that we do not practice perfect abstinence from things if we do not taste them; true abstinence is refraining from things that taste good to the mouth. And with this he had come to such clarity and light of intelligence that even great clerics came to him for solutions to the most difficult questions and obscure passages of Scripture; and he enlightened them on every difficulty.

Because his spirit was entirely set free and removed from earthly things, like the swallows he flew very high through contemplation, and sometimes for twenty days, sometimes for thirty days, he remained alone on the peaks of high mountains, contemplating heavenly things. For this reason Brother Giles used to say about him that others had not received this gift, which had been given to Brother Bernard of Quintavalle, that is, like a swallow, finding food for himself while flying. And because of this outstanding grace that he had from God, Saint Francis often and willingly talked with him by day and by night, so that sometimes they were found together rapt in God the whole night long in the woods where both of them met to speak with God.

The Little Flowers of Saint Francis, 28
The Prophet, 616–7

31 MARCH

Christ's new students ... arrived at a deserted place. They were hungry and exhausted from the weariness of their journey and could not find any food, as that place was far removed from people's homes. But God's grace was looking after them, for suddenly they met a man carrying bread in his hand, and he gave it to them and left. They honestly did not recognize him and, marveling in their hearts, they all eagerly encouraged each other to a greater trust in divine mercy.

After eating the food and being much strengthened by it, they went on to a place near the city of Orte, where they stayed for about fifteen days. Some of them went into the city to acquire the necessary food. They brought back to the other brothers the small amount they managed to obtain by going door-to-door and they ate together with gratitude and joyful hearts. If anything remained, since they could not give it to anyone, they stored it in a tomb, which had once held the bodies of the dead, so they could eat it at another time. The place was deserted and abandoned, and hardly anyone ever visited it.

They had great joy, because they saw nothing and had nothing that could give them empty or carnal delight. There, they began to have commerce with holy poverty. Greatly consoled in their lack of all things of the world, they resolved to adhere to the way they were in that place always and everywhere. Only divine consolation delighted them, having put aside all their cares about earthly things. They decided and resolved that even if buffeted by tribulations and driven by temptations they would not withdraw from its embrace.

Thomas of Celano, The Life of Saint Francis, First Book, XIV, 34–5
The Saint, 213–14

April

1 APRIL

The resolute knight of Christ never spared his body. As if it were a stranger to him, he exposed it to every kind of injury, whether in word or deed. If anyone tried to enumerate everything this man underwent, the list would be longer than that passage where the apostle recounts the tribulations of the saints.

Those enrolled in that first school also subjected themselves to every discomfort. It was even considered criminal to seek any consolation except that of the spirit. Wearing iron belts and breastplates they grew weak from constant fasting and frequent vigils. They would have collapsed many times, were it not for their devoted shepherd's constant warnings that made them relax the rigors of their self-denial.

One night while all were sleeping, one of his flock cried out: "Brothers! I'm dying! I'm dying of hunger!" At once that extraordinary shepherd got up, and hurried to treat the sick lamb with the right medicine. He ordered them to set the table, although filled with everyday fare. Since there was no wine — as often happened — they made do with water. Francis started eating first. Then, he invited the rest of the brothers to do the same, for charity's sake, so their brother would not be embarrassed.

Once they had taken their food in the fear of the Lord, so that nothing would be lacking in this act of charity, the father wove for his sons a long parable about the virtue of discernment. He ordered them to season with salt every sacrifice to God. With concern he reminded them that in offering service to God each one should consider his own strength.

He insisted that it was just as much a sin to deprive the body without discernment of what it really needed as, prompted by gluttony, to offer it too much. And he added: "Dear brothers, realize that, what I just did by eating was not my own choice, but an exception, demanded by fraternal charity. Let the charity, not the food, be an example for you, for the latter feeds the belly while the former feeds the spirit."

Thomas of Celano, The Remembrance of the Desire of a Soul,
First Book, XIV–XV, 21–2
The Founder, 258–9

2 APRIL

Once a little cell was made on a certain mountain. In it the servant of God did penance rigorously for a period of forty days. After that span of time was over he left that place, and the cell remained in its lonely location without anyone taking his place. The small clay cup from which the saint used to drink was left there. Now, some people one time went to that place out of reverence for the saint, and they found that cup full of bees. With wonderful skill they had constructed the little cells of their honeycomb in the cup itself, certainly symbolizing the sweetness of the contemplation which the holy one of God drank in at that place.

Thomas of Celano, The Remembrance of the Desire of a Soul,
Second Book, CXXVIII, 169
The Founder, 356

3 APRIL

The Lord gave me, Brother Francis, thus to begin doing penance in this way: for when I was in sin, it seemed too bitter for me to see lepers. And the Lord Himself led me among them and I showed mercy to them. And when I left them, what had seemed bitter to me was turned into sweetness of soul and body. And afterwards I delayed a little and left the world.

And the Lord gave me such faith in churches that I would pray with simplicity in this way and say: "We adore You, Lord Jesus Christ, in all Your churches throughout the whole world and we bless You because by Your holy cross You have redeemed the world."

Afterwards the Lord gave me, and gives me still, such faith in priests who live according to the rite of the holy Roman Church because of their orders that, were they to persecute me, I would still want to have recourse to them. And if I had as much wisdom as Solomon and found impoverished priests of this world, I would not preach in their parishes against their will. And I desire to respect, love and honor them and all others as my lords. And I do not want to consider any sin in them because I discern the

Son of God in them and they are my lords. And I act in this way because, in this world, I see nothing corporally of the most high Son of God except His most holy Body and Blood which they receive and they alone administer to others.

The Testament, 1-10
The Saint, 124-5

4 APRIL

I want to have these most holy mysteries honored and venerated above all things and I want to reserve them in precious places. Wherever I find our Lord's most holy names and written words in unbecoming places, I want to gather them up and I beg that they be gathered up and placed in a becoming place. And we must honor all theologians and those who minister the most holy divine words and respect them as those who minister to us spirit and life.

And after the Lord gave me some brothers, no one showed me what I had to do, but the Most High Himself revealed to me that I should live according to the pattern of the Holy Gospel. And I had this written down simply and in a few words and the Lord Pope confirmed it for me. And those who came to receive life gave whatever they had to the poor and were content with one tunic, patched inside and out, with a cord and short trousers. We desired nothing more. We clerical [brothers] said the Office as other clerics did; the lay brothers said the Our Father; and we quite willingly remained in churches. And we were simple and subject to all.

And I worked with my hands, and I still desire to work; and I earnestly desire all brothers to give themselves to honest work. Let those who do not know how to work learn, not from desire to receive wages, but for example and to avoid idleness. And when we are not paid for our work, let us have recourse to the table of the Lord, begging alms from door to door. The Lord revealed a greeting to me that we should say: "May the Lord give you peace."

The Testament, 11-23
The Saint, 125-6

5 APRIL

Francis, Christ's bravest soldier, went around the cities and villages, proclaiming the kingdom of God and preaching peace and penance for the remission of sins, not in the persuasive words of human wisdom but in the learning and power of the Spirit.

He acted confidently in all matters because of the apostolic authority granted him. He did not use fawning or seductive flattery. He did not smooth over but cut out the faults of others. He did not encourage but struck at the life of sin with a sharp blow, because he first convinced himself by action and then convinced others by words. Not fearing anyone's rebuke, he spoke the truth boldly, so that even well-educated men, distinguished by fame and dignity, were amazed at his words and were shaken by a healthy fear in his presence.

Men ran, women also ran, clerics hurried, and religious rushed to see and hear the holy one of God, who seemed to everyone a person of another age. People of all ages and both sexes hurried to behold the wonders which the Lord worked anew in the world through his servant.

At that time, through the presence of Saint Francis and through his reputation, it surely seemed a new light had been sent from heaven to earth, driving away all the darkness that had so nearly covered that whole region that hardly anyone knew where to turn. Deep forgetfulness of God and lazy neglect of his commandments overwhelmed almost everyone, so that they could barely be roused from old, deep-seated evils.

Thomas of Celano, The Life of Saint Francis, First Book, XV, 36
The Saint, 214–15

6 APRIL

He gleamed like a shining star in the darkness of night and like the morning spread over the darkness. Thus, in a short time, the appearance of the entire region was changed and, once rid of its earlier ugliness, it revealed a happier expression everywhere. The former dryness was put to rout and a crop sprang up quickly in the untilled field. Even the uncultivated vine began to produce buds with a sweet-smell for the Lord, and when it had produced flowers of sweetness, it brought forth equally the fruit of honor and respectability. Thanks and the voice of praise resounded everywhere, as many, casting aside earthly concerns, gained knowledge of themselves in the life and teaching of the most blessed father Francis and aspired to love and reverence for their Creator.

Many people, well-born and lowly, cleric and lay, driven by divine inspiration, began to come to Saint Francis, for they desired to serve under his constant training and leadership. All of these the holy one of God, like a fertile stream of heavenly grace, watered with showers of gifts and he adorned the field of their hearts with the flowers of perfection.

He is without question an outstanding craftsman, for through his spreading message, the Church of Christ is being renewed in both sexes according to his form, rule and teaching, and there is victory for the triple army of those being saved. Furthermore, to all he gave a norm of life and to those of every rank he sincerely pointed out the way of salvation.

Thomas of Celano, The Life of Saint Francis, First Book, XV, 37
The Saint, 215–17

7 APRIL

At one time the blessed and venerable father Francis, with worldly crowds gathering eagerly every day to hear and see him, sought out a place of rest and secret solitude. He desired to free himself for God and shake off any dust that clung to him from the time spent with the crowds. It was his custom to divide the time given him to merit grace and, as seemed best, to spend some of it to benefit his neighbors and use the rest in the blessed solitude of contemplation. He took with him only a few companions — who knew his holy way of living better than others — so that they could shield him from the interruption and disturbance of people, respecting and protecting his silence in every way.

After he had been there for some time, through unceasing prayer and frequent contemplation, he reached intimacy with God in an indescribable way. He longed to know what in him and about him was or could be most acceptable to the Eternal King. He sought this diligently and devoutly longed to know in what manner, in what way, and with what desire he would be able to cling more perfectly to the Lord God, according to His counsel and the good pleasure of His will. This was always his highest philosophy; this was the highest desire that always burned in him as long as he lived. He asked the simple and the wise, the perfect and the imperfect, how he could reach the way of truth and arrive at his great goal.

Since he was the most perfect among the perfect, he refused to think he was perfect and thought himself wholly imperfect. He could taste and see how pleasing, sweet and good the God of Israel is to those who are of sincere heart and who seek Him in true purity and in pure simplicity.

He felt pouring down on him from above a sweetness and delight rarely given to even a few, and it made him lose himself completely. He was filled with such joy that he wished by any means to pass over entirely to that place where, in passing out of himself, he had already partially gone. This man, having the spirit of God, was ready to endure any suffering of mind and bear any affliction of the body, if at last he would be given the choice that the will of the heavenly Father might be fulfilled mercifully in him.

Thomas of Celano, The Life of Saint Francis, Second Book, II, 91–2
The Saint, 261–2

8 APRIL

So one day he approached the sacred altar which had been built in the hermitage where he was staying and, taking up the volume where the holy Gospels were written, he placed it reverently upon the altar.

Then he prostrated himself with his heart as much as his body in prayer to God, asking in humble prayer that God in His kindness — the Father of mercies and the God of all consolation — be pleased to show him His will. He prayed earnestly that at the first opening of the book he would be shown what was best for him to do, so that he could bring to complete fulfillment what he had earlier simply and devotedly begun. In this he was led by the spirit of the saints and holy ones, as we read they did something similar with sincere devotion in their desire for holiness.

Rising from prayer in a spirit of humility and with a contrite heart, he prepared himself with the sign of the holy cross. He took the book from the altar, and opened it with reverence and fear. When he opened the book, the first passage that met his eye was the passion of our Lord Jesus Christ that tells of the suffering he was to endure. To avoid any suspicion that this was just a coincidence, he opened the book a second and a third time. Every time he found either the same text or one that was similar. This man filled with the spirit of God then understood that he would have to enter into the kingdom of God through many trials, difficulties and struggles.

The brave soldier was not disturbed by oncoming battles, nor was he downcast in his spirit as he was about to fight the wars of the Lord in the camps of this world.

He was not afraid that he would yield to the enemy since he had long struggled beyond human strength not even to give in to himself. He was so filled with fire that, even if in preceding ages there had been someone with a purpose equal to his, no one has been found whose desire was greater than his. He found it easier to do what is perfect than to talk about it; so he was constantly active in showing his zeal and dedication in deeds, not in words, because words do not do what is good, they only point to it. Thus he remained undisturbed and happy, singing songs of joy in his heart to himself and to God. For this reason he was found worthy of a greater revelation, since he rejoiced over a small one; faithful in a small thing, he was placed over greater ones.

Thomas of Celano, The Life of Saint Francis, Second Book, II, 92–3
The Saint, 262–3

9 APRIL

One of those days, withdrawn in this way, while he was praying and all of his fervor was totally absorbed in God, Christ Jesus appeared to him as fastened to a cross. His soul melted at the sight, and the memory of Christ's passion was so impressed on the innermost recesses of his heart that, from that hour, whenever Christ's crucifixion came to his mind, he could scarcely contain his tears and sighs, as he later revealed to his companions when he was approaching the end of his life. Through this the man of God understood as addressed to himself the Gospel text: If you wish to come after me, deny yourself and take up your cross and follow me.

Bonaventure, The Major Legend of Saint Francis, I, 5
The Founder, 534

10 APRIL

While he was staying in that hermitage called La Verna, after the place where it is located, two years prior to the time that he returned his soul to heaven, he saw in the vision of God a man, having six wings like a Seraph, standing over him, arms extended and feet joined, affixed to a cross. Two of his wings were raised up, two were stretched out over his head as if for flight, and two covered his whole body. When the blessed servant of the most High saw these things, he was filled with the greatest awe, but could not decide what this vision meant for him. Moreover, he greatly rejoiced and was much delighted by the kind and gracious look that he saw the Seraph gave him. The Seraph's beauty was beyond comprehension, but the fact that the Seraph was fixed to the cross and the bitter suffering of that passion thoroughly frightened him. Consequently, he got up both sad and happy as joy and sorrow took their turns in his heart. Concerned over the matter, he kept thinking about what this vision could mean and his spirit was anxious to discern a sensible meaning from the vision.

While he was unable to perceive anything clearly understandable from the vision, its newness very much pressed upon his heart. Signs of the nails began to appear on his hands and feet, just as he had seen them a little while earlier on the crucified man hovering over him.

His hands and feet seemed to be pierced through the middle by nails, with the heads of the nails appearing on the inner part of his hands and on the upper part of his feet, and their points protruding on opposite sides. Those marks on the inside of his hands were round, but rather oblong on the outside; and small pieces of flesh were visible like the points of nails, bent over and flattened, extending beyond the flesh around them. On his feet, the marks of nails were stamped in the same way and raised above the surrounding flesh. His right side was marked with an oblong scar, as if pierced with a lance, and this often dripped blood, so that his tunic and undergarments were frequently stained with his holy blood.

Thomas of Celano, The Life of Saint Francis, Second Book, III, 94–5
The Saint, 263–4

11 APRIL

Sadly, only a few merited seeing the sacred wound in his side during the life of the crucified servant of the crucified Lord. Elias was fortunate and did merit somehow to see the wound in his side. Rufino was just as lucky: he touched it with his own hands. For one time, when the same brother Rufino put his hand onto the holy man's chest to rub him, his hand slipped, as often happens, and it chanced that he touched the precious scar in his right side. As soon as he had touched it, the holy one of God felt great pain and pushed Rufino's hand away, crying out for the Lord to spare him.

He hid those marks carefully from strangers, and concealed them cautiously from people close to him, so that even the brothers at his side and his most devoted followers for a long time did not know about them.

Although the servant and friend of the Most High saw himself adorned with such magnificent pearls, like precious stones, and marvelously decorated beyond the glory and honor of all others, still his heart did not grow vain. He did not seek to use this to make himself appealing to anyone in a desire for vainglory. Rather in every way possible he tried to hide these marks, so that human favor would not rob him of the grace given him.

He would never or rarely reveal his great secret to anyone. He feared that his special friends would reveal it to show their intimacy with him, as friends often do, and he would then lose some of the grace given to him. He always carried in his heart and often had on his lips the saying of the prophet: "I have hidden your words in my heart to avoid any sin against You."

Whenever some people of the world approached him and he did not wish to speak with them, he would give this sign to the brothers and sons staying with him: if he recited the verse mentioned above, immediately they would dismiss politely those who had gathered to see him. He had learned through experience that one cannot be a spiritual person unless one's secrets are deeper and more numerous than what can be seen on the face and by their appearance can be judged in different ways by different people. For he had met some people who agreed with him outwardly but inwardly disagreed, applauding him to his face but laughing behind his back. These brought judgment upon themselves and made honest people seem somewhat suspect to him.

So it is that malice often attempts to smear sincerity and because of the lies of many, the truth of the few is not believed.

Thomas of Celano, The Life of Saint Francis, Second Book, III, 95–6
The Saint, 264–5

12 APRIL

You are the holy Lord God Who does wonderful things.

You are strong, You are great, You are the most high,
   You are the almighty king. You holy Father,
   King of heaven and earth.

You are three and one, the Lord God of gods;
   You are the good, all good, the highest good,
   Lord God living and true.

You are love, charity; You are wisdom, You are humility,
   You are patience, You are beauty, You are meekness,
   You are security, You are rest,
   You are gladness and joy, You are our hope,
      You are justice,
   You are moderation, You are all our riches to sufficiency.

You are beauty, You are meekness,
   You are the protector, You are our custodian and defender,
   You are strength, You are refreshment.

You are our hope,
   You are our faith, You are our charity,
   You are all our sweetness, You are our eternal life:
   Great and wonderful Lord, Almighty God,
      Merciful Savior.

The Praises of God
The Saint, 109

13 APRIL

Shining with the splendor of his life and teaching, like the morning star in the midst of clouds, by his resplendent rays he guided into the light those sitting in darkness and in the shadow of death, and like the rainbow shining among clouds of glory he made manifest in himself the sign of the Lord's covenant.

He preached to people the Gospel of peace and salvation, being himself an angel of true peace. Like John the Baptist, he was destined by God to prepare in the desert a way of the highest poverty and to preach repentance by word and example.

First endowed with the gifts of divine grace, he was then enriched by the merit of unshakable virtue; and filled with the spirit of prophecy, he was also assigned an angelic ministry and was totally aflame with a Seraphic fire.

Like a hierarchic man, one lifted up on a fiery chariot, it may be reasonably accepted as true that he came in the spirit and power of Elijah, as will appear quite clearly in the course of his life. And so in the true prophecy of that other friend of the Bridegroom, John the Apostle and Evangelist, he is considered not without reason to be like the angel ascending from the rising of the sun bearing the seal of the living God. For "at the opening of the sixth seal," John says in the Apocalypse, "I saw another Angel ascending from the rising of the sun, having the sign of the living God."

Bonaventure, The Major Legend of Saint Francis, Prologue, 1 5
The Founder, 526–7

14 APRIL

While the holy man was staying in a hermitage near Rieti, a doctor used to visit him every day to treat his eyes. One day the saint said to his brothers: "Invite the doctor, and give him the best to eat." The guardian answered him: "Father, we're embarrassed to say this, but we're ashamed to invite him, because right now we're so poor." But the saint answered: "Do you want me to tell you again?" And the doctor, who was nearby, said: "Dear brothers, I would consider it a treat to share in your poverty."

The brothers hurried to place the whole contents of their storeroom on the table: a little bread, and not much wine, and, to make the meal more lavish, the kitchen provided a few beans. Meanwhile, the table of the Lord took pity on the table of his servants. Someone knocked at the door, and they answered immediately. There was a woman offering a basket filled with beautiful bread, loaded with fish and crabcakes, and with honey and grapes heaped on top. The table of the poor rejoices at this sight, the cheap food is put away, and the delicacies are eaten immediately.

The doctor heaved a sigh and spoke to them: "Neither you, brothers, as you should, nor we lay people, realize the holiness of this man." They would not have been sufficiently filled if the miracle had not fed them even more than the food.

A father's eye never looks down on his own, but rather feeds beggars with greater care the needier they are. The poor enjoy a more generous meal than a prince's, as God is more generous than humans.

Thomas of Celano, The Remembrance of the Desire of a Soul,
Second Book, XV, 44
The Founder, 276

15 APRIL

A pilgrim while in the body, away from the Lord, Francis, the man of God, strove to keep himself present in spirit to heaven, and, being already made a fellow-citizen of the angels, he was separated from them only by the wall of the flesh. With all his soul he thirsted for his Christ: to him he dedicated not only his whole heart but also his whole body. We will tell only a few things, to be imitated by posterity — to the extent that they can be told to human ears — about the wonders of his prayer, things we have seen with our own eyes.

He turned all his time into a holy leisure in which to engrave wisdom on his heart, so that, if he did not always advance, he would not seem to give up. If visits from people of the world or any kind of business intruded, he would cut them short rather than finish them, and hurry back to the things that are within. The world had no flavor to him, fed on the sweetness of heaven, and divine delicacies had spoiled him for crude human fare. He always sought out a hidden place where he could join to God not only his spirit but every member of his body. When it happened that he was suddenly overcome in public by a visitation of the Lord so as not to be without a cell, he would make a little cell out of his mantle. Sometimes, when he had no mantle, he would cover his face with his sleeve to avoid revealing the hidden manna. He would always place something between himself and bystanders so they would not notice the Bridegroom's touch. Even when crowded in the confines of a ship, he could pray unseen. Finally, when none of these things was possible, he made a temple out of his breast. Forgetful of himself he did not cough or groan; and being absorbed in God took away any hard breathing or external movement.

Thomas of Celano, The Remembrance of the Desire of a Soul,
Second Book, LVI, 94 *The Founder,* 308–9

16 APRIL

But when praying in the woods or solitary places he would fill the forest with groans, water the places with tears, strike his breast with his hand, and, as if finding a more secret hiding place, he often conversed out loud with his Lord. There he replied to the Judge, there he entreated the Father; there he conversed with the Friend, there he played with the Bridegroom. Indeed, in order to make all the marrow of his heart a holocaust in manifold ways, he would place before his eyes the One who is manifold and supremely simple. He would often ruminate inwardly with unmoving lips, and, drawing outward things inward, he raised his spirit to the heights. Thus he would direct all his attention and affection toward the one thing he asked of the Lord, not so much praying as becoming totally prayer.

How deeply would you think he was pervaded with sweetness, as he grew accustomed to such things? He knows. I can only wonder. Those with experience will be given this knowledge; but it is not granted to those with no experience. His spirit kindled, with boiling heat, his whole expression, and his whole soul melting. He was already dwelling in the highest homeland, the heavenly kingdom. The blessed Father usually neglected no visitation of the Spirit, but, whenever offered, he would follow it; and for as long as the Lord allowed, he enjoyed the sweetness thus offered him. When he was pressed by some business or occupied with travel, as he began to feel the touch of grace he would enjoy brief tastes, of the sweetest manna here and there. Even on the road, with his companions going on ahead, he would stop in his tracks, as he turned a new inspiration into something useful. He did not receive grace in vain.

Thomas of Celano, The Remembrance of the Desire of a Soul,
Second Book, LVI, 95 *The Founder,* 309–10

17 APRIL

He celebrated the canonical hours with no less awe than devotion. Although he was suffering from diseases of the eyes, stomach, spleen, and liver, he did not want to lean against a wall or partition when he was chanting the psalms. He always fulfilled his hours standing up straight and without a hood, without letting his eyes wander and without dropping syllables.

When he was travelling the world on foot, he always would stop walking in order to say the Hours, and when he was on horseback he would dismount to be on the ground. So, one day when he was returning from Rome and it was raining constantly, he got off his horse to say the Office, and, standing for quite a while, he became completely soaked. He would sometimes say: "If the body calmly eats its food, which along with itself will be food for worms, the soul should receive its food, which is its God, in great peace and tranquility."

Thomas of Celano, The Remembrance of the Desire of a Soul,
Second Book, LVII, 96
The Founder, 311

18 APRIL

Blessed Francis always had this as his highest and main goal: constantly to have in himself spiritual joy, internally and externally, outside the times of prayer and the divine office. This is also what he especially liked in his brothers, and he would, moreover, frequently rebuke them because of their acedia and sadness.

He used to say: "If a servant of God always strives to have and preserve internally and externally the spiritual joy that proceeds from purity of heart and is acquired through the devotion of prayer, the devils could do him no harm. They would say: "Since the servant of God has joy both in tribulation and in prosperity, we are not able to find an entrance to enter him and do him harm." The devils would be delighted when they can extinguish or prevent devotion and joy in the heart of a servant of God which spring from clean prayer and other virtuous deeds.

"For if the devil can have something of his own in a servant of God, he will in a short time make a single hair into a beam, always making it bigger, unless the servant of God is wise and careful, removing and destroying it as quickly as possible by means of the power of holy prayer, contrition, confession, and works of satisfaction.

"Therefore, my brothers, because spiritual joy springs from integrity of heart and the purity of constant prayer, it must be your primary concern to acquire and preserve these two virtues, to possess internal, as well as external joy. I so fervently desire and love to see this both in myself and in you, for the edification of the neighbor and the defeat of the enemy. It is the fate of the devil and his minions to be sad, and it is our lot to rejoice always and be glad in the Lord."

A Mirror of Perfection (The Sabatier Edition), VII, 95
The Prophet, 341–2

19 APRIL

Once at the beginning of the Order Saint Francis was with Brother Leo in a place where they did not have books for saying the Divine Office. When the time for Matins came, Saint Francis said to Brother Leo. "Dearest Brother, we do not have a breviary with which we can say Matins; but so that we may spend the time in praising God, I'll speak and you'll respond as I teach you. And be careful that you don't change the words into something different from what I teach you. I'll say this: "O, Brother Francis, you have done so many evil things and so many sins in the world that you are worthy of hell." And you, Brother Leo, will respond: "That's true: you deserve the lowest place in hell." And Brother Leo with dove-like simplicity responded: "Of course, Father, begin, in the name of God." Then Saint Francis began to say, "O Brother Francis, you have done so many evil things and so many sins in the world that you are worthy of hell." And Brother Leo responded, "God will do so many good things for you that you will go to Paradise." Saint Francis said, "Don't say that, Brother Leo! When I say, "Brother Francis, you have done so many evil things against God that you deserve to be cursed by God," you will respond like this: "Truly, you deserve to be put among the cursed." And Brother Leo responded, "Of course, Father." Then Saint Francis, with many tears and groans and beating his breast said in a loud voice, "O my Lord of heaven and earth, I have committed so many iniquities and sins against you, that I thoroughly deserve to be cursed by You." And Brother Leo responded, "O Brother Francis, God will do so much for you that you will be singularly blessed among the blessed." And Saint Francis, surprised that Brother Leo responded the opposite of what he had told him, rebuked him in this way: "Why don't you respond the way I teach you? I command you by holy obedience to respond as I teach you. I will say this: "O evil little Brother Francis, do you think God will have mercy on you? You have committed so many sins against the Father of mercy and God of every consolation, that you don't deserve to find mercy." And you, Brother Leo, little lamb, will respond: "You in no way deserve to find mercy." But when Saint Francis said, "O evil little Brother Francis," etc., Brother Leo responded: "God the Father, whose mercy is infinitely more than your sin, will have great mercy on you, and on top of this He will add many graces." At this response, Saint Francis, sweetly angered and patiently upset, said to Brother Leo, "And why have you got the presumption to act contrary to obedience? You've already responded several times the opposite of what I've ordered you!" Brother Leo responded very humbly and reverently, "God knows, my Father: each time I tried in my heart to respond as you commanded me, but God makes me speak as it pleases Him, not as it pleases me." Saint Francis was surprised by this, and said to Brother Leo. "I beg you most dearly that you respond this time as I've told you." Brother Leo responded, "In the name of God, say it, and this time for sure I will respond as you want." And Saint Francis said tearfully, "O evil little Brother Francis, do you think that God has mercy on you?" Brother Leo responded, "More than that, you will receive great grace from God and He will exalt you and glorify you forever, since whoever humbles himself will be exalted. And I cannot say anything else, since God speaks through my mouth." And so, in this humble contest, with many tears and much spiritual consolation, they kept vigil until daybreak.

The Little Flowers of Saint Francis, 9
The Prophet, 581–2

20 APRIL

To enumerate and recount all the things our glorious father Francis did and taught while living in the flesh would be a lengthy or an even impossible task. Who could ever express the deep affection he bore for all things that belong to God? Or who would be able to tell of the sweet tenderness he enjoyed while contemplating in creatures the wisdom, power, and goodness of the Creator? From this reflection he often overflowed with amazing, unspeakable joy as he looked at the sun, gazed at the moon, or observed the stars in the sky. What simple piety! What pious simplicity!

Even for worms he had a warm love, since he had read this text about the Savior: I am a worm and not a man [Ps 22:7]. That is why he used to pick them up from the road and put them in a safe place so that they would not be crushed by the footsteps of passers-by.

What shall I say about the other lesser creatures? In the winter he had honey or the best wine put out for the bees so that they would not perish from the cold. He used to extol the artistry of their work and their remarkable ingenuity, giving glory to the Lord. With such an outpouring, he often used up an entire day or more in praise of them and other creatures. Once the three young men in the furnace of burning fire invited all the elements to praise and glorify the Creator of all things, so this man, full of the spirit of God never stopped glorifying, praising, and blessing the Creator and Ruler of all things in all the elements and creatures.

How great do you think was the delight the beauty of flowers brought to his soul whenever he saw their lovely form and noticed their sweet fragrance? He would immediately turn his gaze to the beauty of that flower, brilliant in springtime, sprouting from the root of Jesse. By its fragrance it raised up countless thousands of the dead. Whenever he found an abundance of flowers, he used to preach to them and invite them to praise the Lord, just as if they were endowed with reason.

Fields and vineyards, rocks and woods, and all the beauties of the field, flowing springs and blooming gardens, earth and fire, air and wind: all these he urged to love of God and to willing service. Finally, he used to call all creatures by the name of "brother" and "sister" and in a wonderful way, unknown to others, he could discern the secrets of the heart of creatures like someone who has already passed into the freedom of the glory of the children of God.

O good Jesus, with the angels in heaven he now praises you as wonderful, who, when placed on earth, preached you as lovable to all creatures.

Thomas of Celano, The Life of Saint Francis, First Book, XXIX, 80–1
The Saint, 250–1

21 APRIL

Whenever he used to say your name, O holy Lord, he was moved in a way beyond human understanding. He was so wholly taken up in joy, filled with pure delight, that he truly seemed a new person of another age.

For this reason he used to gather up any piece of writing, whether divine or human, wherever he found it: on the road, in the house, on the floor. He would reverently pick it up and put it in a sacred or decent place because the name of the Lord, or something pertaining to it, might be written there.

Once a brother asked why he so carefully gathered bits of writing, even writings of pagans where the name of the Lord does not appear. He replied: "Son, I do this because they have the letters which make the glorious name of the Lord God. And the good that is found there does not belong to the pagans nor to any human being, but to God alone 'to whom belongs every good thing.'"

What is even more amazing is this: when he had letters written as greetings or admonitions he would not allow a single letter or syllable to be erased from them even when they included a repetition or mistake.

How handsome, how splendid! How gloriously he appeared in innocence of life, in simplicity of words, in purity of heart, in love of God, in fraternal charity, in enthusiastic obedience, in agreeable compliance, in angelic appearance.

Friendly in behavior, serene in nature, affable in speech, generous in encouragement, faithful in commitment, prudent in advice, efficient in endeavor, he was gracious in everything! Tranquil in mind, pleasant in disposition, sober in spirit, lifted in contemplation, tireless in prayer, he was fervent in everything!

Firm in intention, consistent in virtue, persevering in grace, he was the same in everything!

Swift to forgive, slow to grow angry, free in nature, remarkable in memory, subtle in discussing, careful in choices, he was simple in everything!

Strict with himself, kind with others, he was discerning in everything!

Thomas of Celano, The Life of Saint Francis, First Book, XXIX, 82–3
The Saint, 251–3

22 APRIL

For blessed Francis held that to beg for alms for the love of the Lord God was of very great nobility, dignity, and courtesy before God and before the world. He held this because, everything that the heavenly Father has created for a human's use, after the sin, He has given freely, as alms, both to the worthy and the unworthy on account of the love of His beloved Son.

Therefore blessed Francis would say that a servant of God must beg alms for the love of God with greater freedom and joy than someone, who, out of courtesy and generosity, wants to buy something, and goes around saying: "Whoever will give me a penny, I will give him a hundred silver pieces, nay, a thousand times more." Because a servant of God offers the love of God which a person merits when he gives alms; in comparison to which, all things in this world and even those in heaven are nothing.

The Assisi Compilation, 96
The Founder, 199

23 APRIL

"Write that I bless all my brothers, those who are and who will be in the religion until the end of the world." ... "Since I cannot speak much because of weakness and the pain of my illness, I am showing my will to my brothers briefly in these three words: as a sign of remembrance of my blessing and my testament, may they always love each other; may they always love and observe our Lady Holy Poverty; and may they always remain faithful and subject to the prelates and all the clerics of holy Mother Church."

The Siena Testament from *The Assisi Compilation,* 59
The Founder, 162

24 APRIL

We have already said that virginity, humility, and poverty were the outstanding signs of Christ Jesus and of His coming, and the first two have been somewhat examined. The third, poverty, has been constituted the hidden treasure by Jesus, Wisdom of the Father, for the acquiring of which everything must be sold. He himself led others by His example to observe it and decreed that evangelical perfection consists in poverty. For on this rock upon which the evangelical house is founded, no floods dashing into it can swamp it, no winds or downpours can shift it, no gales can knock it down. To this virtue Jesus has consigned the undisturbed possession in this life of the kingdom of heaven; whereas to the others He has merely promised its future possession. Because those who imitate true poverty in fervor of spirit must, of necessity, live off celestial fare. Because they give no thought to earthly wares and relish instead, during their present exile, the delicious crumbs that fall from the table of the angels, this is that most exalted virtue of Christ Jesus on which His unique seal is imprinted on those who strive to observe it throughout the course of their perfection. For the one who shall espouse this virtue with fullness of faith, most fervent love and unsullied observance will be lacking in no perfection. Not only is this poverty a virtue; it is the perfection and queen of all virtues. For she lays the very summits of all the virtues under her surveillance and above all, those who yield to her wishes she shapes to the likeness of Jesus, Son of God, by a renewal in which the perfecting of every state consists.

Ubertino di Casale, The Tree of the Crucified Life of Jesus, V, III, 26
The Prophet, 159–60

25 APRIL

Accordingly Francis, emulator of the likeness of Jesus from the outset of his conversion, applied his every effort to seek out holy Poverty and to follow her totally, ever eager to observe the likeness of Christ. He hesitated before no adversity, feared no menace, shrank from no toil, sought to avoid no physical discomfort, if only he could enjoy the embraces of Lady Poverty.

This inquisitive explorer began his search in the streets and in the squares of the Church, questioning individuals from different states of life on how they loved Gospel poverty. The expression he used seemed obscure, almost uncouth to his listeners. None of them ever heard of it, recoiled from the very mention of it, and practically reviled him for questioning them. "May the poverty you seek always be with you, your children and your seed after you." They said, "We should be allowed to enjoy the good things of life in affluence."

When Francis heard this from those of a common state, he said, "I'll go to the supreme pontiffs, and speak with them. Surely they have long known the way of the Lord and the judgement of God. These commoners perhaps are unknowing and foolish, ignorant of the paths their own Lord Jesus trod." Yet those pontiffs responded more harshly. "What," they said, "is this new teaching we are hearing? Who could exist without temporal possessions? Are you better than our ancestors who gave us temporalities and occupied well-endowed churches? What is this poverty that tells us little? We do not know what you are talking about."

Ubertino di Casale, The Tree of the Crucified Life of Jesus,
V, III, 57, 426a1, 8
The Prophet, 160

26 APRIL

Francis was amazed. Drunk with the spirit of poverty, he turned to the pursuit of prayer and began to invoke Jesus, the teacher of poverty:

"O Lord Jesus show me the pathways of your beloved Poverty. I know that the Old Testament was a figure of the New, and that there you promised: "Wherever the sole of your foot treads will be yours [Dt 11:24]." To tread underfoot is to despise.

Poverty treads on everything, and therefore she is queen of all things. But, my good Lord Jesus, pity me and Lady Poverty. For I, too, languish with love for her nor can I find rest without her. My Lord, you know it, you who loved me because of her. But even she sits in sorrow, rejected by all. How like a widowed woman has she become, she that was great among the nations, abject and pitiful. She, queen of all virtues, is now moaning on her dunghill because her friends have all betrayed her and become her enemies, and these are the very ones who for long have proved themselves adulterers and not spouses.

"Look, Lord Jesus, how poverty is the great queen of the virtues, for the reason that You, leaving the angelic dwelling-places, came down to earth that You could espouse her in perpetual charity and in her, from her, and by her produce all the sons of perfection. And she clung to You with such fidelity that Your esteem for her began in Your own mother's womb, for You had, as is believed, the most diminutive of human bodies which, once it came forth from the womb, found its rest in the holy manger and stable. As long as You lived in the world, You so deprived yourself of everything as to lack even a place to lay Your head. Further, that faithful consort of Yours accompanied You loyally when You came to do battle for our redemption. And in the very conflict of the Passion, she stood by You as Your personal armor-bearer. And though the disciples abandoned You and denied Your name, she did not forsake You. Rather did she keep You, together with the whole company of her princes, close to those who remained faithful.

"At that time Your own mother was alone in devoting herself to You and languishing with love for You as she joined in Your sufferings. Yet even for such a mother the cross was too high to reach and touch you. But Lady Poverty, destitute of everything, like Your dearest handmaid was embracing You more closely than ever before, her whole heart involved in Your torments. She was so deprived that she had leisure neither to smooth the cross nor put it together in rustic fashion, nor to manufacture as many nails as there would be wounds, nor yet to sharpen and refine them. All she could get ready were three, uneven and twisted ones to aid Your torments. Then, when You were dying of burning thirst, that faithful spouse was there to assist You. For when You could not obtain a little water, she made up a drink from what she could get from shameful lackeys, which was so bitter that You could only taste it rather than actually drink it. And so in the close embrace of Your spouse You breathed Your last.

Nor was this loyal spouse absent from Your burial. For she would permit You to have nothing connected with ointments and linen that was not lent by others. Nor yet was Your most holy spouse missing from Your resurrection: for, rising gloriously in her embraces, You left behind in the tomb everything that had been lent for the occasion of Your burial. You carried her with You to heaven, leaving to the worldly all that belonged to the world. And You bequeathed to Lady Poverty the seal of the kingdom of heaven, for the signing of the elect who wished to walk the path of perfection.

"Oh, who is there who would not love this Lady Poverty above all other things? I beg You that I be signed with the entitlement that is hers to give. I desire to be enriched with the treasure she is. O most poor Jesus, I petition You, for the sake of Your name, that this be the property my brothers and I will have for ever, namely, never to be able to own anything under heaven. And let this flesh of mine, as long as it lives, be sustained always, though in utter frugality, by fare that comes from others."

Ubertino di Casale, The Tree of the Crucified Life of Jesus,
V, III, 18, 20, 33, 48, 426b6, 14
The Prophet, 160–2

27 APRIL

The Kindest One granted his petition by putting into his heart and revealing to his mind an understanding of poverty's height and gave him the desire to imitate it to the full. By a singular privilege — beyond all earlier saints — he wished him to transmit this to his followers, so that it would be unique to his religion: never to be able to have anything under heaven whatever as its own, but to live by the strict use of the things of others.

It was never Francis's wish to break his sacred association either with the Lady Poverty or Worldly Persecution, both of whom Christ had as lawful wives. On the contrary he wanted to love them both with an equal amount of charity, or rather with one and the same charity, since they are not really two but one. Therefore, in order completely to gain possession of the kingdom of heaven, which has been given to them both, he would have nothing to do with all those ways in which persecutors can be bypassed. It was because the rights of privilege stifle poverty and annul persecution, thus effectively divorcing a sacred marriage; for this reason, he wanted no papal document, no privilege. All he wished for was that his poverty not be sullied. And now he grieves over being fraudulently despoiled of her by the conduct of his descendants. For this status went down from Jerusalem to Jericho and fell among robbers, who did not leave it half dead, but completely dead! It now gives off a four-day-old stink, since they shut it up in a tomb. And having got what they wanted, they now boast about it in a wild frenzy. This disintegration the saint foresaw and fought to elude in no uncertain fashion his whole life long.

His Legend speaks of what he found most offensive to look at, namely, anything in the brothers that was not completely consistent with poverty. He used to instruct the brothers to build, as poor people have to, poor little houses, which they were not to dwell in as if their own, but more like pilgrims and strangers in places belonging to others. By this he meant that if people wanted to evict them they were to offer no resistance, no right of their own or of another, no ownership, no clever ploy, or delaying tactic. They should simply get off other people's property and clear away, with complete trust in the Lord, in the conviction that they are now called, through the Holy Spirit, to go elsewhere, even if this means facing the fury of persecutors.

And this is why poverty and earthly persecution are sisters and why the keys of the kingdom of heaven are given them, not just in promise but to possess. For persecution is able to sweep away an entire world, while evangelical poverty has no power to defend what is mundane. The most prudent Creator made none of his creatures without its proper place; and since Poverty and Persecution had in this world no place they could call their own, he gave them heavenly mansions. Certainly the unspiritual person cannot take in these thoughts, nor do they make any sense to Lady Poverty's defiler, or to him whose dealings with her are a forced service and who craftily churns up his caricature of "poor use." Yet those that have the spirit of Christ, who taught and lived poverty, have ears for these things and gladly observe them.

Ubertino di Casale, The Tree of the Crucified Life of Jesus,
V, III, 21, 27, 45, 56, 427a1
The Prophet, 162–4

28 APRIL

As the merits of Saint Francis increased, his quarrel with the ancient serpent also increased. The greater his gift, the more subtle the serpent's attempts, and the more violent his attacks on him. Although he had often shown himself to be a mighty warrior who had not yielded in the struggle even for an hour, still the serpent tried to attack the one who always won.

At one time a very serious temptation of spirit came upon the holy father, surely to embellish his crown. Because of it he was filled with anguish and sorrow; he afflicted and chastised his body, he prayed and wept bitterly. He was under attack in this way for several years, until one day while praying at Saint Mary of the Portiuncula, he heard in spirit a voice: "Francis, if you had faith like a mustard seed, you would tell the mountain to move from here, and it would move." The saint replied: "Lord, what is the mountain that I could move?" And again he heard: "The mountain is your temptation." And he said, sobbing: "Lord, be it done to me as you have said!" At once the whole temptation was driven away. He was set free and inwardly became completely calm.

Thomas of Celano, The Remembrance of the Desire of a Soul,
Second Book, LXXXI, 115
The Founder, 324

29 APRIL

Just as our Lord Jesus Christ says in the Gospel: "I know my sheep, and my sheep know me..." [Jn 10:14] so the blessed Father Saint Francis, as a good shepherd, knew by divine inspiration all the merits and virtues of his companions and also knew their failings; therefore he knew how to provide the best remedies for them all, that is: humbling the proud; exalting the humble; reviling vices and praising virtues, just as we read in the amazing revelations he had about his earliest family.

Among these we find that once Saint Francis was in a certain place with that same family conversing about God, and Brother Rufino was not with them for that conversation, but was in the woods in contemplation. As that conversation about God continued, Brother Rufino came out of the woods and passed by, a short distance from them. Then Saint Francis, seeing him, turned to the companions and questioned them, saying: "Tell me, which is the holiest soul that God has in this world?" And they replied that they thought that it was his. And Saint Francis said to them: "My dear brothers, of myself I'm the most vile man that God has in this world. But do you see this Brother Rufino who's now coming out of the woods? God has revealed to me that his soul is one of the three holiest souls in the world. And I tell you confidently that I wouldn't hesitate to call him Saint Rufino during his lifetime, since his soul is confirmed in grace, and sanctified and canonized in heaven by our Lord Jesus Christ." And Saint Francis would never say these words in the presence of that same Brother Rufino.

In a similar way, how Saint Francis knew the faults of his brothers can be clearly seen regarding Brother Elias, whom he often rebuked for his pride; and regarding Brother John de Capella, about whom he predicted that he would hang himself by the neck; and regarding that brother whom the devil held tightly by the throat when he was being corrected for his disobedience; and regarding many other brothers whose secret faults and whose virtues he knew clearly by Christ's revelation.

The Little Flowers of Saint Francis, 31
The Prophet, 621–2

30 APRIL

From the time when this holy man had turned to Christ and cast the things of this world into oblivion, he never wanted to lie on a mattress or place his head on a feather pillow. He never broke this strict resolution, even when he was sick or receiving the hospitality of strangers. But it happened that while he was staying at the hermitage of Greccio his eye disease became worse than usual, and he was forced against his will to use a small pillow. The first night, during the morning vigil, the saint called his companion and said to him: "Brother, I couldn't sleep this whole night, or remain upright and pray. My head was spinning, my knees were giving way, and the whole framework of my body was shaking as if I had eaten bread made from rye grass. I believe," he added, "there's a devil in this pillow I have for my head. Take it away, because I don't want the devil by my head any more."

The brother, sympathizing with the father's complaint, caught the pillow thrown at him to take away. But as he was leaving, he suddenly lost the power of speech. Struck by terror and paralyzed, he could not move his feet from where he stood nor could he move his arms. After a moment, the saint recognized this and called him. He was set free, came back in and told him what he had suffered. The saint said to him: "Last night as I was saying compline I knew for certain that the devil had come into my cell. Our enemy," he added, "is very cunning and subtle; when he can't harm you inside, in your soul, he at least gives you cause for complaint in your body."

Let those listen who prepare little pillows on every side so that wherever they fall they will land on something soft! The devil gladly follows luxury; he delights in standing by elegant beds, especially where necessity does not demand them and profession forbids them. On the other hand the ancient serpent flees from a naked man, either because he despises the company of the poor or because he fears the heights of poverty. If a brother realizes that the devil is underneath feathers he will be satisfied with straw under his head.

Thomas of Celano, The Remembrance of the Desire of a Soul, Second Book, XXXIV, 64
The Founder, 289–90

May

1 MAY

What tongue could tell of this man's compassion for the poor? He certainly had an inborn kindness, doubled by the piety poured out on him. Therefore, Francis's soul melted for the poor, and to those to whom he could not extend a hand, he extended his affection. Any need, any lack he noticed in anyone, with a rapid change of thought, he turned back to Christ. In that way he read the Son of our Poor Lady in every poor person. As she held Him naked in her hands so he carried Him naked in his heart. Although he had driven away all envy from himself, he could not give up his envy of poverty. If he saw people poorer than himself, he immediately envied them and, contending with a rival for poverty was afraid he would be overcome.

It happened one day when the man of God was going about preaching he met a poor man on the road. Seeing the man's nakedness, he was deeply moved and, turning to his companion, said: "This man's need brings great shame on us; it passes a harsh judgment on our poverty." "How so, brother?" his companion replied. The saint answered in a sad voice: "I chose Poverty for my riches and for my Lady, but look: she shines brighter in this man. Don't you know that the whole world has heard that we are the poorest of all for Christ? But this poor man proves it is otherwise!"

Oh enviable envy! Oh rivalry to be rivaled by his children! This is not the envy that is distressed by the good fortune of others; nor that which grows dim in the sun's rays, opposed to piety and tormented by spite. Do you think that Gospel poverty has nothing worth envying? She has Christ himself, and through him has all in all. Why do you pant after stipends, clerics of today? Tomorrow you will know Francis was rich when you find in your hand the stipend of torments.

Thomas of Celano, *The Remembrance of the Desire of a Soul*,
Second Book, LI, 83–4
The Founder, 302–3

2 MAY

Another day, when he was preaching, a sick poor man came to the place. Taking pity on the man's double misfortune — that is, his need and his illness — he began to speak about poverty with his companion. And since suffering with the suffering, he had moved beyond to the depths of his heart, when the saint's companion said to him: "My brother, it is true that he is poor, but it could be that in the whole province there is no one who desires riches more!" At once the saint rebuked him, and as the companion acknowledged his fault, said to him: "Quickly now, strip off your tunic; throw yourself down at the poor man's feet and confess your fault! And, don't just ask his pardon, but also beg for his prayers!" The brother obeyed, made his amends and returned. The saint said to him: "Brother, whenever you see a poor person, a mirror of the Lord and his poor Mother is placed before you. Likewise in the sick, look closely for the infirmities which He accepted for our sake."

Ah! Always a bundle of myrrh abided in Francis. Always he gazed upon the face of his Christ. Always he caressed the Man of Sorrows, familiar with suffering.

Thomas of Celano, The Remembrance of the Desire of a Soul,
Second Book, LI, 85
The Founder, 303

3 MAY

Completely absorbed in the love of God, blessed Francis perfectly discerned the goodness of God not only in his own soul, already adorned in the perfection of every virtue, but also in any creature whatever. Because of this, by a singular and profound love, he was moved toward creatures, especially to those in which something of God or something pertaining to religion was symbolized.

Of all the birds, he particularly loved a little bird called the lark, commonly called the cowled lark. Concerning these, he used to say: "Sister Lark has a capuche like religious, and is a humble bird, because she gladly goes along the road looking for some grain. Even if she finds it in manure, she pecks it out and eats it. While flying, she praises the Lord very sweetly, like good religious looking down on earthly things, whose way of life is always in heaven and intention is always for the praise of God. Her clothes, that is, her feathers, resemble the earth and give an example to religious not to wear colorful and refined clothing, but those of a cheaper price and color, just as the earth is of little worth compared to the other elements."

And because he considered these things in them, he was very glad to see them. Therefore it pleased the Lord that these little birds should show some signs of affection for him at the hour of his death. For on the Saturday evening after vespers, before the night on which he passed to the Lord, a great flock of these birds called larks came over the roof of the house where he lay, and flying low and wheeling in a circle around the roof and singing sweetly, they seemed to praise the Lord.

A Mirror of Perfection, XI, 113
The Prophet, 362–3

4 MAY

The first companions of Saint Francis strove with all their strength to be poor in earthly things and rich in virtues, by which one arrives at true riches, heavenly and eternal.

It happened that one day when they were gathered together to speak about God, one of them gave this example: "There was someone who was a great friend of God, and he had great grace in active life and contemplative life; and with this he had such excessive humility that he thought himself the greatest of sinners. This humility sanctified him and confirmed him in grace, and made him grow constantly in virtues and the gifts of God, and never allowed him to fall into sin." As Brother Masseo heard such wonderful things about humility and realized that this was a treasure of eternal life, he began to be so inflamed with love and desire for this virtue of humility that, raising his face to heaven in great fervor, he made a vow and a very firm promise never to be happy in this world until he felt this virtue perfectly in his soul. And from then on he remained almost constantly enclosed in a cell, mortifying himself with fasting, vigils, prayers and loud weeping before God, to receive from Him this virtue, without which he believed himself worthy of hell, and with which that friend of God was so gifted, as he had heard.

As Brother Masseo remained many days with this desire, he happened one day to go into the woods and, in fervor of spirit, walked through the woods pouring out tears, sighs and cries, asking God for this divine virtue with fervent desire. And since God willingly hears the prayers of the humble and contrite, as Brother Masseo remained in this state a voice came from heaven and called him twice: "Brother Masseo! Brother Masseo!" Knowing in spirit that it was the voice of Christ, he replied: "My Lord!" And Christ said to him: "And what do you want to give to have this grace you ask?" Brother Masseo responded: "Lord, I want to give the eyes in my head." And Christ said to him: "And I want you to have the grace and the eyes too." At these words the voice disappeared; and Brother Masseo remained full of such grace of that desired virtue of humility and of the light of God that from then on he was always jubilant. Often when he was praying, he would constantly make a formless cry of joy with a soft voice like a dove: "Ooo, Ooo, Ooo;" and would remain in contemplation with a happy face and cheerful heart. And with this, having become very humble, he considered himself the least of all the people of the world.

When asked by Brother James of Fallerone why he did not change the tune in his cry of joy he responded with great joy that when in one thing all good is found, there is no need to change the tune.

The Little Flowers of Saint Francis, 32
The Prophet, 622–3

5 MAY

This happy traveler, hurrying to leave the world as the exile of pilgrimage, was helped, and not just a little, by what is in the world. Toward the princes of darkness, he certainly used it as a field of battle. Toward God, however, he used it as the clearest mirror of goodness. In art he praises the Artist; whatever he discovers in creatures he guides to the Creator. He rejoices in all the works of the Lord's hands, and through their delightful display he gazes on their life-giving reason and cause. In beautiful things he discerns Beauty Itself; all good things cry out to him: "The One who made us is the Best." Following the footprints imprinted on creatures, he follows his Beloved everywhere; out of them all he makes for himself a ladder by which he might reach the Throne.

He embraces all things with an intensity of unheard devotion, speaking to them about the Lord and exhorting them to praise Him.

He spares lanterns, lamps, and candles unwilling to use his hand to put out their brightness which is a sign of the eternal light.

He walked reverently over rocks, out of respect for Him who is called the Rock. When he came to the verse "You have set me high upon the rock," in order to express it more respectfully, he would say: "You have set me high under the feet of the Rock."

When the brothers are cutting wood he forbids them to cut down the whole tree, so that it might have hope of sprouting again.

He commands the gardener to leave the edges of the garden undisturbed, so that in their season the green of herbs and the beauty of flowers may proclaim the beautiful Father of all. He even orders that within the garden a smaller garden should be set aside for aromatic and flowering herbs so that those who see them may recall the memory of eternal savor.

He picks up little worms from the road so they will not be trampled underfoot.

That the bees not perish of hunger in the icy winter, he commands that honey and the finest wine should be set out for them.

He calls all animals by a fraternal name, although, among all kinds of beasts, he especially loves the meek.

Who is capable of describing all of this? Truly, that fountain-like goodness, which will be all in all, already shone clearly in all for this saint.

Thomas of Celano, The Remembrance of the Desire of a Soul,
Second Book, CXXIV, 165
The Founder, 353–4

6 MAY

All creatures, therefore, strive to return the saint's love, and to respond to his kindness with their gratitude. They smile at his caress, his requests they grant, they obey his commands.

It may be good to tell of a few cases. At the time of an eye disease, he is forced to let himself be treated by a physician. A surgeon is called to the place, and when he comes he is carrying an iron instrument for cauterizing. He ordered it to be placed in the fire until it became red hot. But the blessed Father, to comfort the body, which was struck with panic, spoke to the fire: "My brother Fire, your beauty is the envy of all creatures, the Most High created you strong, beautiful and useful. Be gracious to me in this hour; be courteous! For a long time I have loved you in the Lord. I pray the Great Lord who created you to temper now your heat that I may bear your gentle burning."

When the prayer is finished, he makes the sign of the cross over the fire and then remains in place unshaken. The surgeon takes in his hands the red-hot glowing iron. The brothers, overcome by human feeling, run away. The saint joyfully and eagerly offered himself to the iron. The hissing iron sinks into tender flesh, and the burn is extended slowly straight from the ear to the eyebrow. How much pain that burning caused can best be known by the witness of the saint's words, since it was he that felt it. For when the brothers who had fled return, the father says with a smile: "Oh, you weak souls of little heart; why did you run away? Truly I say to you, I did not feel the fire's heat, nor any pain in my flesh." And turning to the doctor, he says: "If the flesh isn't well cooked, try again!" The doctor had experienced quite a different reaction in similar situations, exalts this as a divine miracle, saying: "I tell you, brothers; today I have seen wonderful things!" I believe he had returned to primeval innocence, for when he wished, the harshest things grew gentle.

> Thomas of Celano, The Remembrance of the Desire of a Soul,
> Second Book, CXXV, 165
> *The Founder,* 354–5

7 MAY

Let those who wish to stay in hermitages in a religious way be three brothers or, at the most, four; let two of these be "the mother" and have two "sons" or at least one. Let the two who are "mothers" keep the life of Martha and the two "sons" the life of Mary and let one have one enclosure in which each one may have his cell in which he may pray and sleep.

And let them always recite Compline of the day immediately after sunset and strive to maintain silence, recite their Hours, rise for Matins, and seek first the kingdom of God and His justice. And let them recite Prime at the proper hour and, after Terce, they may end their silence, speak with and go to their mothers. And when it pleases them, they can beg alms from them as poor little ones out of love of the Lord God. And afterwards let them recite Sext, None and, at the proper hour, Vespers.

And they may not permit anyone to enter or eat in the enclosure where they dwell. Let those brothers who are the "mothers" strive to stay far from everyone and, because of obedience to their minister, protect their "sons" from everyone so that no one can speak with them. And those "sons" may not talk with anyone except with their "mothers" and with the minister and his custodian when it pleases them to visit with the Lord's blessing.

The "sons," however, may periodically assume the role of the "mothers," taking turns for a time as they have mutually decided. Let them strive to observe conscientiously and eagerly everything mentioned above.

A Rule for Hermitages
The Saint, 61–2

8 MAY

Seeing how some were panting for prelacies, an ambition which even by itself made them unworthy of presiding, he said that they were not Lesser Brothers, but that they had fallen away from glory by forgetting the vocation to which they were called. He criticized the wretched few who were upset when removed from office; they were looking for honors, not burdens.

He once said to his companion: "I would not consider myself a Lesser Brother unless I had the attitude which I will describe to you." And he said: "Here I am, a prelate of the brothers, and I go to the chapter. I preach to the brothers and admonish them, and, in the end, they speak against me: 'An uneducated and despicable man is not right for us; we do not want you to rule over us. You cannot speak; you are simple and ignorant.' So in the end I'm thrown out in disgrace, looked down upon by everyone. I tell you, unless I hear these words with the same expression on my face, with the same joy in my heart, and with the same resolution for holiness, then I am in no sense a Lesser Brother." And he would add: "In a prelacy there is a fall; in praise, a precipice; in the humility of a subject, profit for the soul. Why, then, do we pay attention to danger more than profits, while we have time for making profit?"

Thomas of Celano, The Remembrance of the Desire of a Soul,
Second Book, CVI, 145
The Founder, 340–1

9 MAY

A young man one day caught many doves and was carrying them off to sell. Saint Francis met him and, always having singular kindness for meek animals, looking at those doves with a look of pity, said to the young man: "O good young man, I beg you to give them to me, so that such innocent birds, which are compared in Scripture to chaste, humble and faithful souls, may not fall into the hands of cruel people who will kill them." The young man, inspired by God, gave them all to Saint Francis, and he, taking them to his breast, began to speak sweetly to them: "O my sister doves, simple, chaste and innocent, why did you let yourselves be caught? Now, you see, I want to rescue you from death and make nests for you so that you can bear fruit and multiply according to our Creator's command."

And Saint Francis went and made nests for them all. And they used them, and began to lay eggs and raise their young among the brothers. They stayed and behaved tamely with Saint Francis and the other brothers as if they were chickens that the brothers had always fed. And they never departed unless Saint Francis with his blessing gave them permission to leave.

Saint Francis said to the boy who gave him the doves: "Son, you will yet become a brother in this Order and you will graciously serve Jesus Christ." And so it happened: that young man became a brother, and lived in the Order with great holiness.

The Little Flowers of Saint Francis, 22
The Prophet, 604

10 MAY

This place [the Portiuncula] the holy man loved more than other places in the world; for here he began humbly, here he progressed virtuously, here he ended happily. This place he entrusted to his brothers at his death as the most beloved of the Virgin.

Before his conversion, a certain brother, dedicated to God, had a vision about this church which is worth telling. He saw countless people who had been stricken with blindness, on their knees in a circle around this church, with their faces raised to heaven. All of them, with tearful voices and uplifted hands, were crying out to God, begging for mercy and light. Then a great light came down from heaven and, diffusing itself through them, gave each the sight and health they desired.

This is the place where the Order of Lesser Brothers was begun by Saint Francis under the prompting of divine revelation. For at the bidding of divine providence which guided Christ's servant in everything, he built up three material churches before he preached the Gospel and began the Order not only to ascend in an orderly progression from the sensible to the intelligible, from the lesser to the greater, but also to symbolize mystically in external actions perceived by the senses what he would do in the future. For like the three buildings he built up, so the Church — where there is victory for the triple army of those being saved — was to be renewed in three ways under his leadership: by the form, rule, and teaching of Christ which he would provide. And now we see that this prophecy has been fulfilled.

Bonaventure, The Major Legend of Saint Francis, II, 8
The Founder, 540-1

11 MAY

Many times he was often suspended in such sweetness of contemplation that he was carried away above himself and experienced things beyond human understanding, which he would not reveal to anyone.

However, one incident that did become known shows us how frequently he was absorbed in heavenly sweetness. One time he was riding on a donkey and had to pass through Borgo San Sepolcro, and when he stopped to rest at the dwelling of some lepers, many found out about the visit of the man of God. Men and women came running from every direction to see him, and with their usual devotion wanting to touch him. What then? They touched and pulled him, cut off bits of his tunic, but the man seemed not to feel any of this. He noticed as much of what was happening as if he were a lifeless corpse. They finally came to the place, and were long past Borgo, when that contemplator of heaven, as returning from somewhere else, anxiously inquired when they would be reaching Borgo.

Thomas of Celano, The Remembrance of the Desire of a Soul,
Second Book, LXIV, 98
The Founder, 312

12 MAY

Once he saw a companion with a sad and depressed face and, not taking it kindly, said to him: "It is not right for a servant of God to show himself to others sad and upset, but always pleasant. Deal with your offences in your room, and weep and moan before your God. But when you come back to your brothers, put away your sorrow and conform to the others." A little later he added: "Those who envy the salvation of humankind bear a grudge against me, and when they cannot disturb me, they try to do it among my companions."

He so loved the man filled with spiritual joy, that at one chapter he had these words written down as a general admonition: "Let them be careful not to appear outwardly as sad and gloomy hypocrites but show themselves joyful, cheerful, and consistently gracious in the Lord."

Thomas of Celano, The Remembrance of the Desire of a Soul,
Second Book, XCI, 128
The Founder, 331

13 MAY

A barely seven-year-old son of a notary of the city of Rome wanted in his childish way to follow his mother who was going to the church of San Marco to hear a preacher. He was turned back by his mother and her refusal upset him. By some diabolical impulse — I do not know why — he threw himself from the window of the building and, shaking with a last tremor, he came to know the passing of death, the common lot of all. The mother had not gone far, and the sound of someone falling made her suspect the fall of her treasure. She quickly returned home and saw her son lifeless. She turned avenging hands on herself; her neighbors rushed out at her screams; and doctors were called to the dead boy. But could they raise the dead? The time for prognoses and prescriptions was past. He was in the hands of God: that much the doctors could determine, but could not help. Since all warmth and life were gone, all feeling, movement and strength, the doctors determined he was dead.

Brother Rao, of the Order of Lesser Brothers and a well-known preacher in Rome, was on his way to preach there. He approached the boy and, full of faith, spoke to the father. "Do you believe that Francis, the saint of God, is able to raise your son from the dead because of the love he always had for the Son of God, the Lord Jesus Christ?" The father replied, "I firmly believe and confess it. I will be his lasting servant, and I will regularly visit his holy place." That brother knelt with his companion in prayer and urged all those present to pray. With that the boy began to yawn a little, lift his arms and sit up. His mother ran and embraced her son; the father was beside himself for joy. All the people, filled with wonder, marveled and, shouting, praised Christ and His saint. In the sight of all the boy immediately began walking, restored to full life.

Thomas of Celano, The Treatise on the Miracles of Saint Francis, VII, 42
The Founder, 421

14 MAY

At the time when Brother Conrad and Brother Peter, two shining stars in the Province of the March and both heavenly men, were staying together at the place of Forano, in the custody of Ancona, there was such love and charity between them that it seemed there was one and the same heart and soul between the two of them; they bound each other to this pact: that every consolation which the mercy of God gave to them, they should both reveal to each other in charity.

Having sealed this pact, it happened one day that while Brother Peter was in prayer, thinking devoutly about the Passion of Christ, and how the most Blessed Mother of Christ and the most beloved John the Evangelist and Saint Francis were painted at the foot of the cross, crucified with Christ through suffering of spirit, a desire came to him, to know which of those three had experienced the greatest suffering over the Passion of Christ: the Mother who had given Him birth; or the disciple who had slept on His breast; or Saint Francis who was crucified with Christ. And while he was in this devout thought, there appeared to him the Virgin Mary with Saint John the Evangelist and Saint Francis, clothed in the most noble clothing of blessed glory; but Saint Francis appeared dressed in clothing more beautiful than Saint John's. As Brother Peter was completely startled by this vision, Saint John comforted him and said to him: "Do not fear, dearest Brother, because we have come to console you and clear up your doubt for you. So you should know that the Mother of Christ and I more than any creature suffered over the Passion of Christ; but after us Saint Francis felt greater suffering than any other; and therefore you see him in such glory." And Brother Peter asked him: "Most Holy Apostle of Christ, why does the clothing of Saint Francis appear more beautiful than yours?" Saint John replied: "The reason is this: because when he was in the world he wore more vile clothing than mine." After saying these words, Saint John gave to Brother Peter a glorious robe that he held in his hand and said to him: "Take this robe, which I have brought to give to you." And as Saint John wanted to dress him in that robe, Brother Peter fell to the ground, startled, and began to cry out: "Brother Conrad, Brother Conrad, quick, help me, come and see amazing things!" And at these words, that holy vision disappeared. When Brother Conrad arrived, he told him everything in detail, and they gave thanks to God.

The Little Flowers of Saint Francis, 44
The Prophet, 639–40

15 MAY

Sometimes he used to do this: a sweet melody of the spirit bubbling up inside him would become a French tune on the outside; the thread of a divine whisper which his ears heard secretly would break out in a French song of joy. Other times — as I saw with my own eyes — he would pick up a stick from the ground and put it over his left arm, while holding a bow bent with a string in his right hand, drawing it over the stick as if it were a viola, performing all the right movements, and in French would sing about the Lord. All this dancing often ended in tears, and the song of joy dissolved into compassion for Christ's suffering. Then the saint would sigh without stopping, and sob without ceasing. Forgetful of lower things he had in hand, he was caught up to heaven.

Thomas of Celano, The Remembrance of the Desire of a Soul,
Second Book, XC, 127
The Founder, 331

16 MAY

Because whoever belongs to God hears the words of God, we who are more especially charged with divine responsibilities must not only listen to and do what the Lord says but also care for the vessels and other liturgical objects that contain His holy words in order to impress on ourselves the sublimity of our Creator and our subjection to Him. I, therefore, admonish all my brothers and encourage them in Christ to venerate, as best as they can, the divine written words wherever they find them. If they are not well kept or are carelessly thrown around in some place, let them gather them up and preserve them, inasmuch as it concerns them, honoring in the words the Lord Who spoke them. For many things are made holy by the words of God and the sacrament of the altar is celebrated in the power of the words of Christ.

A Letter to the Entire Order, 34–7
The Saint, 119

17 MAY

As he neared the end of his call to the Lord, a brother who was always concerned about the things of God, asked him a question out of piety for the Order. "Father, you will pass on, and the family of your followers will be left behind in this vale of tears. Point out someone in the Order, if you know one, on whom your spirit may rest, and on whom the weight of the general ministry may safely be laid."

Saint Francis, drawing a sigh with every word, replied as follows: "Son, I find no one adequate to be the leader of such a varied army, or the shepherd of such a widespread flock. But I would like to paint one for you, or make one by hand, as the phrase goes, to show clearly what kind of person the father of this family should be.

"He must be a very dignified person, of great discernment, and of praiseworthy reputation. He must be without personal favorites, lest by loving some more than others, he create scandal for all. He must be a committed friend of holy prayer, who can distribute some hours for his soul and others for the flock entrusted to him. Early in the morning, he must put first the sacrament of the Mass, and with prolonged devotion commend himself and his flock to divine protection. After prayer, he must make himself available for all to pick at him, and he should respond to all and provide for all with meekness. He must be someone who does not create sordid favoritism toward persons, but will take as much care of the lesser and simple brothers as of the learned and greater ones. Even if he should be allowed to excel in gifts of learning, he should all the more bear in his behavior the image of holy simplicity, and nourish this virtue.

"He should loathe money, the principal corrupter of our profession and perfection; as the head of a poor religion, offering himself to others as someone to be imitated, he must never engage in the abuse of using any money pouch. For with his needs," he said, "a habit and a little book should be enough, and, for the brothers' needs, he should have a pen case and seal. He should not be a book collector, or too intent on reading, so he does not take away from his duties what he spends on his studies.

"Let him be someone who comforts the afflicted, and the final refuge of the distressed, so that the sickness of despair does not overcome the sick because he did not offer healing remedies. In order to bend rebels to meekness, let him lower himself, let go of some of his rights that he may gain a soul for Christ. As for runaways from the Order, let him not close a heart of mercy to them, for they are like lost sheep; and he knows how overpowering the temptations can be which can push someone to such a fall."

Thomas of Celano, The Remembrance of the Desire of a Soul,
Second Book, CXXXIX, 184–5
The Founder, 364–5

18 MAY

"I want all to honor him as standing in Christ's place, and I wish that all his needs be provided for with every kindness. He should not enjoy honors, or delight in approval more than insults. If he should need more substantial food when he is sick or tired, he should not eat it in secret but in a public place, so that others may be freed from embarrassment at having to provide for their weak bodies. It especially pertains to him to discern what is hidden in consciences and to draw out the truth from its hidden veins, not lending an ear to gossips. Finally, he must be one who would never allow the desire for preserving honor to weaken the strong figure of justice, and he must feel such a great office more a burden than an honor. And yet, excessive meekness should not give birth to slackness, nor loose indulgence to a breaking down of discipline, so that, loved by all, he is feared, nonetheless, by those who work evil.

"I would like him to have companions endowed with honesty, who, like him, show themselves an example of all good works: stern against pleasures, strong against difficulties, and yet friendly in the right way, so that they receive all who come to them with holy cheerfulness. There," he concluded, "that is the kind of person the general minister of the Order should be."

The blessed Father also demanded all these things in provincial ministers, though each ought to stand out even more in the general minister. He wanted them to be friendly to the lesser ones, and peaceful and kind so that those who committed faults would not be afraid to entrust themselves to their affection. He wanted them to be moderate in commanding, gracious when offended, more willing to bear injuries than to inflict them; enemies of vice but healers of the vice-ridden. In short, he wanted them to be men whose life would be a mirror of discipline for others. He would have them honored and loved in every way, as those who bear the burden of cares and labor. He said they deserved the highest rewards before God if they rule the souls committed to them according to this model and this law.

>Thomas of Celano, The Remembrance of the Desire of a Soul,
>Second Book, CXXXIX–CXL, 186–7
>*The Founder,* 365–6

19 MAY

In this way this man rejected any glory which did not recall Christ: in this way he inflicted everlasting anathema on human favor. He realized that the price of fame is to lose privacy of conscience, and that misusing virtues is much more harmful than not having them. He knew that protecting what you have is as virtuous as seeking what you lack. Ah! Vanity inspires us more than charity; and the world's approval prevails over the love of Christ. We do not discern initiatives; we do not test the spirits. And so, when vanity drives us to do something we imagine it was prompted by charity. Furthermore, if we do even a little good, we cannot bear its weight, while we are living we keep unloading it, and let it slip away as we approach the final shore. We can patiently accept not being good. What we cannot bear is not being considered good, not appearing good. And so we live only for human praise, since we are only human.

>Thomas of Celano, The Remembrance of the Desire of a Soul,
>Second Book, CI, 139
>*The Founder,* 336–7

20 MAY

Humility is the guardian and embellishment of all virtues. Any spiritual building without this foundation may appear to rise higher but is headed for ruin. So that this man, adorned with so many gifts, should lack nothing, this gift filled him more abundantly. In his own opinion he was nothing but a sinner, though he was the beauty and splendor of every kind of holiness.

It was on this that he strove to build himself, to lay the foundation as he had learned from Christ. Forgetting what he had gained, he kept before his eyes only what he lacked, considering that more was lacking in him than present. Not satisfied with his first virtues, his only ambition was to become better and to add new ones. Humble in manner, he was more humble in opinion, and most humble in his own estimation. This prince of God could not be identified as a prelate, except by this sparkling gem: he was the least among the lesser. This virtue, this title, this badge pointed him out as general minister. There was no arrogance in his mouth, no pomp in his gestures, no conceit in his actions. He learned by revelation the meaning of many things, but when he was conversing among others he put the opinions of others ahead of his own. He considered the opinions of his companions safer than his own and the views of others better than his own. He would say that a man had not yet given up everything for God as long as he held on to the moneybag of his own opinions. He would rather hear himself blamed than praised, since the former moved him to change while the latter pushed him to fall.

Thomas of Celano, The Remembrance of the Desire of a Soul,
Second Book, CII, 140
The Founder, 337–8

21 MAY

Once, when he was preaching to the people of Terni, the bishop of that city commended him to everyone at the end of the sermon, saying: "In this last hour God has honored his Church by means of this little, poor, and looked down upon man, simple and unlettered. And because of this we should always praise the Lord, realizing that he has not done this for every nation."

When the saint heard this, he accepted it with deep feeling, for the bishop had so expressly referred to him as a contemptible man. Entering the church, he fell down at the bishop's feet, saying: "My Lord Bishop, in truth you have done me great honor, for you alone have kept safe for me what is my own, while others take it away. You have distinguished between what is precious from what is vile, like a discerning man, giving God the glory and me the scorn."

The man of God not only showed himself humble to the great, but also to his peers and to the lowly, more willing to be admonished and corrected than to admonish others. For example, one day he was riding a donkey, since he was too weak and sickly to walk, and he passed through the field of a peasant who was working there. The peasant ran to him and asked anxiously if he were Brother Francis. When the man of God humbly answered that he was, the peasant said: "Try hard to be as good as everyone says you are, because many people put their trust in you. So I'm warning you; don't ever be different from what people expect!" When the man of God, Francis, heard this, he got down from the donkey on to the ground, and prostrate before the peasant, humbly kissed his feet, thanking him for being so kind to admonish him.

Although so famous that many considered him a saint, he thought himself vile in the sight of God and people. He did not feel proud of his great fame or the holiness attributed to him: not even of the many holy brothers and sons given to him as the down payment of a reward for his merits.

> Thomas of Celano, The Remembrance of the Desire of a Soul,
> Second Book, CIII, 141–2
> *The Founder,* 339

22 MAY

Hail, Queen Wisdom!
May the Lord protect You,
with Your Sister, holy pure Simplicity!
Lady holy Poverty,
may the Lord protect You,
with Your Sister, holy Humility!
Lady holy Charity,
may the Lord protect You,
with Your Sister, holy Obedience.
Most holy Virtues,
may the Lord protect all of You
from Whom You come and proceed.

There is surely no one in the whole world
who can possess any one of You
without dying first.
Whoever possesses one
and does not offend the others
possesses all.
Whoever offends one
does not possess any
and offends all.
And each one confounds vice and sin.

A Salutation of the Virtues, 1–8
The Saint, 164

23 MAY

Holy Wisdom confounds
Satan and all his cunning.
Pure holy Simplicity confounds
all the wisdom of this world
and the wisdom of the body.
Holy Poverty confounds
the desire for riches,
greed,
and the cares of this world.
Holy Humility confounds
pride,
all people who are in the world
and all that is in the world.
Holy Charity confounds
every diabolical and carnal temptation
and every carnal fear.
Holy Obedience confounds
every corporal and carnal wish,
binds its mortified body
to obedience of the Spirit
and obedience to one's brother,
so that it is
subject and submissive
to everyone in the world,
not only to people
but to every beast and wild animal as well
that they may do whatever they want with it
insofar as it has been given to them
from above by the Lord.

A Salutation of the Virtues, 9–14
The Saint, 165

24 MAY

When the appointed day [for a meal with Saint Francis] arrived, Saint Clare with a companion came out from the monastery, was accompanied by companions of Saint Francis, and came to Saint Mary of the Angels. After she devoutly greeted the Virgin Mary in front of her altar, where she had been tonsured and veiled, they took her around to see the place until it was time to eat. And in the meantime Saint Francis had the table prepared on the bare ground, as he usually did. When it was time to eat they sat down together: Saint Clare with Saint Francis; one of the companions of Saint Francis with the companion of Saint Clare; then all the other companions gathered humbly at the table. And as a first course Saint Francis began to speak of God so sweetly, so deeply, and so wonderfully that the abundance of divine grace descended upon them, and all were rapt into God.

And while they were enraptured this way, their eyes and hands lifted up to heaven, the people of Assisi and Bettona and those of the surrounding area saw Saint Mary of the Angels burning brightly, along with the whole place and the forest, which was next to the place. It seemed that a great fire was consuming the church, the place and the forest together. For this reason the Assisians in a great hurry ran down there to put out the fire, believing that everything really was burning. But on arriving at the place, not finding anything burning, they went inside and found Saint Francis with Saint Clare and all their companions sitting around that humble table, rapt into God through contemplation. From this they clearly understood that that was divine, not material fire, which God had made appear miraculously, to demonstrate and signify the fire of divine love, burning in the souls of these holy brothers and holy nuns. Then they departed with great consolation in their hearts and with holy edification.

Then, after a long time, Saint Francis and Saint Clare together with the others returned to themselves; and feeling themselves well comforted by spiritual food, they had little concern for bodily food. And thus finishing that blessed meal, Saint Clare, well accompanied, returned to San Damiano. On seeing her the sisters were very glad, because they feared that Saint Francis might have sent her to govern some other monastery, as he had already sent Sister Agnes, her holy sister, as abbess to govern the monastery of Monticelli in Florence. Saint Francis had once said to Saint Clare, "Prepare yourself, in case I have to send you someplace"; and she, as a daughter of holy obedience had responded, "Father, I'm always prepared to go wherever you send me." So the sisters rejoiced greatly when they had her back; and Saint Clare from then on remained greatly comforted.

The Little Flowers of Saint Francis, 15
The Prophet, 590–1

25 MAY

His constant wish and watchful concern was to foster among his sons the bond of unity so that those drawn by the same Spirit and begotten by the same father should be held peacefully on the lap of the same mother. He wanted to unite the greater to the lesser, to join the wise to the simple in brotherly affection, and to hold together those far from each other with the glue of love.

He once presented a moral parable, containing no little instruction. "Imagine," he said, "a general chapter of all the religious in the Church. Because the literate are present along with those who are unlettered, the learned, as well as those who, without learning, have learned how to please God, a sermon is assigned to one of the wise and another to one of the simple. The wise man, because he is wise, thinks to himself: 'This is not the place to show off my learning, since it is full of understanding scholars. And it would not be proper to make myself stand out for originality, making subtle points to men who are even more subtle. Speaking simply would be more fruitful.'

"The appointed day dawns, the gathering of the saints gathers as one, thirsting to hear this sermon. The learned man comes forward dressed in sackcloth, with head sprinkled with ashes, and to the amazement of all, he spoke briefly, preaching more by his action. 'Great things have we promised,' he said, 'greater things have been promised us; let us observe the former and yearn for the latter. Pleasure is short and punishment is eternal; suffering is slight and glory infinite. Many are called; few are chosen, all are repaid.' The hearts of the listeners were pierced, and they burst into tears, and revered this truly wise man as a saint.

"'What's this?' the simple man says in his heart. 'This wise man has stolen everything I planned to do or say! But I know what I will do. I know a few verses of the psalms; I'll use the style of the wise man, since he used the style of the simple.' The next day's meeting arrives and the simple brother gets up, and proposes a psalm as his theme. Then, inspired with the divine Spirit, he preaches by the inspired gift of God with such fire, subtlety and sweetness that all are filled with amazement and say: 'Yes, He speaks with the simple!'" [Prv 3:32]

The man of God would then explain the moral parable he told: "Our religion is a very large gathering, like a general council gathered together from every part of the world under a single form of life. In it the learned can draw from the simple to their own advantage when they see the unlettered seeking the things of heaven with fiery vigor and those not taught by men knowing spiritual things by the Spirit. In it even the simple turn to their advantage what belongs to the learned, when they see outstanding men, who could live with great honor anywhere in the world, humble themselves to the same level with themselves. Here," he said, "is where the beauty of this blessed family shines; a diverse beauty that gives great pleasure to the father of the family."

Thomas of Celano, The Remembrance of the Desire of a Soul,
Second Book, CXLIV, 191–2
The Founder, 369–71

26 MAY

He [Francis] used to affirm that the Lesser Brothers had been sent from the Lord in these last times to show forth examples of light to those wrapped in the darkness of sins. He would say that he was filled with the sweetest fragrance and anointed with strength from precious ointment whenever he heard of the great deeds of holy brothers in faraway lands....

He was greatly consoled, however, by God's visitations which reassured him that the foundations of the religion would always remain unshaken. He was also promised that the number of those being lost would undoubtedly be replaced by those being chosen. One time he was disturbed by some bad examples. In his disturbance he turned to prayer and received a scolding from the Lord: "Why are you so upset, little man? Have I set you up as shepherd over my religion so that you can forget that I am its main protector? I have entrusted this to you, a simple man, so that the things that I work in you for others to imitate may be followed by those who want to follow. I have called; I will preserve, and I will pasture; and I will raise up others to make up for the fall of some, so that, even if they have not been born, I will have them born! So do not be upset, but work out your salvation, for even if the religion should come to number only three, by my gift it will still remain forever unshaken."

From that time on he used to say that the virtue of a single holy person overwhelms a great crowd of the imperfect, just as the deepest darkness disappears at a single ray of light.

Thomas of Celano, *The Remembrance of the Desire of a Soul*, Second Book, CXV–CVII, 155 & 158
The Founder, 347 & 349

27 MAY

Something marvelous happened to the holy man while he was going to the city of Siena for some urgent reason. Three poor women, who were exactly alike in height, age, and appearance, met him on the great plain between Campiglia and San Quirico and offered him a small gift of a new greeting. "Welcome, Lady Poverty!" they said. When he heard this, the true lover of poverty was filled with unspeakable joy, for he had in himself nothing that he would so gladly have people hail as what these women had chosen.

Once they had abruptly disappeared, considering the remarkable novelty of the likeness among them, of the greeting, of the meeting and of the disappearance, the brothers accompanying him weighed, not without reason, what the mystery meant about the holy man. Clearly, it would seem that through those three poor women so alike in appearance, offering such an unusual greeting, and disappearing so quickly, the beauty of Gospel perfection, consisting in poverty, chastity, and obedience was fittingly revealed to be shining perfectly in the man of God in an equal way. Nonetheless, he had chosen to glory above all in the privilege of poverty which he was accustomed to call his mother, his bride, and his lady.

Bonaventure, The Major Legend of Saint Francis, VII, 6
The Founder, 580–1

28 MAY

In the village of Pomarico, in the mountains of Apulia, a mother and father had an only daughter, tender of age and tenderly loved. And since they did not expect any future offspring, she was the object of all their love, the motive for all their care. When she became deathly ill, the girl's mother and father considered themselves dead. Day and night they kept anxious watch over the child's care, but one morning they found her dead. Perhaps they had been negligent, overcome by sleep or the strain of their vigil. The mother, deprived of her daughter and with no hope of other offspring, seemed to die herself.

Friends and neighbors gathered for a very sad funeral and prepared to bury the lifeless body. The unhappy mother lay grief-stricken, and the depth of her sorrow kept her from noticing what was going on. In the meantime, Saint Francis with one companion visited the desolate woman and spoke these comforting words, "Do not weep, I will rekindle the light of your quenched lamp!" The woman jumped up, told everyone what Saint Francis had told her, and would not allow the body of the deceased to be carried away. Then the mother turned to her daughter, invoked the saint's name, and lifted her up safe and sound. We leave it to others to describe the wonder that filled the hearts of the bystanders and the rare joy of the girl's parents.

Thomas of Celano, The Treatise on the Miracles of Saint Francis, VII, 46
The Founder, 423–4

29 MAY

For love of holy poverty, the servant of almighty God used the alms he had begged from door to door more gladly than those offered spontaneously. For if he were invited by distinguished persons and honored by a more lavish dinner, he would first seek some pieces of bread at the neighboring houses and then, enriched by poverty, sit down at table.

And once he did this, when he was invited by the Lord Bishop of Ostia, who held Christ's poor man in special affection. After the bishop complained that he had disparaged his honor as would be expected when a dinner guest goes out for alms, God's servant replied: "My lord, I showed you great honor while I have honored a greater Lord. For the Lord is pleased by poverty and especially when one freely chooses to go begging for Christ. This is the royal dignity which the Lord Jesus assumed when he became poor for us that he might enrich us by his want and would make us truly poor in spirit, as heirs and kings of the kingdom of heaven. I do not wish to relinquish this royal dignity for a fief of false riches granted for only an hour."

Bonaventure, The Major Legend of Saint Francis, VII, 7
The Founder, 581–2

30 MAY

Almighty, eternal, just and merciful God, give us miserable ones the grace to do for You alone what we know you want us to do and always to desire what pleases You. Inwardly cleansed, interiorly enlightened and inflamed by the fire of the Holy Spirit, may we be able to follow in the footprints of Your beloved Son our Lord Jesus Christ, and, by Your grace alone, may we make our way to You, Most High, Who live and rule in perfect Trinity and simple Unity, and are glorified God almighty, forever and ever. Amen.

A Letter to the Entire Order, 50–2
The Saint, 120–1

31 MAY

And because he had learned in prayer that the presence of the Holy Spirit for which he longed was offered more intimately to those who invoke him, the more it found them far from the noise of worldly affairs.

Therefore seeking out solitary places, he used to go to deserted and abandoned churches to pray at night. There he often endured horrible struggles with devils who would assault him physically, trying to distract him from his commitment to prayer. But armed with heavenly weapons, the more vehemently he was attacked by the enemy, the more courageous he became in practicing virtue and the more fervent in prayer, saying confidently to Christ: "Under the shadow of your wings, protect me from the face of the wicked who have attacked me." To the devils he said: "Do whatever you want to me, you malicious and deceitful spirits! For you cannot do anything unless the heavenly hand relaxes its hold on you. And I am ready to endure with delight whatever He decrees." The demons retreated confused, not tolerating such firmness of mind.

The man of God remaining more alone and at peace would fill the forest with groans, water the places with tears, strike his breast with his hand, and, as if finding a more secret hiding place, would converse with his Lord. There he replied to the Judge, there he entreated the Father, there he conversed with the Friend. There too the brothers who were devoutly observing him heard him on several occasions groan with loud cries, imploring the divine clemency for sinners, and weeping over the Lord's passion as if it were before him. There he was seen praying at night, with his hands outstretched in the form of a cross, his whole body lifted up from the ground and surrounded by a sort of shining cloud, so that the extraordinary illumination around his body was a witness to the wonderful light that shone within his soul. There too, as is proven by certain evidence, the unknown and hidden secrets of divine wisdom were opened up to him, although he never spoke of them outside except when the love of Christ urged him and the good of his neighbor demanded.

> Bonaventure, The Major Legend of Saint Francis, X, 3–4
> *The Founder,* 606–7

June

1 JUNE

He wanted ministers of the word of God to be intent on spiritual study and not hindered by other duties. He said that these men were heralds chosen by a great king to deliver to the people the decrees received from his mouth. For he used to say: "The preacher must first secretly draw in by prayer what he later pours out in sacred preaching; he must first of all grow warm on the inside, or he will speak frozen words on the outside." He said that this office was worthy of reverence and that those who exercised it should be revered by all. As he said, "They are the life of the body, the opponents of demons, the lamp of the world."

He considered doctors of sacred theology to be worthy of even greater honor. Indeed he once had it written as a general rule that "we should honor and revere all theologians and those who minister to us the words of God, as those who minister to us spirit and life." And once, when writing to blessed Anthony, he had this written at the beginning of the letter: "To brother Anthony, my bishop."

He felt deeply sorry for those preachers who often sell what they do for the price of some empty praise. He would sometimes treat the swelling of such people with this antidote: "Why do you boast about people being converted? My simple brothers converted them by their prayers!" And then he would explain the saying while the barren one has given birth to many children [1 Sm 2:5] in this sense: "the barren one is my poor little brother who does not have the duty of producing children in the Church. At the Judgment he will give birth to many children, for then the Judge will credit to his glory those he is converting now by his secret prayers. But the mother of many will languish, because the preacher who rejoices over many as if they were born through his power will then discover that he has nothing of his own in them."

He had little love for those who would rather be praised as orators than as preachers or for those who speak with elegance rather than feeling. He said that they divided things badly, putting everything in preaching and nothing in devotion. But he would praise that preacher who takes time to taste and eat a bit himself.

Thomas of Celano, The Remembrance of the Desire of a Soul,
Second Book, CXXII–CXXIII, 163–4
The Founder, 352–3

ஒ

2 JUNE

Sometimes, as he encouraged the brothers to beg for alms, he would use words such as these: "Go, for in this last hour the Lesser Brothers have been given to the world so that the elect may carry out for them what will be commended by the Judge as they hear those most sweet words: As long as you have done it for one of my lesser brothers, you did it for me [Mt 25:40]." Then he would say that it was a delight to beg with the title of Lesser Brothers, which the Teacher of Gospel truth had so clearly expressed by his own mouth in rewarding the just. When there was an opportunity, he used to go begging even on the principal feasts, saying that, in the holy poor, the prophecy is fulfilled: Man will eat the bread of angels [Ps 77:25].

He used to say that bread is clearly angelic, which holy poverty gathers from door-to-door, which is sought out of God's love and is given out of His love by the blessed prompting of angels.

Bonaventure, The Major Legend of Saint Francis, VII, 8
The Founder, 582

ஒ

3 JUNE

Walking before God with simplicity and among people with confidence, the brothers merited at that time to rejoice in a divine revelation. They were on fire with the Holy Spirit and with prayerful voices sang the "Our Father" in the melody of the Spirit. They did this at all hours and not simply those assigned, since earthly concerns and the nagging anxiety of cares troubled them little.

One night the blessed father Francis was away from them in body. About midnight, some of the brothers were sleeping and others were praying in silence with deep feeling, when a brilliant fiery chariot entered through the little door of the house, and moved here and there through the little house two or three times. On top of it sat a large ball that looked like the sun, and it made the night bright as day. Those who were awake were dumbfounded, while those sleeping woke up in a fright, for they sensed the brightness with their hearts as much as with their bodies. They gathered together and began to ask each other what all this meant. From the strength and grace of such great light, the conscience of each was revealed to the others.

At last they understood, realizing that the soul of the holy father radiated with great brilliance. Thus, thanks to the gift of his outstanding purity and his deep concern for his sons, he merited the blessing of such a gift from the Lord.

Thomas of Celano, The Life of Saint Francis, First Book, XVIII, 47
The Saint, 224

4 JUNE

One time the abbot of the monastery of San Giustino in the diocese of Perugia happened to meet Christ's servant. When he saw him, the devout abbot quickly dismounted from his horse to show reverence to the man of God and to converse with him a bit about the salvation of his soul. Finally, after a pleasant conversation, the abbot, as he left, humbly asked him to pray for him. The dear man of God replied: "I will willingly pray." When the abbot had ridden away a short distance, the faithful Francis said to his companion: "Wait a little, brother, because I want to pay the debt I promised." As he prayed, suddenly the abbot felt in spirit unusual warmth and sweetness like nothing he felt before, and rapt in ecstasy, he totally fainted away into God. This lasted for a short time, and then he returned to his senses and realized the power of Saint Francis's prayer. From that time on, he always burned with ever greater love for the Order, and told many about this miraculous event.

Bonaventure, The Major Legend of Saint Francis, X, 5
The Founder, 582

※

5 JUNE

At the time that Saint Francis was staying in the city of Gubbio, in the district of Gubbio there appeared a very big wolf, fearsome and ferocious, which devoured not only animals but even human beings, so that all the citizens were in great fear, because many times he came near the city. All would go armed when they went out of the city as if they were going to combat, yet with all this, those who were alone and encountered him could not defend themselves from him. And out of fear of this wolf it came to the point that no one dared to leave that town. For this reason Saint Francis had compassion on the people of the town, and decided to go out to this wolf, even though all the citizens advised against it. Making the sign of the most holy Cross, he went out of the town, he and his companions, placing all his confidence in God. As the others hesitated to go any further, Saint Francis took the road toward the place where the wolf was. Then that wolf, seeing many citizens who had come to see this miracle, ran toward Saint Francis with his mouth open. Drawing close to him, Saint Francis made the sign of the most holy cross on him and called him to himself and said this: "Come here, Brother Wolf. I command you on behalf of Christ that you do no harm to me or to anyone." An amazing thing to say! Immediately, when Saint Francis had made the sign of the cross, the fearsome wolf closed his mouth and stopped running; and once the command was given, it came meekly as a lamb, and threw itself to lie at the feet of Saint Francis. And Saint Francis spoke to him thus: "Brother Wolf, you do much harm in this area, and you have done great misdeeds, destroying and killing the creatures of God without His permission. And not only have you killed and devoured beasts, but you have dared to kill people, made in the image of God. For this reason you are worthy of the gallows as a thief and the worst of murderers. And all the people cry out and complain against you, and all this town is your enemy. But I, Brother Wolf, want to make peace between you and these people, so that you do not offend them any more, and they may pardon you every past offence, and so neither the people nor the dogs will persecute you anymore." And after these words were said, the wolf showed that he accepted what Saint Francis said and wanted to observe it, by movement of his body and tail and ears and by bowing his head. Then Saint Francis said, "Brother Wolf, since it pleases you to make this pact of peace and keep it, I promise that I will have food given to you constantly, as long as you live, by the people of this town, so that you will no longer suffer hunger, since I know very well that you did all this harm because of hunger. But in order for me to obtain this grace for you, I want you, Brother Wolf, to promise me that you will never harm any human person nor any animal. Do you promise me this?" And the wolf, bowing his head, made a clear sign that he promised it. And Saint Francis said this: "Brother Wolf, I want you to guarantee this promise, so that I can truly trust it." Saint Francis reached out his hand to receive his guarantee, the wolf lifted his right paw in front of him, and tamely placed it on top of the hand of Saint Francis, giving the only sign of a guarantee that he was able to make.

Then Saint Francis said, "Brother Wolf, I command you in the name of Jesus Christ: come with me now without any hesitation, and we will go to seal this peace-pact in the name of God." And the obedient wolf went with him like a tame lamb; and the citizens, seeing this, were greatly amazed.

The Little Flowers of Saint Francis, 21
The Prophet, 601–2

6 JUNE

Immediately this news was known throughout the whole city; and because of it all the people, men and women, great and small, young and old, poured into the piazza to see the wolf with Saint Francis. And once all the people were fully assembled Saint Francis got up and preached to them, saying, among other things, that God allows such things and pestilences because of sins; and the flame of hell, which lasts forever for the damned, is much more dangerous than the fierceness of the wolf, which can only kill the body. "How much should the mouth of hell be feared when the mouth of a little animal holds such a great multitude in fear! Dear people, return to God, therefore, and do fitting penance for your sins, and God will free you from the wolf in the present, and from hell's fire in the future." When he finished the sermon, Saint Francis said, "Listen, my brothers! Brother Wolf, who is here before you, has promised me, and given me his guarantee, to make peace with you, and never to offend you in anything, if you promise him to give him every day the things he needs. And I make myself trustee for him that he will firmly observe the peace-pact." Then all the people with one voice promised to feed him regularly. And Saint Francis, in front of them all, said to the wolf: "And you, Brother Wolf, do you promise to observe the peace-pact with these people, that you will not harm the people, the animals, nor any creature?" And the wolf knelt down and bowed his head and with gentle movements of his body and tail and ears showed, as much as possible, that he wished to observe every part of the pact with them. Saint Francis said: "Brother Wolf, as you gave me a guarantee of this promise outside the gate, I also want you to give me in front of all the people a guarantee of your promise, that you will not deceive me in my promise and the guarantee that I gave for you." Then the wolf, lifting his right paw, placed it in the hand of Saint Francis. Because of this action, and the others mentioned above, there was such rejoicing and wonder among all the people, both for the devotion of the Saint and for the novelty of the miracle and for the peace of the wolf, that they all began to cry out to heaven, praising and blessing God who sent Saint Francis to them who, through his merits, had freed them from the jaws of the cruel beast.

Afterwards that same wolf lived in Gubbio for two years, and he tamely entered the houses, going from door to door, without doing harm to anyone and without any being done to him; and he was kindly fed by the people, and as he went this way through the town and the houses, no dog barked at him. Finally after two years Brother Wolf died of old age, at which the citizens grieved very much, because when they saw him going through the city so tamely, they better recalled the virtue and holiness of Saint Francis.

The Little Flowers of Saint Francis, 21
The Prophet, 602–3

7 JUNE

The Lord Jesus says to his disciples: I am the way, the truth and the life; no one comes to the Father except through me. If you knew me, you would also know my Father; and from now on, you do know him and have seen him. Philip says to him: Lord, show us the Father and it will be enough for us. Jesus says to him: Have I been with you for so long a time and you have not known me? Philip, whoever sees me sees my Father as well [Jn 4:6–9].

The Father dwells in inaccessible light, and God is spirit, and no one has ever seen God. Therefore He cannot be seen except in the Spirit because it is the Spirit that gives life; the flesh has nothing to offer. But because He is equal to the Father, the Son is not seen by anyone other than the Father or other than the Holy Spirit.

All those who saw the Lord Jesus according to the humanity, therefore, and did not see and believe according to the Spirit and the Divinity that He is the true Son of God, were condemned. Now in the same way, all those who see the sacrament sanctified by the words of the Lord upon the altar at the hands of the priest in the form of bread and wine, and who do not see and believe according to the Spirit and the Divinity that it is truly the Body and Blood of our Lord Jesus Christ, are condemned. [This] is affirmed by the Most High Himself Who says: This is my

Body and the Blood of my new covenant [which will be shed for many]; and Whoever eats my flesh and drinks my blood has eternal life [Mk 14:23–24]. It is the Spirit of the Lord, therefore, That lives in Its faithful, That receives the Body and Blood of the Lord. All others who do not share in this same Spirit and presume to receive Him eat and drink judgment on themselves.

Therefore: children, how long will you be hard of heart? Why do you not know the truth and believe in the Son of God? Behold, each day He humbles Himself as when He came from the royal throne into the Virgin's womb; each day He Himself comes to us, appearing humbly; each day He comes down from the bosom of the Father upon the altar in the hands of a priest.

As He revealed Himself to the holy apostles in true flesh, so He reveals Himself to us now in sacred bread. And as they saw only His flesh by an insight of their flesh, yet believed that He was God as they contemplated Him with their spiritual eyes, let us, as we see bread and wine with our bodily eyes, see and firmly believe that they are His most holy Body and Blood living and true. And in this way the Lord is always with His faithful, as He Himself says: Behold I am with you until the end of the age [Mt 28:20].

The Admonitions, I
The Saint, 128–9

8 JUNE

The saint once arrived with a companion at a church located far from any inhabited area. He wanted to offer solitary prayer, and so he notified his companion: "Brother, I would like to spend the night here alone. Go to the hospice and come back to me at dawn." When he was alone, he poured out long and devout prayers to the Lord. Finally he looked around for a place to lay his head so he could sleep. Suddenly he was disturbed in spirit and began to feel fear and loathing, and to shake in every part of his body. He clearly felt diabolical attacks against him and heard packs of devils running across the roof of the house with a great clatter. He quickly got up, went outside, traced the sign of the cross on his forehead and said: "On behalf of Almighty God I tell you, demons, do to my body whatever is permitted to you: I will gladly bear it. I have no greater enemy than the body, so you will be avenging me on my opponent when you exercise vengeance on it in my place." And so those who had gathered to terrify his spirit discovered a willing spirit in weak flesh and quickly vanished in shame and confusion.

When morning came his companion returned to him, and finding the saint lying prostrate before the altar, waited for him outside the choir, praying fervently before the cross. He passed into an ecstasy! He saw many thrones in heaven, and one of them was more noble than the rest, adorned with precious stones and glittering with great glory. He wondered within himself about that noble throne, and silently thought about whose it might be. Then he heard a voice saying to him: "This throne belonged to one of those who fell, and now it is reserved for the humble Francis." Finally the brother came back to himself, and saw the blessed Francis coming away from prayer. Immediately he prostrated himself in the form of a cross and spoke to him as if he were already reigning in heaven, not still living in the world: "Father, pray for me to the Son of God, that he may not consider my sins!" Extending his hand the man of God lifted him up, realizing that something must have been shown him in prayer. As they were leaving the brother asked blessed Francis: "Father, what is your own opinion about yourself?" And he replied: "I see myself as the greatest of sinners. For if God had pursued any criminal with so much mercy, he would be ten times more spiritual than I am." At this point the Spirit said within that brother's heart: "Now you know that the vision was true. Humility will lift the humblest one to the seat that was lost by pride."

Thomas of Celano, The Remembrance of the Desire of a Soul,
Second Book, LXXXVI, 122–3
The Founder, 327–8

9 JUNE

A certain brother, a spiritual man, an elder in religion, was afflicted with a great tribulation of the flesh, and seemed to be swallowed into the depth of despair. His sorrow doubled daily, as his conscience, more delicate than discerning, made him go to confession over nothing. Certainly there is no need to confess having a temptation, but only giving in to it, even a little. But he was so shamed that he was afraid to reveal the whole thing, even though it was nothing, to a single priest. Instead, dividing up these thoughts, he confided different pieces to different priests. One day as he was walking with blessed Francis, the saint said to him: "Brother, I tell you that from now on you do not have to confess your tribulation to anyone. Do not be afraid. Whatever happens to you that is not your doing will not be to your blame, but to your credit. Whenever you are troubled, I give you my permission just to say seven Our Fathers." The brother wondered how the saint could have known about this; smiling and overjoyed, he got over the temptation in a short time.

Thomas of Celano, The Remembrance of the Desire of a Soul,
Second Book, LXXXVII, 124
The Founder, 329

10 JUNE

This holy man insisted that spiritual joy was an infallible remedy against a thousand snares and tricks of the enemy. He used to say: "The devil is most delighted when he can steal the joy of spirit from a servant of God. He carries dust which he tries to throw into the tiniest openings of the conscience, to dirty a clear mind and a clean life. But if spiritual joy fills the heart, the serpent casts its poison in vain. The devils cannot harm a servant of Christ when they see him filled with holy cheerfulness. But when the spirit is teary-eyed, feeling abandoned and sad, it will easily be swallowed up in sorrow, or else be carried away toward empty enjoyment." The saint therefore always strove to keep a joyful heart, to preserve the anointing of the spirit and the oil of gladness.

He avoided very carefully the dangerous disease of acedia, so that when he felt even a little of it slipping into his heart, he quickly rushed to prayer. For he used to say: "When a servant of God gets disturbed about something, as often happens, he must get up at once to pray and remain before the most High Father until he gives back to him the joy of his salvation. But if he delays, staying in sadness, that Babylonian sickness will grow and, unless scrubbed with tears, it will produce in the heart permanent rust."

Thomas of Celano, The Remembrance of the Desire of a Soul,
Second Book, LXXXVIII, 125
The Founder, 329–30

11 JUNE

Once when the Lord's servant was gravely ill at Nocera, he was brought back to Assisi by formally appointed representatives sent for that purpose out of devotion by the people of Assisi. As they carried Christ's servant back, they came to a poor little village called Satriano where, since their hunger and the hour called for food, they went out, and finding nothing for sale, returned empty-handed. The holy man told them: "You didn't find anything, because you trust more in those flies of yours than in God." For he used to call coins "flies." "But go back," he said, "to the houses which you have visited and, offering the love of God as a reward, humbly ask for an alms. Do not consider this shameful or cheap out of false esteem, for after sin everything is bestowed as alms, for that great Almsgiver, out of his abundant piety, gives to both the worthy and the unworthy."

The knights overcame their embarrassment, readily begged for alms, and bought more with the love of God than with money. Since their hearts were struck with compunction by the divine nod, the poor villagers generously gave not only what was theirs, but also themselves. And so it happened that Francis's wealthy poverty supplied the need which money could not alleviate.

Bonaventure, The Major Legend of Saint Francis, VII, 10
The Founder, 583

12 JUNE

Let all of us, clergymen, consider the great sin and the ignorance some have toward the most holy Body and Blood of our Lord Jesus Christ and His most holy names and written words that consecrate His Body. We know It cannot be His Body without first being consecrated by word. For we have and see nothing corporally of the Most High in this world except [His] Body and Blood, [His] names and words through which we have been made and redeemed from death to life.

Let all those who administer such most holy ministries, however, especially those who administer them without discernment, consider how very dirty the chalices, corporals and altar-linens are upon which the Body and Blood of our Lord are sacrificed. It is left in many dirty places, carried about unbecomingly, received unworthily, and administered to others without discernment. Even His names and written words are at times left to be trampled under foot; for the carnal person does not perceive the things of God.

Are we not moved by piety at these things when the pious Lord offers Himself into our hands and we touch Him and receive Him daily with our mouth? Do we refuse to recognize that we must come into His hands? Let us, therefore, amend our ways quickly and firmly in these and all other matters. Wherever the most holy Body and Blood of our Lord Jesus Christ has been illicitly placed and left, let It be moved from there, placed in a precious place and locked up. Likewise, wherever the names and written words of the Lord may be found in unclean places, let them be gathered up and placed in a becoming place.

We know that we are bound to observe above all else all of these matters according to the precepts of the Lord and the constitutions of holy mother Church. Whoever does not do this, let him know that, on the day of judgment, he will be bound to render an account of himself before our Lord Jesus Christ.

Let whoever makes copies of this writing so that it may be better observed know that they will be blessed by the Lord God.

Exhortations to the Clergy (Later Edition)
The Saint, 54–5

13 JUNE

Sir Saint Anthony of Padua, that wonderful vessel of the Holy Spirit and one of the chosen disciples and companions of Saint Francis, whom Saint Francis called his bishop, was preaching one time before the pope and the cardinals in a consistory, and in that consistory there were men of different nations, Greek, Latin, French, German, Slavs, English and many others of diverse languages of the world. Inflamed by the Holy Spirit, he proclaimed the word of God so effectively, so devoutly, so subtly, so sweetly, so clearly, and so understandably that all those who were in the Consistory, though of different languages, understood clearly his every word, as if he had spoken in the language of each of them; and all were amazed, and it seemed that the ancient miracle of the Apostles at the time of Pentecost had been renewed, as they had spoken in every language by virtue of the Holy Spirit.

Together they said to each other in amazement: "The one who is preaching, is he not from Spain? Then how do we all hear in his words the language of our own countries?" The pope also, reflecting and marvelling at the profundity of his words, said: "He is truly the Ark of the Covenant and the Library of Holy Scripture."

The Little Flowers of Saint Francis, 39
The Prophet, 631

14 JUNE

Toward the sacrament of the Lord's Body he burned with fervor to his very marrow, and with unbounded wonder of that loving condescension and condescending love. He considered it disrespectful not to hear, if time allowed, at least one Mass a day. He received Communion frequently and so devoutly that he made others devout. Following that which is so venerable with all reverence he offered the sacrifice of all his members, and receiving the Lamb that was slain he slew his own spirit in the fire which always burned upon the altar of his heart.

Because of this he loved France as a friend of the Body of the Lord, and even wished to die there, because of its reverence for sacred things.

He once wanted to send brothers throughout the world with precious pyxes, so that wherever they should find the price of our redemption in an unsuitable place they might put it away in the very best place.

He wanted great reverence shown to the hands of priests, since they have the divinely granted authority to bring about this mystery. He often used to say: "If I should happen at the same time to come upon any saint coming from heaven and some little poor priest, I would first show honor to the priest, and hurry more quickly to kiss his hands. For I would say to the saint: 'Hey, Saint Lawrence, a wait! His hands may handle the Word of Life, and possess something more than human!' "

Thomas of Celano, The Remembrance of the Desire of a Soul,
Second Book, CLII, 201
The Founder, 375–6

15 JUNE

In the town of Pofi, located in Campagna, a priest named Tommaso went with many others to repair a mill belonging to his church. Below the mill was a deep gorge, and the raised channel flowed rapidly. The priest carelessly walked along the edge of the channel, and accidentally fell into it. In an instant he was thrust by force against the wooden blades that turned the mill. There he remained, pinned against the wood, unable to move at all. Because he was lying face down the flow of water pitiably muffled his voice and blocked his sight. But his heart, if not his tongue, was free to call plaintively on Saint Francis.

He remained there a long time, and his companions, rushing back to him, nearly despaired of his life. "Let's turn the mill by force in the opposite direction," said the miller, "so it will release the corpse." With a struggle they turned the mill in reverse, and they saw the trembling body thrown into the water.

The priest, still half-alive, was being rolled around in the pool, when suddenly there appeared a Lesser Brother in a white tunic bound with a cord. With great gentleness he drew the unfortunate man by the arm out of the water, and said, "I am Francis, the one you called." The man was stunned to be freed in this way and began to run here and there saying, "Brother, Brother!" and asking the bystanders, "Where is he? Which way did he go?" But they were terrified: they fell prostrate to the ground and gave glory to God and to his saint.

Thomas of Celano, The Treatise on the Miracles of Saint Francis, VIII, 50
The Founder, 425–6

16 JUNE

Let the brothers who are the ministers and servants of the others visit and admonish their brothers and humbly and charitably correct them, not commanding them anything that is against their soul and our rule. Let the brothers who are subject, however, remember that, for God's sake, they have renounced their own wills. Therefore, I strictly command them to obey their ministers in everything they have promised the Lord to observe and which is not against their soul or our Rule.

Wherever the brothers may be who know and feel they cannot observe the Rule spiritually, they can and should have recourse to their ministers. Let the ministers, moreover, receive them charitably and kindly and have such familiarity with them that these same brothers may speak and deal with them as masters with their servants, for so it must be that the ministers are the servants of all the brothers.

Moreover, I admonish and exhort the brothers in the Lord Jesus Christ to beware of all pride, vainglory, envy and greed, of care and solicitude for the things of this world, of detraction and murmuring.

The Later Rule (With Papal Approval), X
The Saint, 105

17 JUNE

As an angel announced to him, blessed Francis said that he had obtained from the Lord four things. Namely, the religion and the profession of the Lesser Brothers will last until the day of judgment. In addition, no one who deliberately persecutes the Order will live long. Furthermore, no evil person, intending to live an evil life in it, will be able to remain in it for long. Likewise, whosoever loves the Order wholeheartedly, however great a sinner, will obtain mercy in the end.

A Mirror of Perfection, IV, 79
The Prophet, 324

18 JUNE

After blessed Francis had obtained that place of Saint Mary from the abbot of Saint Benedict, he ordered that a chapter be held there twice a year, that is, on Pentecost and on the Dedication of Saint Michael.

At Pentecost, all the brothers used to gather at the church of Saint Mary and discuss how they could better observe the Rule. They appointed brothers throughout the various provinces who would preach to the people, and assigned other brothers in their provinces. Saint Francis, however, used to give admonitions, corrections, and directives as it seemed to him to be according to the Lord's counsel. Everything that he said to them in word, however, he would show them in deed with eagerness and affection.

He used to revere prelates and priests of the holy Church, and honored the elderly, the noble, and the wealthy. Moreover, he intimately loved the poor, suffering deeply with them, and he showed himself subject to all.

Although he was more elevated than all the brothers, he still appointed one of the brothers staying with him as his guardian and master. He humbly and eagerly obeyed him, in order to avoid any occasion of pride. For in the presence of people, he lowered his head even to the ground; so that now in the presence of God's saints and chosen ones, he merits to be exalted in the divine sight.

He zealously used to admonish the brothers to observe the holy Gospel and the Rule which they had firmly promised; and particularly to be reverent and devoted about divine services and ecclesiastical regulations, hearing Mass devotedly, and adoring the Body of the Lord even more devoutly. He wanted priests who handle the tremendous and greatest sacraments to be honored uniquely by the brothers, so that wherever they met them, as they bowed their heads to them, they would kiss their hands. And if they found them on horseback, he wanted them not only to kiss their hands but, out of reverence for their power, even the hooves of the horses upon which they were riding.

The Legend of the Three Companions, XIV, 57
The Founder, 100–1

19 JUNE

He also admonished the brothers not to judge anyone, nor to look down upon those who live with refinement and dress extravagantly or fashionably. For, he would say, their God is ours, the Lord Who is capable of calling them to Himself and justifying those called. He also used to tell them he wanted the brothers to show reverence to these people as their brothers and lords. They are brothers, because we were all created by one Creator; they are lords, because they help the good to do penance by providing them with the necessities of life. He added: "The brothers' way of life among the people should be such that whoever hears or sees them glorifies and praises the heavenly Father with dedication."

For his great desire was that he, as well as his brothers, would abound in such good deeds for which the Lord would be praised. He used to tell them: "As you announce peace with your mouth, make sure that greater peace is in your hearts. Let no one be provoked to anger or scandal through you, but may everyone be drawn to peace, kindness, and harmony through your gentleness. For we have been called to this: to heal the wounded, bind up the broken, and recall the erring. In fact, many who seem to us to be members of the devil will yet be disciples of Christ."

The Legend of the Three Companions, XIV, 58
The Founder, 101–2

20 JUNE

Moreover, the pious father used to reprove his brothers who to him were too austere, exerting too much effort in those vigils, fasts and corporal punishments. Some of them afflicted themselves so harshly to repress within them every impulse of the flesh, that they seemed to hate themselves. The man of God forbade them, admonishing them with kindness, reprimanding them with reason, and binding up their wounds with the bandages of wholesome precepts.

Among the brothers who had come to the chapter, no one dared to discuss worldly matters, but they spoke of the lives of the holy fathers, and how they could better and more perfectly find the grace of the Lord Jesus Christ. If some of the brothers who came to the chapter experienced any temptation or tribulation, upon hearing blessed Francis speaking so sweetly and fervently, and on seeing his penance, they were freed from their temptations and were miraculously relieved of the tribulations. For, while suffering with them, he spoke to them, not as a judge, but as a merciful father to his children, or a good doctor to the sick, knowing how to be sick with the sick and afflicted with the afflicted. Nevertheless he duly rebuked all delinquents, and restrained the obstinate and rebellious with an appropriate punishment.

When a chapter had ended, he would bless all the brothers and assign each of them to individual provinces. To anyone possessing the Spirit of God and an eloquence suitable for preaching, whether cleric or lay, he gave permission to preach. When those men received his blessing with great joy of spirit, they went throughout the world as pilgrims and strangers, taking nothing on their way except the books in which they could say their Hours. Whenever they found a priest, rich or poor, good or bad, bowing humbly they paid him their respect. When it was time to seek lodging, they more willingly stayed with priests rather than with seculars.

The Legend of the Three Companions, XIV, 59
The Founder, 102–3

☙

21 JUNE

In the March of Ancona there was a man of the world who had forgotten himself and did not know God, and who had prostituted himself entirely to vanity. He was known as the "King of Verses," because he was prince of bawdy singers and creator of worldly ballads. To be brief I will just say worldly glory had raised the man so high that he had been pompously crowned by the Emperor himself. While in this way, he was walking in darkness and in the harness of vanity pulling iniquity, the divine piety had pity on him and decided to call back the miserable man, so the outcast would not perish. By God's providence blessed Francis and this man met each other at a monastery of poor enclosed women; the blessed father had come there with his companions to visit his daughters, while that man had come with many of his comrades to see one of his women relatives.

Then the hand of the Lord came upon him, and, with his bodily eyes, he saw Saint Francis marked with two bright shining swords intersecting in the shape of a cross. One of them stretched from his head to his feet, and the other across his chest from one hand to the other.

He did not know blessed Francis, but once when he had been pointed out by such a miracle, he recognized him immediately. Struck at once by what he saw, he began to promise to live better at some future date. But although the blessed Father at first preached generally to everyone there, he pointed the sword of God's word on that man. He took him aside and gently reminded him about the vanity of society and contempt of the world, and then pierced his heart warning him about divine judgment. At once the man replied: "What's the point of piling up any more words? Let's move on to deeds! Take me away from people, and give me back to the Great Emperor!" The next day the saint invested him, and, since he had been brought back to the peace of the Lord, named him Brother Pacifico. His conversion was all the more edifying to many because the crowd of his vain comrades had been so widespread.

Enjoying the company of the blessed father, Brother Pacifico began to experience anointings he had never felt before. Repeatedly he was allowed to see what was veiled to others. For, shortly after that, he saw the great sign of the Tau on the forehead of blessed Francis, which displayed its beauty with the multi-colored circles of a peacock.

Thomas of Celano, The Remembrance of the Desire of a Soul,
Second Book, LXXII,106
The Founder, 316–17

22 JUNE

Another time, at Saint Mary's of the Portiuncula, the man of God began to consider how the benefit of prayer is lost through idle words. And so he established the following remedy: "Whenever a brother utters a useless or idle word, he must admit his fault at once, and for each idle word he must say one Our Father. Further, if he accuses himself of what he did, let him say the Our Father for his own soul, but if someone else corrected him first, let him say it for the soul of the one who corrected him."

He used to say that the lukewarm, who do not apply themselves constantly to some work, would be quickly vomited out of the Lord's mouth. No idler could appear in his presence without feeling the sharp bite of his criticism. This exemplar of every perfection always worked, and worked with his hands, not allowing the great gift of time to go to waste. And so he would often say: "I want all my brothers to work and keep busy, and those who have no skills to learn some." And he gave this reason: "That we may be less of a burden to people, and that in idleness the heart and tongue may not stray into what is forbidden." But he would not have profit or payment for work left to the whim of the worker, but entrusted it to the guardian or the family.

Thomas of Celano, The Remembrance of the Desire of a Soul,
Second Book, CXIX–CXX, 160-1
The Founder, 350-1

23 JUNE

Some young people from the town of Celano went out together to cut grass in some fields where an old well lay hidden, its opening covered with plant growth, holding water with a depth of almost four paces. While the children ran about, each going a different direction, one accidentally fell into the well. As the deep pit was swallowing his body, his soul's spirit rose up to call on the aid of blessed Francis, calling out with faith and confidence even as he was falling, "Saint Francis, help me!" The others turned around this way and that, and when they noticed that the other boy was missing they went in search of him, shouting and crying. When they discovered that he had fallen into the well, they ran crying back to the town, explained what had happened and begged for help. They returned with a large crowd of people, and a man was lowered by a rope into the well. He found the boy floating on the surface of the water totally unharmed. When the boy was lifted out of the well, the boy said to all the bystanders, "When I suddenly fell, I called for Saint Francis's protection, and he instantly arrived while I was still falling. He reached out his hand and gently held me and did not leave until, along with you, he pulled me from the well."

Bonaventure, The Major Legend of Saint Francis:
the Miracles, III, 3
The Founder, 660

24 JUNE

While many were joining the brothers, as already related, the blessed father Francis was travelling through the Spoleto valley. He reached a place near Bevagna, in which a great multitude of birds of different types gathered, including doves, crows, and others commonly called monaclae. When Francis, the most blessed servant of God, saw them, he ran swiftly toward them, leaving his companions on the road. He was a man of great fervor, feeling much sweetness and tenderness even toward lesser, irrational creatures. When he was already very close, seeing that they awaited him, he greeted them in his usual way. He was quite surprised, however, because the birds did not take flight, as they usually do. Filled with great joy, he humbly requested that they listen to the word of God.

Among many other things, he said to them: "My brother birds, you should greatly praise your Creator, and love Him always. He gave you feathers to wear, wings to fly, and whatever you need. God made you noble among His creatures and gave you a home in the purity of the air, so that, though you neither sow nor reap, He nevertheless protects and governs you without your least care." He himself, and those brothers who were with him, used to say that, at these words, the birds rejoiced in a wonderful way according to their nature. They stretched their necks, spread their wings, opened their beaks and looked at him. He passed through their midst, coming and going, touching their heads and bodies with his tunic. Then he blessed them, and having made the sign of the cross, gave them permission to fly off to another place. The blessed father, however, went with his companions along their way rejoicing and giving thanks to God, Whom all creatures revere by their devout confession.

He was already simple by grace, not by nature. After the birds had listened so reverently to the word of God, he began to accuse himself of negligence because he had not preached to them before. From that day on, he carefully exhorted all birds, all animals, all reptiles, and also insensible creatures, to praise and love the Creator, because daily, invoking the name of the Savior, he observed their obedience in his own experience.

> Thomas of Celano, The Life of Saint Francis, First Book, XXI, 58
> *The Saint*, 234

25 JUNE

One day he came to a village called Alviano to preach the word of God. Going up to a higher place where all could see him, he called for silence. All remained silent and stood reverently. But a large number of swallows nesting there were shrieking and chirping. Since blessed Francis could not be heard by the people, he said to the noisy birds: "My sister swallows, now it is time for me also to speak, since you have already said enough. Listen to the word of the Lord and stay quiet and calm until the word of the Lord is completed." Immediately those little birds fell silent — to the amazement and surprise of all present — and did not move from that place until the sermon was over. Those men who saw this sign were filled with great wonder, saying: "Truly, this man is holy, and a friend of the Most High."

With great devotion they hurried to touch at least his clothes, while praising and blessing God. It was certainly a marvel that even irrational creatures recognized his feeling of tenderness toward them, and sensed the sweetness of his love. Once while he was staying near the town of Greccio, a certain brother brought him a live rabbit caught in a trap. Seeing it, the most blessed man was moved with tenderness. "Brother rabbit," he said, "come to me. Why did you let yourself get caught?" As soon as the brother holding it let go, the rabbit, without any prompting, took shelter with the holy man, as in a most secure place, resting in his bosom. After it had rested there for a little while, the holy father, caressing it with motherly affection, let it go, so that now free it would return to the woods. As often as it was put on the ground, it rushed back to the holy man's lap, so he told the brothers to carry it away to the nearby forest. Something similar happened with another little rabbit, a wild one, when he was on the island in the Lake of Perugia.

He had the same tender feeling toward fish. When he had the chance he would throw back into the water live fish that had been caught, and he warned them to be careful not to be caught again. One time while he was sitting in a little boat at the port on the Lake of Rieti, a fisherman caught a large fish, commonly called a tinca, and reverently offered it to him. He accepted it gladly and gratefully, calling it "brother." He put it back in the water next to the little boat, and with devotion blessed the name of the Lord. For some time that fish did not leave the spot but stayed next to the boat, playing in the water where he put it until, at the end of his prayer, the holy man of God gave it permission to leave.

Thus the glorious father Francis, walking in the way of obedience, and embracing the yoke of complete submission to God, was worthy of the great honor before God of having the obedience of creatures. Water was changed into wine for him once at the hermitage of Sant' Urbano when he was suffering from a severe illness. Once he tasted it, he recovered so easily that everyone believed it was a divine miracle, as it indeed was. He is truly a saint, whom creatures obey in this way: at his wish the very elements convert themselves to other uses.

Thomas of Celano, The Life of Saint Francis, First Book, XXI, 59–61
The Saint, 235–6

26 JUNE

At the time the venerable father Francis preached to the birds, as reported above, he went around the towns and villages, sowing the seed of divine blessings everywhere, until he reached the city of Ascoli. There he spoke the word of God with his usual fervor. By a change of the right hand of the Most High, nearly all the people were filled with such grace and devotion that they were trampling each other in their eagerness to hear and see him. Thirty men, cleric and lay, at that time received the habit of holy religion from him.

So great was the faith of men and women and so great the devotion of their hearts towards the holy one of God, that a person was considered fortunate who was able to touch at least his clothing. When he entered a city, clergy rejoiced, bells rang, men exulted, women rejoiced, and children clapped. Often taking branches from trees and singing psalms, they went out to meet him. The perversity of heretics was shamed, the faith of the Church was extolled and, as believers rejoiced, heretics hid.

The marks of his holiness were so clear in him that no one dared to speak against him, as the assembly of the people paid attention to him alone. He put the faith of the Holy Roman Church above and beyond all things, preserving, honoring and following it, since the salvation of all who would be saved was found in it alone. He honored priests and affectionately embraced every ecclesiastical order.

The people used to bring him loaves of bread to bless, which they kept for a long time, and, on tasting them, they were cured of various diseases.

Driven by great faith, people often tore his habit until sometimes he was left almost naked. Even more remarkable is that health was restored to some people through something that the holy father had touched with his hands.

There was a pregnant woman living on a small farm in the Arezzo area. At the time of childbirth she was in labor with such excruciating pain that she hovered between life and death. Her neighbors and relatives heard that the blessed Francis was going to pass by there on his way to a hermitage. While they were waiting the blessed Francis went to that place by another route. He had gone on horseback because he was weak and sick. When he reached that place, he sent one of the brothers, named Peter, to return the horse to the man who had lent it to him out of sincere charity.

When returning the horse brother Peter went down the road near the house where the woman was suffering. The men of that area saw him and raced to meet him, thinking that he was blessed Francis. When they realized that he was not, they were sorely disappointed. They began to inquire among themselves if they could find some item that blessed Francis's hand had touched. They had spent quite a bit of time in this search, when they finally discovered the bridle reins which he had held in his hand while riding. Pulling the bridle from the horse's mouth, they placed on the woman the reins which he had held in his very hands. At this, the danger passed, and the woman gave birth in great joy and good health.

Thomas of Celano, The Life of Saint Francis, First Book, XXII, 62–3
The Saint, 236–9

27 JUNE

The faithful servant of Christ, Saint Francis, once held a General Chapter at Saint Mary of the Angels, and at that chapter five thousand brothers gathered. Saint Dominic came there, the head and foundation of the Order of Brother Preachers, as he was then going from Burgundy to Rome. Hearing of the gathering of the General Chapter that Saint Francis was holding on the plane of Saint Mary of the Angels, he went to see it with seven brothers of his Order. Also at that Chapter there was a cardinal very devoted to Saint Francis whom he had prophesied would become pope, and that is what happened. That cardinal had come especially to Assisi from Perugia, where the Court was staying. He came every day to see Saint Francis and his brothers, and he sometimes sang Mass and sometimes preached a sermon to the brothers in the Chapter. And that Cardinal experienced great delight and devotion when he came to visit that holy gathering. He saw the brothers sitting on that plain around Saint Mary of the Angels, group by group, forty here, there a hundred, further on eighty together, all busy in speaking of God, in prayer, in works of charity. And they remained in such silence with such modesty that no sound or loud noise could be heard. Marveling over such a crowd gathered as one in such order, he said with tears and great devotion: "This is truly the camp and the army of the knights of God!" In that great multitude no one was heard telling stories or lies, but wherever a group of brothers gathered, they either prayed or said the Office, or wept over their own sins or those of their benefactors or spoke about the salvation of souls. There in that field there were huts of mats and reeds, separated into groups for the brothers of different Provinces. For this reason, that Chapter was called the Chapter of Mats or of Reeds. Their beds were the bare ground and some had a little straw; their pillows were stones or pieces of wood. For this reason there was such devotion toward them among those who heard or saw them, and such was their reputation for holiness that many came from the pope's Court, which was then at Perugia; and from other areas of the Spoleto Valley came many counts, barons, knights and noblemen, common people, cardinals, bishops, abbots and many other clerics, to see such a holy and great and humble gathering of so many holy men together, the likes of which the world had never seen. They came particularly to see the head and most holy father of that holy people, who had robbed the world of such beautiful prey and gathered such a lovely and devout flock to follow the footprints of the true shepherd, Jesus Christ.

After the whole General Chapter was gathered, the holy father of all and general minister, Saint Francis, in fervor of spirit proclaimed the word of God in a loud voice, preaching what the Holy Spirit gave him to say. And he offered these words as the theme of the sermon: "My sons, we have promised great things to God; greater things are promised to us by God if we observe what we have promised Him: let us await confidently those promised to us. Brief is the delight of the world; but the punishment that follows is eternal. The suffering of this life is small, but the glory of the other life is infinite." He preached most devoutly on these words, comforting and encouraging all the brothers to obedience and reverence for Holy Mother Church, to brotherly love; to pray to God for all the people, to have patience in the hardships of the world and temperance in prosperity, to keep purity and angelic chastity, to have harmony and peace with God, the people and their own conscience, to love and observance of most holy poverty. Then he said to them, "By virtue of holy obedience, I command all you gathered here: have no care or anxiety about what to eat or drink or other things necessary for the body, but to concentrate only on praying and praising God; and leave all care for your body to Him, since He has a special care for you." They all received this command with joyful hearts and glad faces. And when Saint Francis finished the sermon, they all hurried to prayer.

The Little Flowers of Saint Francis, 18
The Prophet, 595–7

28 JUNE

One day when blessed Francis was sitting at table with the brothers, little birds, male and a female, came over and took some crumbs from the saint's table as they pleased. They did this every day, anxious to feed their newly hatched chicks. The saint rejoiced over them, and caressed them, as was his custom, and offered them a reward for their efforts. One day the father and mother offered their children to the brothers, as if they had been raised at their expense; and once they entrusted their fledglings to the brothers, they were never seen again in that place. The chicks grew tame with the brothers and used to perch on their hands. They stayed in the house, not as guests but as members of the family. They hid at the sight of people of the world, showing they were the foster children of the brothers alone.

The saint noticed this, surprised, and invited the brothers to rejoice: "See," he said, "what our brothers the robins have done, as if they were endowed with reason! They have said to us: "Brothers, we present to you our babies, who have been fed by your crumbs. Do with them as you please; we will go off to another home." "The young birds became completely tame with the brothers, and all ate together peacefully. But greed broke up this harmony, for a bigger one grew arrogant and harassed the smaller ones. When the big one had already eaten his fill, he still pushed the others away from the food. "Look now," said the father, "at what this greedy one is doing! He's full to bursting, but he's still jealous of his hungry brothers. He will die an evil death." The punishment followed soon after the saint's word. The one who disturbed his brothers climbed on the edge of a water pitcher to take a drink, and suddenly fell into it and drowned ....

When so punished in birds, is not avarice an evil to be feared when found in mortals! And is not the judgment of the saint to be feared when punishment ensues with such ease!

Thomas of Celano, The Remembrance of the Desire of a Soul,
Second Book, XVIII, 47
The Founder, 279

29 JUNE

The power of love had made him a brother to other creatures; no wonder the charity of Christ made him even more a brother to those marked with the image of the Creator. He would say that nothing should be placed ahead of the salvation of souls and would often demonstrate this with the fact that the Onlybegotten Son of God saw fit to hang on the cross for the sake of souls. From this arose his effort in prayer, his frequent travel in preaching and his extraordinary behavior in giving example.

He would not consider himself a friend of Christ unless he loved the souls which He loved. For him this was the principal cause for revering the doctors of theology: they are the helpers of Christ, who carry out with Christ this office. With all the unbounded affection of the depths of his heart, he embraced the brothers themselves as fellow members in the household of the same faith, united by a share in an eternal inheritance.

Whenever somebody criticized him for the austerity of his life, he would reply that he was given to the Order as an example, as an eagle that prompts her young to fly. His innocent flesh, which already submitted freely to the spirit, had no need of the whip because of any offence. Still he renewed its punishments because of example, staying on hard paths only for the sake of others. And he was right.

In prelates what the hand does is notice more than what the tongue says. By your deeds, Father, you convinced more gently; you persuaded more easily, you proved things more certainly. For if they were to speak in the tongues of men and angels, but without showing examples of charity, it profits little; they profit nothing. For if the one who gives correction is not feared, and gives his will as the reason to act, will the trappings of power suffice for salvation? Still, what they thunder about should be done: as water flows to the gardens in empty canals. Meanwhile, let the rose be gathered from thorns, that the greater may serve the lesser.

Thomas of Celano, The Remembrance of the Desire of a Soul,
Second Book, CXXXI, 172
The Founder, 358–9

30 JUNE

Once a brother who was tempted was sitting alone with the saint and said to him: "Pray for me, kind father, for I firmly believe if you should be good enough to pray for me, I'll be freed from my temptation immediately. I really am tormented beyond my strength, and I know this is not hidden from you." Saint Francis said to him: "Believe me, son, I believe you are even more a servant of God because of this. And you should know the more you're tempted, the more I will love you." He added: "I tell you the truth, no one should consider himself a servant of God until he has passed through temptations and tribulations. A temptation overcome is like a ring with which the Lord betroths the soul of his servant. Many flatter themselves over their many years of merit and rejoice at never having suffered any temptations. But sheer fright would knock them out before a battle even started. So they should know that the Lord has kept in mind their weakness of spirit. Hard fights are rarely fought except by those with the greatest strength."

Thomas of Celano, The Remembrance of the Desire of a Soul,
Second Book, LXXXVIII, 118
The Founder, 325–6

July

1 JULY

Another time when God's servant was preaching on the seashore at Gaeta, out of devotion, crowds rushed upon him in order to touch him. Horrified at people's acclaim, the servant of Christ jumped alone into a small boat that was drawn up on the shore. The boat began to move, as if it had both intellect and motion of itself, and, without the help of any oars, glided away from the shore, to the wonderment of all who witnessed it. When it had gone out some distance into the deep water, it stood motionless among the waves, as long as the holy man preached to the attentive crowd on the shore. When, after hearing the sermon, seeing the miracle, and receiving his blessing, the crowd went away and would no longer trouble him, the boat returned to land on its own.

Who, then, would be so obstinate and lacking in piety as to look down upon the preaching of Francis? By his remarkable power, not only creatures lacking reason learned obedience, but even inanimate objects served him when he preached, as if they had life.

Bonaventure, The Major Legend of Saint Francis, XII, 6
The Founder, 625

2 JULY

He used to say the psalms with such attention of mind and spirit, as if he had God present. When the Lord's name occurred in the psalms, he seemed to lick his lips because of its sweetness.

He wanted to honor with special reverence the Lord's name not only when thought but also when spoken and written. He once persuaded the brothers to gather all pieces of paper wherever they were found and to place them in a clean place so that if that sacred name happened to be written there, it would not be trodden underfoot. When he pronounced or heard the name Jesus, he was filled with an inner joy and seemed completely changed exteriorly as if some honey-sweet flavor had transformed his taste or some harmonious sound had transformed his hearing.

Bonaventure, The Major Legend of Saint Francis, X, 6
The Founder, 609

3 JULY

A servant of God can be known to have the Spirit of the Lord in this way: if, when the Lord performs some good through him, his flesh does not therefore exalt itself, because it is always opposed to every good. Instead he regards himself the more worthless and esteems himself less than all others.

Blessed are the peacemakers, for they will be called children of God.

A servant of God cannot know how much patience and humility he has within himself as long as he is content. When the time comes, however, when those who should make him content do the opposite, he has as much patience and humility as he has at that time and no more.

Blessed are the poor in spirit, for theirs is the kingdom of heaven.

There are many who, while insisting on prayers and obligations, inflict many abstinences and punishments upon their bodies. But they are immediately offended and disturbed about a single word which seems to be harmful to their bodies or about something which might be taken away from them. These people are not poor in spirit, for someone who is truly poor in spirit hates himself and loves those who strike him on the cheek.

Blessed are the peacemakers, for they will be called children of God.

Those people are truly peacemakers who, regardless of what they suffer in this world, preserve peace of spirit and body out of love of our Lord Jesus Christ.

Blessed are the clean in heart, for they will see God.

The truly clean of heart are those who look down upon earthly things, seek those of heaven, and, with a clean heart and spirit, never cease adoring and seeing the Lord God living and true.

Blessed is that servant who no more exalts himself over the good the Lord says or does through him than over what He says or does through another.

A person sins who wishes to receive more from his neighbor than what he wishes to give of himself to the Lord God.

The Admonitions, XII–XVII
The Saint, 133–4

&

4 JULY

The brothers at that time begged him to teach them how to pray, because, walking in simplicity of spirit, up to that time they did not know the Church's office. Francis told them: "When you pray, say "Our Father" and "We adore you, O Christ, in all your churches throughout the whole world, and we bless you, for by your holy cross you have redeemed the world." "The brothers, devout disciples of their master, strove diligently to observe this. For they attempted to fulfill completely not only the things he told them as brotherly advice or fatherly commands, but even those things he thought or meditated upon, if they could know them by some indication. The blessed father told them that true obedience is not about just what is spoken but also about what is thought, not just what is commanded but what is desired, that is: 'If a brother subject to a prelate not only hears his words but understands his will, he should immediately ready himself fully for obedience, and do whatever by some sign he knows the other wants.'"

For this reason, in whatever place a church had been built, even when they were not near it, but could glimpse it from a distance, they would turn toward it. Prostrate on the ground, bowing inwardly and outwardly, they would adore the Almighty saying, "We adore you, O Christ, in all your churches…" just as their holy father taught them. What is just as striking is that wherever they saw a cross or the sign of a cross, whether on the ground, on a wall, in the trees or roadside hedges they did the same thing.

    Thomas of Celano, The Life of Saint Francis, First Book, XVII, 45
The Saint, 222

5 JULY

In this way holy simplicity filled them, innocence of life taught them, and purity of heart so possessed them that they were completely ignorant of duplicity of heart. For just as there was in them one faith, so there was one spirit, one will, one charity, continual unity of spirit, harmony in living, cultivation of virtues, agreement of minds, and loyalty in actions.

For example, they often used to confess their sins to a certain secular priest, even when his wickedness had been reported to them by many people. He had a very bad reputation and was despised by everyone else because of the enormity of his misdeeds. But they did not wish to believe it; so they did not stop confessing their sins to him as usual, nor stop showing him proper reverence.

One day he, or another priest, said to one of the brothers, "Watch out, brother, don't be a hypocrite!" The brother immediately believed that he was a hypocrite because of the priest's statement. For this reason, he was crying and weeping day and night, moved by deep sorrow. When the brothers asked him what caused such grief and unusual gloom, he answered, "A priest told me something that has upset me so much that I can hardly think about anything else." The brothers kept trying to console him and urged him not to believe it. But he said, "How can you say that, brothers? A priest told me this. Could a priest lie? Since a priest does not lie, we must believe what he said." Remaining for a long time in this simplicity, he finally gave in to the words of the blessed father who explained to him the priest's statement and wisely excused his intention. For in almost any case of disturbance of mind in one of the brothers, at his burning words the clouds would break up and clear weather would return.

Thomas of Celano, The Life of Saint Francis, First Book, XVII, 46
The Saint, 223

6 JULY

One time when Saint Francis was seriously ill and Brother Leo was taking care of him, that same Brother Leo was near Saint Francis and was praying, and he was rapt in ecstasy and led in spirit to a very great river, wide and turbulent. As he was watching those crossing over, he saw some brothers with heavy loads entering that river. They were immediately overwhelmed by the force of the river and drowned. Several others went a third of the way across the river, and some as far as the middle of the river, and some as far as the shore; but all of them, because of the force of the river and the loads they carried with them, finally fell in and drowned. Brother Leo, seeing this, felt great compassion for them; and suddenly, as he stood there, a great multitude of brothers arrived, without any loads or burdened by anything at all, and in whom shone holy poverty. They entered the river and crossed it without any harm at all. Having seen this, Brother Leo returned to himself.

Then Saint Francis, sensing in spirit that Brother Leo had seen a vision, called him to himself, and asked him what he had seen. And the same Brother Leo told him the whole vision in detail, and Saint Francis said: "What you saw is true. The great river is this world; the brothers who drowned in the river are those who do not follow their evangelical profession especially in regard to the highest poverty. Those who crossed without danger are those brothers who neither seek nor possess anything earthly or anything of the flesh, but are content having only basic food and clothing, following Christ naked on the Cross and willingly and happily carrying the burden and the gentle yoke of Christ and of holy obedience; and therefore they cross easily from temporal life to eternal life."

The Little Flowers of Saint Francis, 36
The Prophet, 627

7 JULY

Sylvester was a secular priest of the city of Assisi. The man of God once bought from him some stones for repairing a church. At that time, this man Sylvester, inflamed with consuming greed, saw Brother Bernard — who was the first small sprout of the Order of Lesser Ones after the holy one of God, perfectly giving up what he had, and giving it to the poor. He lodged a complaint with the man of God that the price of stones he once sold to him had not been paid in full. Francis smiled when he saw that the priest's mind was infected with the poison of avarice. Wishing to offer something to cool that man's cursed heat, he filled his hands with money, without even counting it. The priest Sylvester rejoiced at this gift, but even more he was amazed at the generosity of the giver. When he returned home, he kept thinking about what happened. Under his breath he grumbled a contented complaint that, although he was already getting old, he still loved this world; it was amazing that that younger man despised it all. At last, he was filled with a pleasant fragrance, and Christ opened the bosom of His mercy.

He showed him in a vision how much the deeds of Francis were worth; how eminently they shone in His presence; how magnificently they filled the frame of the whole world. He saw in a dream a golden cross coming out from Francis's mouth. "Its top touched the heavens," its outstretched arms circled the world on every side with their embrace. Struck to the heart by what he saw, the priest cast off harmful delay, left the world and became a perfect imitator of the man of God. He began perfectly his life in the Order, and by the grace of Christ completed it more perfectly.

Is it surprising that Francis appeared crucified when he was always so much with the cross? Is it any wonder that the wondrous cross, taking root inside him, and sprouting in such good soil should bear remarkable flowers, leaves, and fruit? Nothing of a different kind could come to be produced by such soil, which that wonderful cross from the beginning claimed entirely for itself.

Thomas of Celano, The Remembrance of the Desire of a Soul,
Second Book, LXXV,109
The Founder, 319–20

8 JULY

Great was his compassion towards the sick and great his concern for their needs. If lay people's piety sent him tonics he would give it to the others who were sick even though he had greater need of them. He had sympathy for all who were ill and when he could not alleviate their pain he offered words of compassion. He would eat on fast days so the weak would not be ashamed of eating, and he was not embarrassed to go through the city's public places to find some meat for a sick brother.

However, he also advised the sick to be patient when things were lacking and not stir up a scandal if everything was not done to their satisfaction. Because of this he had these words written in one of the rules: "I beg all my sick brothers that in their illness they do not become angry or upset at God or the brothers. They should not anxiously seek medicine, or desire too eagerly to free the flesh, that is soon to die and is an enemy of the soul. Let them give thanks for all things and let them desire, however, to be as God wills them to be. For God teaches with the rod of punishment and sicknesses those whom he has destined to eternal life as he himself has said: 'Those I love, I correct and chastise.'"

He once realized that a sick brother had a craving to eat grapes, so he took him into the vineyard and, sitting under a vine, in order to encourage him to eat, began to eat first himself.

Thomas of Celano, The Remembrance of the Desire of a Soul, Second Book, CXXXIII, 175–6
The Founder, 359–60

9 JULY

With even greater mercy and patience he would bear with and comfort those sick brothers whom he knew were like wavering children, agitated with temptations and faint in spirit. Avoiding harsh corrections when he saw no danger he spared the rod so as to spare the soul. He would say that it was proper for a prelate, who is a father, not a tyrant, to prevent occasion for failure and not allow one to fall who, once fallen can be lifted up only with difficulty.

Woe to the pitiful madness of our age! Not only do we not lift up or even hold the tottering, but often enough we push them to fall! We consider it nothing to take away from that greatest shepherd, one little lamb for whose sake he offered loud cries and tears on the cross.

On the contrary you, holy father, preferred to correct the strays rather than lose them. We know that in some the disease of self-will is so deeply rooted that they need cauterizing, not salve. It is clear that for many it is healthier to be broken with a rod of iron than to be rubbed down with hands. Still, to every thing there is a season; oil and wine; rod and staff; zeal and pity, burning and salving, prison and womb. All of these are demanded by the God of vengeance, and Father of mercies, who desires mercy more than sacrifice.

Thomas of Celano, The Remembrance of the Desire of a Soul,
Second Book, CXXXIII, 177
The Founder, 360

10 JULY

The holy man abhorred pride, the source of all evil, and disobedience, its worst offspring, but he welcomed the humility of repentance with no less intensity.

It happened once that a brother, who had done something against the law of obedience, was brought to him to be punished according to justice. Seeing that the brother showed clear signs of being truly sorry, the man of God was drawn to be easy on him out of love of humility. However, so this easy forgiveness might not be an incentive for others to fail in their duty, he ordered that the brother's hood be taken off and thrown into the midst of a fire, so that all could see what and how harsh a punishment the offence of disobedience deserved. When the hood had been within the fire for a while, he ordered that it be pulled out of the flames and returned to the humbly repentant brother. What a marvel! The hood was pulled out of the middle of the flames, showing no trace of a burn. This was done so that, with this one miracle, God might so commend both the holy man's virtue and the humility of repentance.

Therefore, worthy of being followed is the humility of Francis that obtained such marvelous honor even on earth that, at his mere nod, it inclined God to his wish, changed the attitude of a human being, repulsed the obstinacy of demons at his command, and restrained the greed of flames. In truth, as it exalts its possessors, this is what wins honor from all, while it exhibits reverence to all.

Bonaventure, The Major Legend of Saint Francis, VI, 11
The Founder, 576

11 JULY

The faithful servant and perfect imitator of Christ, Francis, sensing himself most powerfully transformed into Christ through the virtue of holy humility, desired that humility in his brothers before all other virtues. And that they would love, desire, acquire, and preserve it unceasingly, he would more passionately stimulate them by word and example, and would especially admonish and incite the ministers and preachers to exercise works of humility.

For he used to say that, because of the office of prelacy or of zeal for preaching, they should not abandon holy and devout prayer, going for alms, working at times with their hands, and performing other humble tasks like the other brothers, for good example and for the benefit of their souls, as well as others.

He said: "The brothers who are subjects will be very edified when their ministers and preachers devote themselves freely to prayer, and give themselves to humble and lowly tasks. Otherwise they cannot admonish the other brothers about these things without confusion, prejudice, and blame. For we must, after Christ's example, first act and then teach, or act and teach simultaneously."

A Mirror of Perfection, III, 73
The Prophet, 321

12 JULY

The blessed Christ, wishing to show the great holiness of his most faithful servant, Sir Saint Anthony, and how devoutly his preaching and holy teaching should be heeded, refuted the foolishness of unbelieving heretics by using irrational animals, one time among others, by using fish, just as in ancient times in the Old Testament He had refuted the foolishness of Balaam by the mouth of the ass. For once when Saint Anthony was in Rimini, where there was a great number of heretics, and wishing that they return to the light of the true faith and the way of truth, he preached to them for many days and discussed the faith of Christ and the Holy Scriptures. But as they not only did not agree with his holy speeches, but actually became hardened and obstinate, and did not want to hear him, by divine inspiration Saint Anthony went one day to the mouth of the river close by the sea, and standing on the bank between the river and the sea, he began, as if preaching, calling the fish on behalf of God: "Listen to the Word of God, you fish of the sea and the river, because the unbelieving heretics refuse to listen." And as soon as he said this, immediately such a multitude of large fish came to him at the bank that such a great multitude had never been seen there. They all held their heads above the water, all turned to face Saint Anthony, and all in great peace and meekness and order: in front of the bank and closer in were the little fish, and behind them the medium fish, and then behind them, where the water was deepest, the biggest fish.

When all the fish were arranged and lined up in this way, Saint Anthony began to preach solemnly and said: "My brother fish, you have a great obligation, according to your ability, to give thanks to your Creator, who has given you such a noble element for your home. You have fresh or salt water, as you like. And he has given you many shelters to avoid storms. Moreover, He has given you an element that is clear and transparent, and food to eat by which you can live. God, your courteous and kind Creator, when He created you, gave you a commandment to increase and multiply, and He gave you His blessing. Then when there was the Flood over everything, and all the other animals died, God preserved only you without harm. Furthermore,

He has given you fins so you can go anywhere you please. By the command of God you were allowed to preserve Jonah *the prophet,* and after the third day to spit him onto the land, safe and sound. You presented the tax-coin to our Lord Jesus Christ when, as a little poor man, he did not have any way to pay. You were the food of the Eternal King Jesus Christ before the Resurrection and after it, by a singular mystery. Because of all these things you are greatly bound to praise and bless God, Who has given you so many and such great gifts, more than to other creatures." At these and similar words the fish began to open their mouths and bowed their heads, and with these and other signs of reverence, according to what was possible to them, they praised God. Then Saint Anthony, seeing the great reverence of the fish toward God the Creator, rejoicing in spirit, cried out in a loud voice: "Blessed be the Eternal God, because aquatic fish honor God more than heretic humans, and unreasoning animals hear His word better than unbelieving people!" And the more Saint Anthony preached, the more the number of fish increased, and not one left the place which it had taken.

The people of the city began to run toward this miracle, and among them were even those same heretics who, on seeing such an amazing and clear miracle, stricken to the heart, threw themselves at the feet of Saint Anthony to hear his sermon. And then Saint Anthony began to preach about the Catholic faith, and he preached about it so nobly that he converted all those heretics and they returned to the true faith of Christ; and all the faithful were filled with joy, comforted and strengthened in the faith. Having done this, Saint Anthony dismissed the fish with God's blessing, and all of them departed with amazing gestures of joy, and the people too. And then Saint Anthony stayed for many days in Rimini, preaching and producing great spiritual fruit of souls.

The Little Flowers of Saint Francis, 40
The Prophet, 632–3

13 JULY

Burning with divine love, the blessed father Francis was always eager to try his hand at brave deeds, and walking in the way of God's commands with heart wide-open, he longed to reach the summit of perfection.

In the sixth year of his conversion, burning with the desire for holy martyrdom, he wished to take a ship to the region of Syria to preach the Christian faith and repentance to the Saracens and other unbelievers. But after he had boarded a ship to go there, contrary winds started blowing, and he found himself with his fellow travelers on the shores of Slavonia.

When he realized that he had been cheated of what he desired, after a little while he begged some sailors going to Ancona to take him with them, since there were hardly any ships that could sail that year to Syria. But the sailors stubbornly refused to do so since he could not pay them. The holy one of God, trusting God's goodness, secretly boarded the ship with his companion. By divine providence, a man arrived unknown to anyone, who brought the food needed. He called over a person from the ship, a God-fearing man. "Take with you all these things," he said, "and in their time of need faithfully give them to those poor men hiding on your ship."

A great storm arose and they had to spend many days laboring at the oars. They had used up all their food. Only the food of the poor Francis remained. Owing to divine grace and power, his food multiplied so much that, although there were still many days of sailing remaining, it fully supplied the needs of them all until they reached the port of Ancona. When the sailors realized that they had escaped the dangers of the sea through God's servant Francis, they gave thanks to almighty God, who is always revealed through his servants as awesome and loving.

Thomas of Celano, The Life of Saint Francis, First Book, XX, 55
The Saint, 229–30

14 JULY

Francis, the servant of the most high, left the sea and began to walk the earth. Furrowing with the plough of the word, he sowed the seed of life, bearing blessed fruit. Soon many good and suitable men, cleric and lay, fleeing the world and courageously escaping the devil, by the grace and will of the Most High, followed him devoutly in his life and proposal.

Though the shoot of the gospel was producing choice fruit in abundance, it did not stifle his highest purpose, the burning desire for martyrdom. Not too long after this, he began to travel towards Morocco to preach the gospel of Christ to the Miramamolin and his retinue. He was so carried away with desire that he would sometimes leave behind his companion on the journey and hurry ahead, intoxicated in spirit, in order to carry out his purpose. But the good God, out of pure kindness, was pleased to be mindful of him and many others. After he reached Spain God withstood him to his face, striking him with illness, and called him back from the journey he had begun.

Shortly afterwards when Francis returned to the Church of Saint Mary of the Portiuncula, some literate men and nobles gladly joined him. He received such men with honor and dignity, since he himself was very noble and distinguished in spirit, and respectfully gave to each his due. In fact, since he was endowed with outstanding discernment, he wisely considered in all matters the dignity of rank of each one.

But still he would not rest from carrying out fervently the holy impulse of his spirit. Now in the thirteenth year of his conversion, he journeyed to the region of Syria, while bitter and long battles were being waged daily between Christians and pagans. Taking a companion with him, he was not afraid to present himself to the sight of the Sultan of the Saracens.

Who is equal to the task of telling this story? What great firmness he showed standing in front of him! With great strength of soul he spoke to him, with eloquence and confidence he answered those who insulted the Christian law.

Before he reached the Sultan, he was captured by soldiers, insulted and beaten, but was not afraid. He did not flinch at threats of torture nor was he shaken by death threats. Although he was ill-treated by many with a hostile spirit and a harsh attitude, he was received very graciously by the Sultan. The Sultan honored him as much as he could, offering him many gifts, trying to turn his mind to worldly riches. But when he saw that he resolutely scorned all these things like dung, the Sultan was overflowing with admiration and recognized him as a man unlike any other. He was moved by his words and listened to him very willingly.

In all this, however, the Lord did not fulfill his desire, reserving for him the prerogative of a unique grace.

Thomas of Celano, The Life of Saint Francis, First Book, XX, 56–7
The Saint, 230–1

15 JULY

After ... [Pope Gregory had made his wise decision], he hurried to Assisi, where a glorious treasure was being kept for him, to make all his suffering and pressing trials disappear. On his arrival, the whole region rejoiced, the city was filled with gladness, a great crowd of people joined the joyful celebration, and the bright day grew brighter with new lights. Everyone went forth to meet him and joined in solemn vigil. The devoted group of poor brothers went out to meet him, each one singing sweet songs to the Lord's anointed. The Vicar of Christ reached the place and first going down to the tomb of Saint Francis, he eagerly paid his respects with great reverence. Groaning deeply, he struck his breast, and breaking into tears, he bowed his venerable head in an outpouring of devotion.

Meanwhile, a solemn assembly was called for the canonization of the saint and the eminent body of cardinals met frequently to consider the matter. Many who had been freed from their illnesses through the holy man of God came from far and wide, and from here and there countless miracles gleamed: these miracles were heard, verified, accepted, and approved.

But then a new problem arose and, obliged by the duties of office, the blessed Pope had to go to Perugia, only in order to be able to return once again to Assisi with more abundant and special grace for the most important task. Another meeting was called in Perugia. The sacred consistory of cardinals met in the chambers of the Lord Pope to consider the cause. All were in agreement. They read the miracles with great reverence; they extolled the life and conduct of the holy man with the highest praise.

"The holy life of this holy man," they said, "does not require the evidence of miracles for we have seen it with our eyes and touched it with our hands and tested it with truth as our guide." They all leapt to their feet with tears of joy; and in their tears there was a great blessing. They immediately fixed the blessed date when they would fill the whole world with blessed joy.

Thomas of Celano, The Life of Saint Francis, Third Book, XX, 123–4
The Saint, 293

16 JULY

The solemn day arrives, "A day held in reverence by every age," showering the earth and even the heavenly mansions with ecstatic rejoicing. Bishops gather, abbots arrive, prelates from the most remote areas appear; a king's presence is noticed, with a noble crowd of counts and dukes. All accompany the lord of the whole earth, and with him enter the city of Assisi in a happy procession. They come to the place prepared for this solemn meeting and the glorious crowd of cardinals, bishops, and abbots gathers around the blessed pope. A distinguished assembly of priests and clerics is there, a happy and sacred gathering of religious men, and the modest presence of veiled consecrated women, a great crowd from every people: an almost numberless multitude of both sexes. They are running from all over, and in this crowd every age is represented enthusiastically. The small and the great are there; the servants and those freed from their masters.

The supreme pontiff, bridegroom of the Church of Christ is standing, surrounded with such variety of children, a crown of glory on his head marked with the sign of holiness. He stands adorned with the pontifical regalia and clothed in holy vestments with settings of gold, the work of a jeweler. He stands there, the Lord's anointed, gilded in magnificence and glory and covered with precious stones cut and sparkling, catching the eyes of all. Cardinals and bishops surround him, clothed with jewels glittering on garments gleaming white as snow, offering an image of the beauty of heaven, displaying the joy of the glorified. All the people are waiting for the cry of joy, the song of gladness, a new song, a song full of sweetness, a song of praise, a song of everlasting blessing.

Pope Gregory first preaches to all the people with deeply felt words sweeter than honey, proclaiming the praises of God in a resonant voice. He praises the holy father Francis in noble words. Recalling his way of life and speaking of his purity, he is drenched in tears. His sermon begins with the text: "Like the morning star in the midst of clouds, like the full moon, like the shining sun, so in his days did he shine in the temple of God."

At the end of this speech, so true and worthy of complete acceptance, one of the subdeacons of the lord Pope, Ottaviano by name, reads in a loud voice the miracles of the Saint to the whole assembly. Lord Ranieri, a Cardinal-deacon, a man of keen intelligence, of outstanding devotion and conduct, speaks about them with sacred eloquence, his eyes welling with tears. The shepherd of the Church is overcome with joy, with deep sighs rising from the bottom of his heart and, often sobbing, breaks out in tears. The other prelates of the Church were also pouring out a flood of tears that dripped onto their sacred vestments. Then all the people are weeping, tired out with eager expectation.

At that moment the blessed Pope cries out in a ringing voice, and raising his hands to heaven proclaims: "To the praise and glory of God almighty, Father, Son, and Holy Spirit, the glorious Virgin Mary, the blessed Apostles Peter and Paul, to the honor of the glorious Roman Church! On the advice of our brothers and other prelates, we decree that the most blessed father Francis, whom the Lord has glorified in heaven and we venerate on earth, shall be enrolled in the catalogue of saints, and his feast is to be celebrated on the day of his death." At this announcement, the reverend cardinals join the pope in singing the Te Deum laudamus in a loud voice.

And there rises the cry of many peoples praising God; the earth echoes the booming sound, the air is filled with jubilation, and the ground is soaked with tears. They sing new songs and the servants of God rejoice in the melody of the Spirit. Sweet sounding instruments are playing as hymns are sung with musical voices. A very sweet fragrance is flowing there and an even more pleasant melody is echoing there, moving everyone deeply. The day is breaking, colored with radiant sunbeams. There are green branches of olive and fresh boughs of other trees. There all are dressed in festive clothing, shining brightly, while the blessing of peace gladdens the spirits of all.

The blessed Pope Gregory then comes down from the high throne, and by the lower steps enters the sanctuary to offer prayers and sacrifices, and with his blessed lips kisses the tomb holding the sacred body dedicated to God. He offers many prayers and celebrates the sacred mysteries. Around him stands a ring of brothers, praising, adoring and blessing almighty God, who has done wondrous things through all the earth.

All the people echoed the praise of God, offering gifts of thanks to Francis in honor of the Most High Trinity. Amen.

These things happened in the city of Assisi, in the second year of the pontificate of the Lord Pope Gregory the Ninth, on the seventeenth day of the calends of the month of August [that is, on 16 July 1228].

Thomas of Celano, The Life of Saint Francis, Third Book, XX, 124–6
The Saint, 294–7

17 JULY

The ... evangelical man Francis resembled the blessed Jesus ... in the prophetic wonders he wrought. Hence fittingly can that line of Ecclesiasticus be cited in his regard: He made him like the saints in glory [Sir 45:2]. To be like the saints in glory, in this life, is to be renowned for miracles; by this the blessed Francis resembled Jesus in a very special way. Let us turn to what has been written down.

Like Jesus he changed water into wine, multiplied loaves of bread. From a boat — which had miraculously stayed still, surrounded by waves — after he had brought it to land, he taught the crowds on the shore who had come to listen. Every creature was seen to obey his command, as though in him primordial innocence had been restored.

Ubertino di Casale, The Tree of the Crucified Life of Jesus,
V, III, 10–15
The Prophet, 185

18 JULY

[F rancis's] resemblance to Jesus lay [also] in his possessing privileged authorization. Most fittingly can that verse of the third chapter of Daniel be cited in his regard: the form of the fourth is like the son of God [Dn 3:42]. He was fourth among the chief Levites: Stephen, Lawrence, Vincent, and Francis. He was also fourth among the founding fathers of Orders: Benedict, Augustine, Dominic, and Francis, as far as the Latins are concerned; for among the Greeks, it was the renowned Basil who first composed a Rule, and his appears to come closest to the perfection of the Gospel.

This, then, is Francis the standard-bearer, holding the seal of authority, the standard of activity, and the signet of charity.

Ubertino di Casale, The Tree of the Crucified Life of Jesus,
V, III, 27
The Prophet, 185

19 JULY

The man of God, the blessed Francis, had been taught not to seek his own salvation, but what he discerned would help the salvation of others. More than anything else he desired to be set free and to be with Christ. Thus his chief object of concern was to live free from all things that are in the world, so that his inner serenity would not be disturbed even for a moment by contact with any of its dust. He made himself insensible to all outside noise, gathering his external senses into his inner being and checking the impetus of his spirit, he emptied himself for God alone.

In the clefts of the rock he would build his nest and in the hollow of the wall his dwelling. With blessed devotion he visited the heavenly mansions; and, totally emptied of himself, he rested for a long time in the wounds of the Savior. That is why he often chose solitary places to focus his heart entirely on God.

But he was not reluctant, when he discerned the time was right, to involve himself in the affairs of his neighbors, and attend to their salvation. For his safest haven was prayer; not prayer of a fleeting moment, empty and proud, but prayer that was prolonged, full of devotion, peaceful in humility. If he began at night, he was barely finished at morning. Walking, sitting, eating, drinking, he was focused on prayer. He would spend the night alone praying in abandoned churches and in deserted places where, with the protection of divine grace, he overcame his soul's many fears and anxieties.

Thomas of Celano, The Life of Saint Francis, First Book, XXVII, 71
The Saint, 243–4

20 JULY

He used to struggle hand to hand with the devil who, in those places, would not only assault him internally with temptations but also frighten him externally with ruin and undermining. The brave soldier of God knew that his Lord could do all things in all places; thus he did not give in to the fears but said in his heart: "You, evil one! You cannot strike me with your evil weapons here anymore than if we were in front of a crowd in a public place."

He was extremely determined and paid no attention to anything beyond what was of the Lord. Though he often preached the word of God among thousands of people, he was as confident as if he were speaking with a close friend. He used to view the largest crowd of people as if it were a single person, and he would preach fervently to a single person as if to a large crowd. Out of the purity of his mind he drew his confidence in preaching and, even without preparation, he used to say the most amazing things to everyone. Sometimes he prepared for his talk with some meditation, but once the people gathered he could not remember what he had meditated about and had nothing to say. Without any embarrassment he would confess to the people that he had thought of many things before, but now he could not remember a thing. Sometimes he would be filled with such great eloquence that he moved the hearts of his hearers to astonishment. When he could not think of anything, he would give a blessing and send the people away with this act alone as a very good sermon.

Thomas of Celano, The Life of Saint Francis, First Book, XXVII, 72
The Saint, 244–5

21 JULY

Once he came to the city of Rome on a matter concerning the Order, and he greatly yearned to speak before the Lord Pope Honorius and the venerable cardinals. Lord Hugo, the renowned bishop of Ostia, venerated the holy man of God with special affection. When he learned of his arrival, Lord Hugo was filled with fear and joy, admiring the holy man's fervor yet aware of his simple purity. Trusting to the mercy of the Almighty that never fails the faithful in time of need, he led the holy man before the Lord Pope and the venerable cardinals.

As he stood in the presence of so many princes of the Church, blessed Francis, after receiving permission and a blessing, fearlessly began to speak.

He was speaking with such fire of spirit that he could not contain himself for joy. As he brought forth the word from his mouth, he moved his feet as if dancing, not playfully but burning with the fire of divine love, not provoking laughter but moving them to tears of sorrow. For many of them were touched in their hearts, amazed at the grace of God and the great determination of the man.

The venerable lord bishop of Ostia was waiting fearfully, praying to God that they would not despise the blessed man's simplicity; for both the glory and the disgrace of the holy man would reflect on himself, since he was the father set over the saint's household.

For Saint Francis clung to the bishop as a son does to his father and an only child to its mother, safely resting and sleeping in the lap of his kindness. The bishop filled the role and did the work of a shepherd, but left the name of shepherd to the holy man. Blessed Francis would foresee needs, but that blessed lord would deliver what was foreseen. There were many who plotted to destroy the new planting of the Order at its beginning. There were many trying to suffocate the chosen vineyard which the Lord's hand had so kindly planted anew in the world. There were many trying to steal and eat its first fresh fruit. But all of these opponents were slain with the sword of the venerable father and lord and their efforts came to naught. For he was a river of eloquence, a wall of the Church, a spokesman for truth, and a lover of the humble.

That was a memorable and blessed day when the holy man of God committed himself to such a venerable lord.

Thomas of Celano, The Life of Saint Francis, First Book, XXVII, 73–4
The Saint, 245–6

22 JULY

In the love that is God, therefore, I beg all my brothers — those who preach, pray, or work, cleric or lay — to strive to humble themselves in everything, not to boast or delight in themselves or inwardly exalt themselves because of the good words and deeds or, for that matter, because of any good that God sometimes says or does or works in and through them, in keeping with what the Lord says: Do not rejoice because the spirits are subject to you [Lk 10:20]. We may know with certainty that nothing belongs to us except our vices and sins. We must rejoice, instead, when we fall into various trials and, in this world, suffer every kind of anguish or distress of soul and body for the sake of eternal life.

Therefore, let all the brothers, beware of all pride and vainglory. Let us guard ourselves from the wisdom of this world and the prudence of the flesh. Because the spirit of the flesh very much desires and strives to have the words but cares little for the activity; it does not seek a religion and holiness in an interior spirit, but wants and desires to have a religion and a holiness outwardly apparent to people. They are the ones of whom the Lord says: Amen, I say to you, they have received their reward [Mt 6:2].

The Spirit of the Lord, however, wants the flesh to be mortified and looked down upon, considered of little worth and rejected. It strives for humility and patience, the pure, simple and true peace of the spirit. Above all, it desires the divine fear, the divine wisdom and the divine love of the Father, Son and Holy Spirit.

Let us refer all good to the Lord, God Almighty and Most High, acknowledge that every good is His, and thank Him, "from Whom all good comes, for everything." May He, the Almighty and Most High, the only true God, have, be given, and receive all honor and respect, all praise and blessing, all thanks and glory, to Whom all good belongs, He Who alone is good. When we see or hear evil spoken or done or God blasphemed, let us speak well and do well and praise God Who is blessed forever.

The Earlier Rule (The Rule without a Papal Seal), XVII, 5–19
The Saint, 75–6

23 JULY

The holy man overflowed with the spirit of charity, bearing within himself a deep sense of concern not only toward other humans in need but also toward mute, brute animals: reptiles, birds, and all other creatures whether sensate or not. But among all the different kinds of creatures, he loved lambs with a special fondness and spontaneous affection, since in Sacred Scripture the humility of our Lord Jesus Christ is frequently and rightly compared to the lamb. He used to embrace more warmly and to observe more gladly anything in which he found an allegorical likeness to the Son of God.

Once he was making a journey through the Marches of Ancona and preached the word of the Lord in the city. Then he took the road toward Osimo, with lord Paul, the one whom he had appointed minister of all the brethren in that province. He came upon a shepherd in the fields pasturing a flock of goats. There was one little sheep walking humbly and grazing calmly among these many goats. When blessed Francis saw it, he stopped in his tracks, and touched with sorrow in his heart, he groaned loudly, and said to the brother accompanying him: "Do you see that sheep walking so meekly among those goats? I tell you, in the same way our Lord Jesus Christ, meek and humble, walked among the Pharisees and chief priests. So I ask you, my son, in your love for Him to share my compassion for this little sheep. After we have paid for it, let us lead this little one from the midst of these goats."

Brother Paul was struck by his sorrow and also began to feel that sorrow himself. They had nothing except the cheap tunics they wore and they were concerned about how to pay for the sheep, when suddenly a travelling merchant arrived and offered to pay for what they wanted. Taking up the sheep, they gave thanks to God and after reaching Osimo made their way to the bishop of the city, who received them with great reverence. Now the lord bishop was surprised both at the sheep the man of God was leading and at the affection for it that was leading him to do this. But when the servant of Christ recounted the long parable of the sheep, the bishop was touched in his heart by the purity of the man of God, and gave thanks to God.

The next day, on leaving the city, the man of God began to wonder what to do with the sheep. On the advice of his companion and brother, he entrusted it to the care of the maidservants of Christ in the cloister of San Severino. The venerable servants of Christ gladly received the little sheep as a great gift from God. They devotedly cared for the sheep for a long time and made a tunic from its wool, a tunic they sent to the blessed father Francis at the church of Saint Mary of the

Portiuncula at the time of a chapter meeting. The holy man of God received the tunic with great reverence and high spirits, hugging and kissing it, and invited all those around him to share this great joy.

Thomas of Celano, The Life of Saint Francis, First Book, XXVIII, 77–8
The Saint, 248–9

24 JULY

Relying on divine grace and papal authority, with great confidence, Francis took the road to the Spoleto valley, that he might fulfill and teach Christ's Gospel. On the way he discussed with his companions how they might sincerely keep the rule they had accepted, how they might advance in all holiness and justice before God, how they should improve themselves and be an example for others.

The hour was already late as they continued their long discussion. Since they were exhausted from their prolonged activity, the hungry men stopped in a place of solitude. When there seemed to be no way for them to get the food they needed, God's providence immediately came to their aid. For suddenly a man carrying bread in his hand appeared, which he gave to Christ's little poor, and then suddenly disappeared. They had no idea where he came from or where he went.

From this the poor brothers realized that while in the company of the man of God they would be given assistance from heaven, and so they were refreshed more by the gift of divine generosity than by the food they had received for their bodies. Moreover, filled with divine consolation, they firmly decided and irrevocably resolved never to withdraw from the promise to holy poverty, be it from starvation or from trial.

Bonaventure, The Major Legend of Saint Francis, IV, 1
The Founder, 550

25 JULY

When they arrived in the Spoleto valley, going back to their holy proposal, they began to discuss whether they should live among the people or go off to solitary places. But Christ's servant Francis, putting his trust in neither his own efforts nor in theirs, sought the pleasure of the divine will in this matter by the fervor of prayer. Enlightened by a revelation from heaven, he realized that he was sent by the Lord to win for Christ the souls which the devil was trying to snatch away. Therefore he chose to live for everyone rather than for himself alone, drawn by the example of the one who deigned to die for all.

Bonaventure, The Major Legend of Saint Francis, IV, 2
The Founder, 550

26 JULY

A boy who was very pure and innocent was received into the Order while Saint Francis was living; and he was staying in a small place where the brothers, out of necessity, slept outside on the ground. Saint Francis once came to this place and in the evening after saying compline, he went off to sleep as he usually did, so he could get up at night to pray when the other brothers were asleep. The boy had in mind to spy attentively on Saint Francis's movements in order to find out about his holiness and especially to know what the saint did at night when he arose. To make sure that sleep would not overcome him, he lay down to sleep at Saint Francis's side and tied his cord to that of Saint Francis, so he would feel when the saint arose. And Saint Francis did not feel any of this. That night, during the first time of sleep, when all the other brothers were sleeping, Saint Francis got up and found his cord tied that way. He gently untied it so that the boy did not feel it, and Saint Francis went alone into the woods near the place, entering a little cell there and set himself to pray. The boy awoke after a while and found the cord untied and Saint Francis gone, so he got up to look for him. When he found the gate to the woods open, he thought that Saint Francis had gone out there, so he entered the woods. Reaching the place where Saint Francis was praying, he began to hear a great sound of voices. Going closer so that he might see and understand what he heard, he saw a wonderful light surrounding Saint Francis on all sides, and in it he saw Christ and the Virgin Mary and Saint John the Baptist and the Evangelist and a great multitude of angels speaking with Saint Francis. When the boy saw and heard this, he fell to the ground as if dead. Then, when the mystery of that holy apparition ended, Saint Francis was returning to the place. And his foot bumped into the boy lying almost dead on the path. Out of compassion, he lifted him up, took him in his arms and carried him back, as a good shepherd does with his little sheep.

Learning from him later about how he saw the vision, he ordered him never to tell anyone, that is, while he lived. The boy, growing in the grace of God and devotion to Saint Francis, was an important man in the Order, and, after the death of Saint Francis, he revealed that vision to the brothers.

The Little Flowers of Saint Francis, 17
The Prophet, 594–5

27 JULY

As the holy man was returning from overseas, with Brother Leonard of Assisi as his companion, he rode on a donkey for a while, because he was weak and tired from his journey. His companion walked behind, and was also quite tired. Thinking in human terms, he began to say to himself: "His parents and mine did not socialize as equals, and here he is riding while I am on foot leading this donkey." As he was thinking this, the holy man immediately got off the donkey. "No, brother," he said. "It is not right that I should ride while you go on foot, for in the world you were more noble and influential than I." The brother was completely astonished, and overcome with embarrassment: he knew the saint had caught him. He fell down at his feet and, bathed in tears, he exposed his naked thought and begged forgiveness.

Thomas of Celano, The Remembrance of the Desire of a Soul,
Second Book, V, 31
The Founder 266

⁂

28 JULY

There was another brother esteemed by the people for his good reputation. Because of his holiness, he was even more esteemed before God. The father of all envy was jealous of his virtue. He planned to cut down this tree which already touched the heavens and to snatch the crown from his hands. He scavaged, searched, shredded, and sifted everything about that brother, looking for the right way to make him stumble. He stirred up in him, under the appearance of greater perfection, a yearning to isolate himself. Then that jealous one could swoop down on him while he was alone and quickly make him fall. And if someone falls while alone, there is no one to lift him up.

What happened?

Separating himself from the religion of the brothers, he went about the world as a guest and a pilgrim. He wore a short tunic made from his habit and a hood not sown to the tunic; and, in this way, he wandered the countryside, despising himself in all things. As he went about in this way, it came to pass, that all divine comfort was taken from him. Soon he was awash in the waves of temptation. The waters climbed up into his soul. Desolate in body and spirit, he marched on like a bird that hurries toward a snare. Already near the abyss he was driven to the brink. Then for his own good, the eye of fatherly Providence looked mercifully on this miserable man. In his panic he regained understanding. Coming to his senses, he said: "Oh, miserable one! Go back to religion! That's where your salvation is." Immediately he jumped up and ran to his mother's lap.

He went to the brothers' place in Siena, and Saint Francis was staying there. As soon as he saw that brother — and this is extraordinary — the saint ran away from him and quickly closed himself in a cell. The brothers were thrown into confusion and wondered why he ran away. "Why are you surprised that I ran away?" the saint asked. "Didn't you see the cause? I fled to the protection of prayer to set free the one who strayed. I saw in my son something that displeased me, and rightly so. But now, by the grace of my Christ, the whole delusion has vanished."

The brother fell on his knees and declared with shame that he was guilty. "May God be kind to you, brother," the saint said to him. "But I warn you: Never again separate yourself from religion and your brothers, under some pretext of holiness." From then on that brother became a friend of company and camaraderie. He was especially devoted to those groups where regular observance flourished. Great are the works of the Lord in the gathering and the assembly of the just! There the shaken are held, the fallen are lifted and the lukewarm are roused; there iron sharpens iron and a brother helped by his brother, stands like a strong city. And even if you cannot see Jesus because of the worldly crowds, the heavenly crowd of angels will never block your view. Just do not run away! Be faithful unto death and you will receive the crown of life.

Thomas of Celano, The Remembrance of the Desire of a Soul,
Second Book, VI, 32–33
The Founder, 267–8

29 JULY

Gagliano is a populous and noble town in the diocese of Valva. A woman named Maria lived there who, through the difficult ways of this world, was converted to God and she subjected herself completely to the service of Saint Francis.

One day she went out to a mountain that was totally deprived of water to prune maple trees, and she forgot to take water along with her. The heat was unbearable and she began to faint from thirst. When she could no longer work and was lying nearly lifeless on the ground, she began intently to call upon her patron, Saint Francis. In her exhaustion she drifted off to sleep. And there was Saint Francis, who called her by name. "Get up," he said, "and drink the water that is provided by divine gift for you and for many!" At the sound the woman yawned but, overcome by drowsiness, fell back asleep. She was called again, but fell back on the ground in her weariness. But the third time, strengthened by a command of the saint, she got up. She grabbed a fern next to her and pulled it from the earth. When she saw that its root was all wet, she began to dig around it with her finger and a twig. Immediately the hole was filled with water and the little puddle grew into a spring. The woman drank, and when she had had enough, she washed her eyes. They were clouded by a long illness, and she could see nothing clearly. Her eyes were enlightened, their old roughness removed, and were flooded as if with new light.

The woman ran home and told everyone about the great miracle, to the glory of Saint Francis. News of the miracle spread and reached the ears of everyone, even in other regions. Many troubled by various diseases came running from every direction, and putting the health of their souls first, through confession, they were then freed of their illnesses. The blind recovered their sight, the lame their walk, the swollen grew slim, and for various illnesses their appropriate remedy was offered. That clear spring still flows, and a chapel in honor of Saint Francis has been built there.

Thomas of Celano, The Treatise on the Miracles of Saint Francis, III, 16
The Founder, 409–10

30 JULY

In the name of the Lord!

Let all the brothers who have been designated the ministers and servants of the other brothers assign their brothers in the provinces and places where they may be, and let them frequently visit, admonish and encourage them spiritually. Let all my other brothers diligently obey them in those matters concerning the well-being of their soul and which are not contrary to our life.

Let them behave among themselves according to what the Lord says: "Do to others what you would have them do to you" [Mt 7:12]; and "Do not do to another what you would not have done to you."

Let the ministers and servants remember what the Lord says: I have not come to be served, but to serve; and because the care of the brothers' souls has been entrusted to them, if anything is lost on account of their fault or bad example, they will have to render an account before the Lord Jesus Christ on the day of judgment.

The Earlier Rule (The Rule without a Papal Seal), IV, 1–6
The Saint, 66–7

31 JULY

Once blessed Francis wanted to travel to a certain hermitage so that he could more freely spend time in contemplation. Because he was very weak, he got a donkey to ride from a poor man. It was summer, and as the peasant went up the mountain following the man of God, he was worn out from the journey over such a rough and long road. And before they came to the place, he was exhausted, fainting with a burning thirst. He urgently cried out after the saint, begging him to have pity on him. He swore he would die if he was not revived by something to drink. The holy one of God, always compassionate to the distressed, immediately leaped down from the donkey, knelt down on the ground, and raised his hands to heaven, praying unceasingly until he sensed he had been heard. "Hurry now," he said to the peasant, "and over there you will find living water which at this very hour Christ has mercifully brought forth from the rock for you to drink." How amazingly kind God is, so easily bowing to his servants! By the power of prayer a peasant drinks water from the rock and draws refreshment from the hard flint. There was no flow of water there before this; and even after a careful search, none was found there afterwards.

Why should we be surprised that this one, so filled with the Holy Spirit, re-enacts the marvelous deeds of all the just! If one is joined to Christ by a gift of special grace, it is not wonderful that he, like other saints, should do similar things.

Thomas of Celano, The Remembrance of the Desire of a Soul,
Second Book, XVII, 46
The Founder, 278

August

1 AUGUST

Once, when Saint Francis was passing by a village near Assisi, a certain John, a very simple man, was ploughing in the field. He ran to him, saying: "I want you to make me a brother, for a long time now I have wanted to serve God." The saint rejoiced noticing the man's simplicity, and responded to his intention: "Brother, if you want to be our companion, give to the poor if you have anything, and once rid of your property, I will receive you." He immediately unyoked the oxen and offered one to Saint Francis saying: "Let's give this ox to the poor! I am sure I deserve to get this much as my share of my father's things." The saint smiled, but he heartily approved his sense of simplicity. Now, when the parents and younger brothers heard of this, they hurried over in tears, grieving more over losing the ox than the man. The saint said to them: "Calm down! Here, I'll give you back the ox and only take away the brother." And so he took the man with him, and, dressed in the clothing of the Order, he made him his special companion because of his gift of simplicity.

Whenever Saint Francis stayed in some place to meditate, simple John would immediately repeat and copy whatever gestures or movements the saint made. If he spat, John would spit too, if he coughed, he would cough as well, sighing or sobbing along with him. If the saint lifted up his hands to heaven, John would raise his too, and he watched him intently as a model, turning himself into a copy of all his actions. The saint noticed this, and once asked him why he did those things. He replied: "I promised to do everything you do. It is dangerous for me to leave anything out." The saint delighted in this pure simplicity, but gently told him not to do this anymore. Shortly after this the simple man departed to the Lord in this same purity. The saint often proposed his life as worth imitating and merrily calling him not Brother John, but Saint John.

Note that it is typical of holy simplicity to live by the norms of the elders and always to rely on the example and teaching of the saints. Who will allow human wisdom to follow him, now reigning in heaven, with as much care as holy simplicity conformed herself to him on earth! What more can I say? She followed the saint in life, and went before the saint to Life.

Thomas of Celano, The Remembrance of the Desire of a Soul,
Second Book, CXLIII, 190
The Founder, 368–9

ॐ

2 AUGUST

The apostle says: No one can say: Jesus is Lord, except in the Holy Spirit [1 Cor 12:3] ; and: There is not one who does good, not even one [Rom 3:12].

Therefore, whoever envies his brother the good that the Lord says or does in him incurs a sin of blasphemy because he envies the Most High Himself Who says and does every good thing.

The Lord says: Love your enemies [do good to those who hate you and pray for those who persecute and slander you] [Mt 5:44]. For that person truly loves his enemy who is not hurt by an injury done to him, but, because of love of God, is stung by the sin of his soul. Let him show him love by his deeds....

Nothing should displease a servant of God except sin. And no matter how another person may sin, if a servant of God becomes disturbed and angry because of this and not because of charity, he is storing up guilt for himself. That servant of God who does not become angry or disturbed at anyone lives correctly without anything of his own. Blessed is the one for whom nothing remains except for him to return to Caesar what is Caesar's and to God what is God's.

The Admonitions, VIII, IX, XI
The Saint, 132–3

ॐ

3 AUGUST

There was a woman in Monte Marano near Benevento who clung to Saint Francis with special devotion, and she went the way of all flesh. The clergy came at night with their psalters to sing the wake and vigils. Suddenly, in the sight of all, the woman sat up in bed and called to one of them, a priest who was her godfather, "I want to confess, Father, hear my sin! I have indeed died, and was destined for a harsh prison because I had never confessed the sin I will reveal to you. But Saint Francis prayed for me as I served him with a devout spirit while I was alive. I have now been permitted to return to my body so that after confessing my sin I might merit eternal life. So now, as all of you watch, after I reveal that to you I will hurry off to my promised rest." She then shakily confessed to the shaken priest, and after receiving absolution, composed herself peacefully on the bed and happily fell asleep in the Lord.

Bonaventure, The Major Legend of Saint Francis: the Miracles, II, 1
The Founder, 655–6

4 AUGUST

One time as the man of God was travelling with a companion through Apulia, near Bari he found a large bag lying on the road; the kind they call a fonda, apparently bursting with coins. His companion alerted the poor man of Christ and urged him to pick the purse up from the ground and distribute the money to the poor. The man of God refused, declaring there was a trick of the devil in this purse they had found, and that the brother was recommending something sinful rather than meritorious, that is, to take what belonged to another and give it away. They left the place and hurried to finish the journey they had begun. But the brother was not yet at peace, deluded by empty piety, bothering the man of God as if he had no concern to relieve the destitution of the poor. The gentleman agreed to return to the place, not to carry out the brother's wish, but to uncover the devil's trickery. So he returned to the fonda with the brother and a young man who was on the road, and after they had prayed, he ordered his companion to pick it up. The trembling brother was dumbfounded, sensing beforehand a diabolical omen. Nevertheless, because of the command of holy obedience, as he was casting out hesitation from his heart, he stretched out his hand toward the bag. Behold, a large snake slid out of the bag and, suddenly disappearing along with it, showed the brother the diabolical deceit. After the enemy's trickery and cunning were grasped, the holy man said to his companion: "To God's servants, brother, money is nothing but a devil and a poisonous snake."

Bonaventure, The Major Legend of Saint Francis, VII, 5
The Founder, 579–80

5 AUGUST

He strove to hide the good things of the Lord in the secrecy of his heart, not wanting to display for his own glory what could be the cause of ruin. Often, when many were calling him blessed, he would reply with these words: "Don't praise me as if I were safe; I can still have sons and daughters! No one should be praised as long as his end is uncertain. Whenever something is on loan and the lender wants it back, all that's left is body and soul — and even non-believers have that much!" This he would say to those who praised him. But he would say to himself: "If the Most High had given so much to a thief, he would be more grateful than you, Francis!"

Thomas of Celano, The Remembrance of the Desire of a Soul,
Second Book, XCVI, 133
The Founder, 333–4

6 AUGUST

He would often say to the brothers: "No one should flatter himself with big applause for doing something a sinner can do. A sinner can fast," he said, "he can pray, he can weep, he can mortify his flesh. But this he cannot do: remain faithful to his Lord. So this is the only reason for boasting: if we return to God the glory that is his; if we serve him faithfully and credit him for what he has given us.

"A person's worst enemy is the flesh; it does not know how to remember what it should regret and it doesn't know how to foresee what it should fear. All its concern is how to squander the present. What is worse," he said, "it claims for itself and takes credit for what was given not to it, but given to the soul. It grabs the praise for virtues and outsiders' applause for vigils and prayers. It leaves nothing for the soul, and even expects to be paid for its tears."

> Thomas of Celano, The Remembrance of the Desire of a Soul,
> Second Book, XCVII, 134
> *The Founder,* 334

7 AUGUST

It would not be right to pass over in silence the marks of the Crucified, worthy of the reverence of the highest spirits. How thickly he covered them! How carefully he concealed them! From the very first, when true love of Christ transformed the lover into his very image, even those closest to him were not aware of them. But Divine Providence did not want them to be forever hidden, never meeting the eyes of those dear to him. In fact, they were on parts of the body that were plainly visible and could not be hidden.

One time a companion saw the marks on his feet, and said to him: "What is this, good brother?" But he replied: "Mind your own business!"

Another time the same brother asked him for his tunic in order to clean it, and noted the blood. When he returned it, he said to the saint: "Whose blood is this that has stained your habit?" The saint put a finger to his eye and said to him: "Ask what this is, if you don't know it's an eye!"

He rarely washed his hands completely; he would only wash his fingers, so as not to allow those standing nearby to see the wounds. He washed his feet very infrequently, and no less secretly than rarely. When someone would ask to kiss his hand, he offered it halfway, putting out only his fingers; sometimes instead of the hand he offered his sleeve.

He began to wear woollen socks so his feet could not be seen, placing a piece of leather over the wounds to soften the wool's roughness. And while the holy Father was not able to hide completely the stigmata on his hands and feet from his companions, he was vexed if someone stared at them. So even his close companions, filled with prudence of spirit, would avert their eyes when he had to uncover his hands or feet for any reason.

Thomas of Celano, The Remembrance of the Desire of a Soul,
Second Book, XCVIII, 135–6
The Founder, 334–5

8 AUGUST

Those two bright lights of the world, Saint Dominic and Saint Francis, were once in the City with the Lord of Ostia, who later became Supreme Pontiff. As they took turns pouring out honey-sweet words about the Lord, the bishop finally said to them: "In the early Church the Church's shepherds were poor, and men of charity, not on fire with greed. Why don't we make bishops and prelates of your brothers who excel more than others in teaching and example?"

There arose a disagreement between the saints about answering — neither wishing to go first, but rather each deferring to the other. Each urged the other to reply. Each seemed superior to the other, since each was devoted to the other. At last humility conquered Francis as he did not speak first, but it also conquered Dominic, since in speaking first, he humbly obeyed.

Blessed Dominic therefore answered the bishop: "My Lord, my brothers are already raised to a good level, if they will only realize it, and as much as possible I would not allow them to obtain any other mark of dignity."

As this brief response ended, Blessed Francis bowed to the bishop and said: "My Lord, my brothers are called 'lesser' precisely so they will not presume to become 'greater.' They have been called this to teach them to stay down to earth, and to follow the footprints of Christ's humility, which in the end will exalt them above others in the sight of the saints. If you want them to bear fruit in the Church of God, keep them in the status in which they were called and hold them to it. Bring them back down to ground level even against their will. And so I beg you, Father, never allow them to rise to become prelates, otherwise they will just be prouder because they're poorer, and treat the others arrogantly." These were the replies of those blessed men....

When the servants of God finished their replies, narrated above, the Lord of Ostia was greatly edified by the words of both, and gave unbounded thanks to God. And as they left that place, blessed Dominic asked Saint Francis to be kind enough to give him the cord he had tied around him. Francis was slow to do this, refusing out of humility what the other was requesting out of charity. At last the happy devotion of the petitioner won out, and he devoutly put on the gift under his inner tunic. Finally they clasped hands, and commended themselves to each other with great sweetness. And so one saint said to the other: "Brother Francis, I wish your Order and mine might become one, so we could share the same form of life in the Church." At last, when they had parted from each other, Saint Dominic said to the many bystanders: "In truth I tell you, the other religious should follow this holy man Francis, as his holiness is so perfect."

Thomas of Celano, The Remembrance of the Desire of a Soul,
Second Book, CIX–CX, 148–50
The Founder, 342–4

9 AUGUST

What do you say, sons of the saints? Your jealousy and envy show you are degenerates, and your ambition for honors proves you are illegitimate. You bite and devour each other, and these conflicts and disputes arise only because of your cravings. Your struggles must be against the forces of darkness, a hard struggle against armies of demons — and instead you turn your weapons against each other!

Your fathers, full of knowledge, look at each other as friends, their faces turned to the Mercy Seat, but their sons are full of envy, and find it hard even to see each other! What will the body do, if its heart is divided? Surely the teaching of piety would flourish more throughout the whole world if the ministers of God's word were more closely joined by the bond of charity! What we say or teach becomes suspect especially because evident signs show the leaven of hatred in us. I know this is not about the good men on both sides, but about the bad ones who, I believe, should be rooted out so they will not infect the holy ones.

Finally, what should I say about those concerned with higher matters? It was by way of humility, not by haughtiness, that the fathers reached the Kingdom; but their sons walk in circles of ambition and do not ask the way to an inhabited town. What should we expect? If we do not follow their way, we will not reach their glory! Far be it from us, Lord! Make the disciples humble under the wings of their humble masters. Make those who are brothers in spirit kind to each other, and may you see your children's children. Peace upon Israel!

> Thomas of Celano, The Remembrance of the Desire of a Soul,
> Second Book, CIX–CX, 149
> *The Founder,* 343

10 AUGUST

Let all the brothers always strive to exert themselves in doing good works, for it is written: "Always do something good that the devil may find you occupied." And again: "Idleness is an enemy of the soul." Servants of God, therefore, must always apply themselves to prayer or some good work.

Wherever the brothers may be, either in hermitages or other places, let them be careful not to make any place their own or contend with anyone for it. Whoever comes to them, friend or foe, thief or robber, let him be received with kindness.

Wherever the brothers may be and in whatever place they meet, they should respect spiritually and attentively one another, and honor one another without complaining. Let them be careful not to appear outwardly as sad and gloomy hypocrites but show themselves joyful, cheerful and consistently gracious in the Lord.

The Earlier Rule (The Rule without a Papal Seal), VII, 10–16
The Saint, 69

11 AUGUST

The first work that blessed Francis undertook, after he had gained his freedom from the hands of his carnally-minded father, was to build a house of God. He did not try to build a new one, but he repaired an old one, restored an ancient one. He did not tear out the foundation, but he built upon it, always reserving to Christ his prerogative, although unaware of it, for no one can lay another foundation, but that which has been laid, which is Christ Jesus.

When he had returned to the place mentioned where the church of San Damiano had been built in ancient times, he repaired it zealously within a short time, aided by the grace of the Most High. This is the blessed and holy place where the glorious religion and most excellent Order of Poor Ladies and holy virgins had its happy beginning, about six years after the conversion of the blessed Francis and through that same blessed man.

The Lady Clare, a native of the city of Assisi, the most precious and strongest stone of the whole structure, stands as the foundation for all the other stones. For after the beginning of the Order of Brothers, when this lady was converted to God through the counsel of the holy man, she lived for the good of many and as an example to countless others. Noble by lineage, but more noble by grace, chaste in body, most chaste in mind, young in age, mature in spirit, steadfast in purpose and most eager in her desire for divine love, endowed with wisdom and excelling in humility, bright in name, more brilliant in life, most brilliant in character. A noble structure of precious pearls arose above this woman, whose praise comes not from mortals but from God, since our limited understanding is not sufficient to imagine it, nor our scanty vocabulary to utter it.

First of all, the virtue of mutual and continual charity that binds their wills together flourishes among them. Forty or fifty of them can dwell together in one place, wanting and not wanting the same things forming one spirit in them out of many. Second, the gem of humility, preserving the good things bestowed by heaven so sparkles in each one that they merit other virtues as well. Third, the lily of virginity and chastity diffuses such a wondrous fragrance among them that they forget earthly thoughts and desire to meditate only on heavenly things. So great a love of their eternal Spouse arises in their hearts that the integrity of their holy feelings keeps them from every habit of their former life. Fourth, all of them have become so distinguished by their title of highest poverty that their food and clothing rarely or never manage to satisfy extreme necessity. Fifth, they have so attained the unique grace of abstinence and silence that they scarcely need to exert any effort to check the prompting of the flesh and to restrain their tongues. Sixth, they are so adorned with the virtue of patience in all these things, that adversity of tribulation, or injury of vexation never breaks or changes their spirit. Seventh, and finally, they have so merited the height of contemplation that they learn in it everything they should do or avoid, and they know how to go beyond the mind to God with joy, persevering night and day in praising Him and praying to Him.

Thomas of Celano, The Life of Saint Francis, First Book, VIII, 18–20
The Saint, 196–9

12 AUGUST

The truly faithful servant and minister of Christ, Francis, in order to do everything faithfully and perfectly, directed his efforts chiefly to the exercise of those virtues which, by the prodding of the sacred Spirit, he knew pleased his God more.

In this matter it happened that he fell into a great struggle over a doubt which, after he returned from many days of prayer, he proposed for resolution to the brothers who were close to him.

"What do you think, brothers, what do you judge better? That I should spend my time in prayer, or that I should travel about preaching? I am a poor little man, simple and unskilled in speech; I have received a greater grace of prayer than of speaking. Also in prayer there seems to be a profit and an accumulation of graces, but in preaching a distribution of gifts already received from heaven.

"In prayer there is a purification of interior affections and a uniting to the one, true and supreme good with an invigorating of virtue; in preaching, there is a dust on our spiritual feet, distraction over many things and relaxation of discipline.

"Finally, in prayer we address God, listen to Him, and, as if living an angelic life, we associate with the angels. In preaching, it is necessary to practice great self-emptying for people and, by living humanly among them, to think, see, speak, and hear human things.

"But there is one thing to the contrary that seems to outweigh all these considerations before God, that is, the only begotten Son of God, who is the highest wisdom, came down from the bosom of the Father for the salvation of souls in order to instruct the world by His example and to speak the word of salvation to people, whom He would redeem by the price of His sacred blood, cleanse with its washing and sustain with its draught, holding back for Himself absolutely nothing that He could freely give for our salvation. And because we should do everything according to the pattern shown to us in Him as on the heights of the mountain, it seems more pleasing to God that I interrupt my quiet and go out to labor."

When he had mulled over these words for many days with his brothers, he could not perceive with certainty which of these he should choose as more acceptable to Christ. Although he understood extraordinary things through the spirit of prophecy, this question he could not resolve with clarity on his own.

But God's providence had a better plan, that the merit of preaching would be shown by a sign from heaven, thus preserving the humility of Christ's servant.

Bonaventure, The Major Legend of Saint Francis, XII, 1
The Founder, 622–3

13 AUGUST

He was not ashamed to ask advice in small matters from those under him, true Lesser Brother that he was, though he had learned great things from the supreme Teacher. He was accustomed to search with special eagerness in what manner, and in what way he could serve God more perfectly according to His good pleasure.

As long as he lived, this was his highest philosophy, this his highest desire: to ask from the wise and the simple, the perfect and the imperfect, the young and the old, how he could more effectively arrive at the summit of perfection.

Choosing, therefore, two of the brothers, he sent them to Brother Sylvester, who had seen the cross coming out from his mouth, and, at that time, spent his time in continuous prayer on the mountain above Assisi. He was to ask God to resolve his doubt over this matter, and to send him the answer in God's name. He also asked the holy virgin Clare to consult with the purest and simplest of the virgins living under her rule, and to pray herself with the other sisters in order to seek the Lord's will in this matter. Through a miraculous revelation of the Spirit, the venerable priest and the virgin dedicated to God came to the same conclusion: that it was the divine good will that the herald of Christ should preach.

When the two brothers returned and told him God's will as they had received it, he rose at once, girded himself and without the slightest delay took to the roads. He went with such fervor to carry out the divine command, just as he ran along so swiftly as if the hand of God were upon him, giving him new strength from heaven.

Bonaventure, The Major Legend of Saint Francis, XII, 2
The Founder, 623.4

❦

14 AUGUST

The Spirit of the Lord, who had anointed and sent him, and also Christ, the power and the wisdom of God, were with their servant Francis wherever he went so that he might abound with words of sound teaching and shine with miracles of great power. For his word was like a blazing fire, reaching the deepest parts of the heart, and filling the souls of all with wonder, since it made no pretence at the elegance of human composition, but exuded the breath of divine revelation.

Once when he was to preach before the pope and cardinals at the suggestion of the lord of Ostia, he memorized a sermon which he had carefully composed. When he stood in their midst to offer his edifying words, he went completely blank and was unable to say any thing at all. This he admitted to them in true humility and directed himself to invoke the grace of the Holy Spirit. Suddenly he began to overflow with such effective eloquence and to move the minds of those high-ranking men to compunction with such force and power that it was clearly evident it was not he, but the Spirit of the Lord, who was speaking.

Because he first convinced himself by action and then convinced others by word, he did not fear rebuke, but spoke the truth boldly. He did not encourage, but struck at the life of sin with a sharp blow, nor did he smooth over, but struck at the faults of sinners with harsh reproaches. He spoke with the same constancy of mind to the great and the small, and would speak with the same joy of spirit to the few as to the many.

People of all ages and both sexes hurried to see and hear this new man given to the world by heaven. Moving about through various regions, he preached the Gospel ardently, as the Lord worked with him and confirmed his preaching with the signs that followed. For in the power of His name Francis, the herald of truth, cast out devils and healed the sick, and, what is greater, he softened the obstinate minds of sinners and moved them to penance, restoring at the same time health to their bodies and hearts.

                        Bonaventure, The Major Legend of Saint Francis, XII, 7–8
                                                    The Founder, 625–6

15 AUGUST

He embraced the Mother of Jesus with inexpressible love, since she made the Lord of Majesty a brother to us. He honored her with his own Praises, poured out prayers to her, and offered her his love in a way that no human tongue can express. But what gives us greatest joy is that he appointed her the Advocate of the Order, and placed under her wings the sons to be left behind, that she might protect and cherish them to the end.

                      Thomas of Celano, The Remembrance of the Desire of a Soul,
                                                  Second Book, CL, 198
                                                           The Founder, 347

16 AUGUST

Among all the lesser and inanimate creatures, he loved fire with singular affection because of its beauty and usefulness. That is why he never wanted to impede its function.

    Once when he was sitting close to a fire, without being aware of it, his linen pants or breeches next to the knee caught fire. Although he felt the heat of the fire, he did not want to extinguish it. His companion, however, seeing that the fire was burning his pants, ran to him, wanting to put out the fire. Blessed Francis prohibited him saying: "No, dearest brother, do not hurt Brother Fire." And thus, in no way did he want him to extinguish it.

    So the brother quickly ran to the brother who was his guardian, and brought him to blessed Francis. At once, contrary to the will of blessed Francis, he began to extinguish the fire. Because of this, however urgent the need, he never wanted to extinguish a fire, a lamp, or a candle, moved as he was with such piety for it.

He also did not want a brother to throw fire or smouldering wood from one place to another, as is usually done, but wanted him simply to place it on the ground, out of reverence for Him who created it....

Next to fire he had a singular love for water through which holy penance and tribulation is symbolized and by which the filth of the soul is washed clean and because of which the first cleansing of the soul takes place through the waters of Baptism.

Because of this, when he washed his hands, he chose a place where the water that fell to the ground would not be trampled underfoot.

Whenever he had to walk over rocks, he would walk with great fear and reverence out of love for Him who is called "the rock." Whenever he recited the verse of the psalm, "You have set me high upon the rock," he would say, out of great reverence and devotion: "You have set me high at the foot of the rock."

He also told the brother who cut and prepared the wood for the fire never to cut down the whole tree, but to cut the tree in such a way that one part always remained intact out of love for Him Who willed to accomplish our salvation on the wood of the cross.

In the same way he used to tell the brother who took care of the garden not to cultivate all the ground in the garden for vegetables, but to leave a piece of ground that would produce wild plants. Thus, in their season, they would produce "Brother Flowers" out of love of Him Who is called "the flower of the field" and "the lily of the valley."

Moreover, he used to tell the brother gardener that he should always make a beautiful flower bed in some part of the garden, planting and cultivating every variety of fragrant plants and those producing beautiful flowers. Thus, in their time they would invite all who saw those herbs and those flowers to the praise of God. For every creature says and exclaims: "God made me for you, O mortal!"

We who were with him saw him rejoice so much, inwardly and outwardly, in all creatures, that touching and looking at them, his spirit seemed no longer on earth but in heaven. And because of the many consolations he had and continued to have in creatures, shortly before his death, he composed the Praises of the Lord in His creatures to move the hearts of his listeners to the praise of God, and so that in His creatures the Lord might be praised by everyone.

A Mirror of Perfection, X1, 116 & 118
The Prophet, 365–6

17 AUGUST

At that time Saint Francis and his brothers felt great gladness and unique joy whenever one of the faithful, led by the Spirit of God, came and accepted the habit of holy religion, whoever the person might be: rich or poor, noble or insignificant, wise or simple, cleric or illiterate, a layman of the Christian people. This was a great wonder to those of the world and an example of humility, challenging them to the way of a more reformed life and to penance for sins.

No lowliness of birth, no weakness of poverty stood in the way of building up in God's work the ones God wanted to build up, a God who delights to be with the simple and those rejected by the world.

Thomas of Celano, The Life of Saint Francis, First Book, XII, 31
The Saint, 209–10

18 AUGUST

When he presented himself and his followers before Pope Innocent to request a rule for his life, it seemed to the pope that their proposal for a way of life was beyond their strength. A man of great discernment, he said to Francis: "My son, pray to Christ that through you he may show us his will, so that, once we know it, we may confidently approve your holy desire."

The saint accepted the command of the supreme shepherd and hurried to Christ. He prayed intently, and devoutly exhorted his companions to appeal to God.

What next? In praying, the answer came to him and he told his sons the news of salvation. Thus, Christ's familiar speaking in parables is recognizable.

"Francis," He said, "say this to the pope: 'Once upon a time there was a poor but lovely woman who lived in a desert. A king fell in love with her because of her great beauty; he gladly betrothed her and with her had lovely children. When they had grown up, having been nobly raised, their mother said: "Dear children, do not be ashamed because you are poor, for you are all children of a great king. Go joyfully to his court, and ask him for what you need." Hearing this they were amazed and overjoyed. At the thought of being royalty, their spirits were lifted. Knowing they would be the king's heirs, they reckoned all their poverty riches. They presented themselves boldly to the king: they were not afraid to look at him since they bore his very image. When the king saw his likeness in them, he was surprised, and asked whose sons they might be. When they said they were the children of the poor woman who lived in the desert, the king embraced them. "You are my heirs," he said, "and my sons; have no fear! If strangers are fed at my table, it is only right that I feed you; for by law my whole inheritance belongs to you." The king then sent orders to the woman to send all his sons to be fed at his court.'" This parable made the saint happy, and he promptly reported this holy message to the pope.

Francis himself was this woman, not because he was soft in his deeds, but because he was fruitful and bore many children. The desert was the world, which was then wild and sterile, with no teaching of virtue. The many beautiful children were the large number of brothers, clothed with every virtue. The king was the Son of God, whom they resemble by their holy poverty. They were fed from the king's table, refusing to be ashamed of their lowliness, when, in imitation of Christ, they were content to live on alms and realized that because of the world's contempt they would be blessed.

The lord pope was amazed at the parable presented to him, and recognized without a doubt that Christ had spoken in this man.

He remembered a vision he had seen only a few days earlier, and instructed by the Holy Spirit, he now believed it would come true in this man. He saw in a dream the Lateran basilica almost ready to fall down. A religious man, small and scorned, was propping it up with his own bent back so it would not fall. "I'm sure," he said, "he is the one who will hold up Christ's Church by what he does and what he teaches!" Because of this the lord pope easily bowed to his request; from then on, filled with devotion to God, he always loved Christ's servant with a special love. He quickly granted what was asked and promised even more.

Visiting towns and villages, Francis began, with the authority now granted him, to preach passionately and to scatter the seeds of virtue.

Thomas of Celano, The Remembrance of the Desire of a Soul,
First Book, XI, 16–17
The Founder, 254–6

19 AUGUST

Presiding over God's Church at that time was the lord Pope Innocent the Third, a glorious man, prolific in learning, brilliant in speech, burning with zeal for justice in matters which the cause of the Christian faith demanded. When he recognized the wish of the men of God, he first considered the matter and then gave his assent to their request, something he completed by a subsequent action. Exhorting and then warning them about many things, he blessed Saint Francis and his brothers and said to them: "Go with the Lord, brothers, and as the Lord will see fit to inspire you, preach penance to all. When the almighty Lord increases you in numbers and grace, come back to me with joy, and I will grant you more things than these and, with greater confidence, I will entrust you with greater things."

The Lord was truly with Saint Francis wherever he went, gladdening him with revelations and encouraging him with gifts. For when he had gone to sleep one night, he seemed to be walking down a road, and alongside it stood a tree of great height. That tree was lovely and strong, thick and exceedingly high. It came about that when he approached the tree and stood under it and marveled at its beauty and height, the holy man himself rose to so great a height that he touched the top of the tree. Taking it into his hand, he easily bent it to the ground. It really happened this way, when the lord Innocent, a very high and lofty tree in the world, bent himself so kindly to his wish and request.

Thomas of Celano, The Life of Saint Francis, First Book, XIII, 33
The Saint, 212–3

20 AUGUST

The apostle says: The letter kills, but the spirit gives life [2 Cor 3:6].

Those people are put to death by the letter who only wish to know the words alone, that they might be esteemed wiser than others and be able to acquire great riches to give to their relatives and friends.

And those religious are put to death by the letter who are not willing to follow the spirit of the divine letter but, instead, wish only to know the words and to interpret them for others.

And those people are brought to life by the spirit of the divine letter who do not attribute every letter they know, or wish to know, to the body but, by word and example, return them to the most high Lord God to Whom every good belongs.

The Admonitions, VII
The Saint, 132

21 AUGUST

At one time robbers used to come sometimes to the hermitage of the brothers above Borgo San Sepolcro to ask the brothers for bread. They hid in the thick forest of that region, coming out from time to time to rob travelers on the streets and footpaths. Some of the brothers of that place said: "It is not right to give them alms because they are robbers and they do many very great evil things to people." Others, taking into consideration that they begged humbly and were compelled by great necessity, used to give them alms sometimes, always admonishing them to be converted to penance.

Meanwhile blessed Francis arrived at that place. The brothers asked him whether they should give them bread, or not. "If you do as I tell you," blessed Francis told them, "I trust in the Lord that you will win their souls. Go get some good bread and good wine and take it to them in the woods where you know they are staying, and cry out: 'Come, Brother Robbers, come to us, because we are brothers and we are bringing you some good bread and good wine.' They will immediately come to you. Then you spread out a table cloth on the ground, placing the bread and wine on it, and, while they are eating, humbly and joyfully wait on them. After the meal, speak to them some words of the Lord. Finally, for the love of the Lord ask them for this first request: make them promise you that they will not strike anyone or injure anyone's person. Do not ask for everything all at once, or they will not listen to you. Because of the humility and charity you show them, they will at once make you this promise. The next day, get up and, because of the promise they made to you, besides eggs and cheese, bring them the bread and wine, and take these to them, and wait on them while they eat. After the meal, say to them: 'Why do you stay here all day long, dying of hunger, suffering many evil things and in your actions doing many evil things for which you will lose your souls unless you are converted? It is better to serve the Lord, who will both supply your bodily needs in this world and save your souls in the end.' Then the Lord in His mercy will inspire them to convert and they will be converted because of the humility and charity you show them."

So the brothers got up and did everything as blessed Francis told them. And by the mercy of God and His grace which descended on them, those men listened and observed to the letter point by point all the requests which the brothers asked of them. Further, because of the friendliness and charity the brothers showed them, they began carrying wood on their shoulders to the hermitage. By the mercy of God, through the charity and friendliness that the brothers showed them, some entered religion, others embraced penance, promising in the hands of the brothers no longer to commit these evil deeds, but to live by the work of their hands.

The brothers and others who heard or knew about this, were quite amazed, as they reflected on the holiness of blessed Francis, how he had predicted the conversion of these men who had been perfidious and wicked, and how quickly they converted to the Lord.

The Assisi Compilation, 115 5
The Founder, 221–2

22 AUGUST

In the province of Rieti a very serious plague broke out and so cruelly took the lives of cattle and sheep that no remedy could be found. A certain Godfearing man was told in a vision at night to hurry to the hermitage of the brothers and get the water in which God's servant Francis, who was staying there at that time, had washed his hands and feet, and to sprinkle it on all the animals. He got up in the morning, came to the place, secretly got the water from the companions of the holy man, and sprinkled it on the sheep and cattle. Marvelous to say, the moment that water touched the animals, which were weak and lying on the ground, they immediately recovered their former vigor, stood up and, as if they had had nothing wrong with them, hurried off to pasture. Thus through the miraculous power of that water, which had touched his sacred wounds, the plague ceased and deadly disease fled from the flocks.

Bonaventure, *The Major Legend of Saint Francis*, XIII, 6
The Founder, 634

23 AUGUST

Saint Clare, a most devoted disciple of the Cross and noble plant of Sir Saint Francis, was of such holiness that not only the bishops and cardinals but even the pope desired with great affection to see her and listen to her, and often visited her personally.

One time among others the Holy Father went to her at the monastery to hear her speak of heavenly and divine things; and as they were speaking together about various things, Saint Clare had the tables prepared and bread placed on them, so that the Holy Father might bless it. So, when their spiritual conversation was finished, Saint Clare knelt down with great reverence, and asked him to be kind enough to bless the bread placed on the table. The Holy Father replied: "My most faithful Sister Clare, I want you to bless this bread, and make over it the sign of the most holy Cross, to which you have given your whole self." And Saint Clare said: "Most Holy Father, forgive me, because I would be worthy of the greatest rebuke if in front of the Vicar of Christ I, who am a vile little woman, should presume to give such a blessing." And the pope replied: "So that this may not be attributed to presumption but to the merit of obedience, I command you under holy obedience to make the sign of the most holy Cross over this bread and bless it in the name of God." Then Saint Clare, as a true daughter of obedience, very devoutly blessed that bread with the sign of the most holy Cross of Christ. An amazing thing happened! Immediately the sign of the Cross appeared, beautifully cut into each loaf. And then some of these loaves were eaten and others were kept because of the miracle. And the Holy Father, having seen the miracle, took some of that bread and, giving thanks to God, departed, leaving Saint Clare with his blessing.

At that time living in that monastery were Sister Ortulana, mother of Saint Clare, and Sister Agnes, her sister, both together, with Saint Clare, filled with virtues and with the Holy Spirit, and many other holy nuns. To them Saint Francis sent many sick people; and with their prayers and the sign of the most holy Cross they returned them all to health.

The Little Flowers of Saint Francis, XXXIII
The Prophet, 624

24 AUGUST

At the time of his last illness, and in the dark of night, he wanted to eat some parsley and humbly asked for it. The cook was called so he could bring it, but he replied that he could not pick any in the garden at that time. "I've been picking parsley every day," he said, "and I've cut off so much of it that even in broad daylight I can hardly find any. Even more so now that darkness has fallen, I won't be able to distinguish it from the other herbs." "Brother," the saint replied, "don't worry, bring me the first herbs your hand touches." The brother went into the garden, unable to see anything, and tore up the first wild herbs he came upon, and brought them back into the house. The brothers looked at the wild herbs, and sorting through them carefully, they found a leafy, tender stock of parsley in the middle of them. The saint then ate a bit of it and felt much better. Then the father said to the brothers: "Dear brothers, do what you're commanded the first time you're told, and don't wait for it to be repeated. Don't pretend that something is impossible; for even if what I command is beyond your strength, obedience will find the strength." Thus to a high degree the Spirit entrusted to him the spirit of prophecy.

Thomas of Celano, The Remembrance of the Desire of a Soul,
Second Book, XXII, 51
The Founder, 281

25 AUGUST

It should not seem strange to anyone that this prophet of our own time should shine with such great privileges. Truly freed from the darkness of earthly things and not subjected to the lusts of the flesh, free, his understanding flew up to the heights; pure, it stepped into the light.

Thus, illumined by the flashes of light eternal, he drew from the Word what echoed in words. Ah, how different we are today! Wrapped in darkness we are ignorant even of what we need to know. And what do you think is the reason for this? Are we not also friends of the flesh, wallowing in the dust of worldly things? Surely, if we would only raise our hearts as well as our hands to heaven, if we would choose to depend on the eternal, maybe we would know what we do not know: God and ourselves. Mired in mud, we see only mud. For the eye fixed on heaven, it is impossible not to see heavenly things.

Thomas of Celano, The Remembrance of the Desire of a Soul,
Second Book, XXIV, 54
The Founder, 283–4

26 AUGUST

Placed in a vale of tears the blessed father scorned the usual riches of the children of men as no riches at all and, eager for higher status, with all his heart, he coveted poverty. Realizing that she was a close friend of the Son of God, but nowadays an outcast throughout the whole world, he was eager to espouse her in an everlasting love. He became the lover of her beauty and not only left his father and his mother but gave up everything he owned so that he might cling to his wife more closely, and the two might be in one spirit. He held her close in chaste embraces and could not bear to cease being her husband even for an hour. He told his sons that she is the way of perfection. She is the pledge and guarantee of eternal wealth. No one coveted gold as avidly as he coveted poverty; no one was as careful to guard a treasure as he was to watch over this pearl of the Gospel. In this especially would his sight be offended: if he saw in the brothers — whether at home or away from it — anything that was contrary to poverty. Truly, from the beginning of his religious life until his death, his entire wealth was a single tunic, cord and breeches; he had nothing else. His poor clothing showed where he stored his riches. This was the reason he was happy; he was carefree. He was ready for the race. He was glad to exchange perishable treasure for the hundredfold.

He taught his own to build poor little dwellings out of wood, and not stone, and how to build these according to a crude sketch. Often, when he spoke to the brothers about poverty, he would insist on that saying of the Gospel: "The foxes have holes and the birds of the air have nests, but the Son of God has no place on which to rest his head [Mt 6:20; Lk 9:58]."

Thomas of Celano, The Remembrance of the Desire of a Soul,
Second Book, XXV–VI, 55–6
The Founder, 284–5

27 AUGUST

The saint used to enjoy staying in the brothers' place at Greccio. He found it rich in poverty and there, in a remote little cell on a cliff, he could give himself freely to heavenly things. This is the place where he had earlier recalled the birth of the Child of Bethlehem, becoming a child with the Child.

Now, it happened that the people there had been stricken by multiple disasters. A pack of raging wolves devoured not only animals, but even people. And every year hailstorms destroyed their wheat fields and vineyards. One day, while preaching to them, blessed Francis said: "To the praise and honor of Almighty God, listen to the truth which I proclaim to you. If each of you will confess your sins, and bear worthy fruit of genuine repentance, I swear to you that all these disasters will cease, and the Lord looking down upon you, will multiply your earthly goods. But also hear this," he said. "I tell you again, if you are ungrateful for these gifts, and return to your vomit, the disasters will return, the punishment will double, and greater wrath will rage against you."

And so it happened: at that very hour the disasters ceased, and through the merits and prayers of our holy father, all dangers vanished. The wolves and hailstorms caused no more harm. And even more remarkable, whenever the hail, falling on neighboring fields, reached the boundaries of Greccio, either it would stop or move off in a different direction.

Thomas of Celano, The Remembrance of the Desire of a Soul,
Second Book, VII, 35–6
The Founder, 269–70

28 AUGUST

If any one of the brothers, at the instigation of the enemy, shall have sinned mortally, let him be bound by obedience to have recourse to his guardian. Let all the brothers who know that he has sinned not bring shame upon him or slander him; let them, instead, show great mercy to him and keep the sin of their brother very secret because those who are well do not need a physician, but the sick do. In a similar way let them be bound by obedience to send him to his custodian with a companion. And let that custodian provide for him with mercy as he would wish to be provided for were he in a similar position. If he falls into some venial sin, let him confess to his brother who is a priest. If there is no priest there, let him confess to his brother until he has a priest who may canonically absolve him, as it has been said. And let them not have the power to impose any other penance on them except this: Go and sin no more [Jn 8:11].

A Letter to a Minister, 14–20
The Saint, 98

29 AUGUST

Some sailors were placed in grave danger at sea when a fierce storm came up while they were ten miles out from the port of Barletta. Anxious for their lives, they let down the anchors. But the stormy wind swelled the sea more violently, breaking the ropes and releasing the anchors. They were tossed about the sea on an unsteady and uncertain course. Finally at God's pleasure the sea was calmed, and they prepared with all their strength to recover their anchors, whose lines were floating on the surface. So they put their full effort into retrieving the anchors. They invoked the help of all the saints and were worn down by their exertion, but could not recover even one after a whole day.

One of the sailors was named Perfetto, though he was perfectly good for nothing. He despised everything that belongs to God. With malice he scoffed and said to his companions, "You have invoked the aid of all the saints, and as you see not one of them has helped. Let's call that Francis. He's a new saint; let him dive into the sea with his capuche and get our anchors back. We can give an ounce of gold to his church, which is just being built in Ortona, if we decide he helped." The others fearfully agreed with the scoffer, but they rebuked him by making a vow. At that very moment the anchors were suddenly floating on the water with no support, as if the nature of iron had been changed into the lightness of wood.

Thomas of Celano, The Treatise on the Miracles of Saint Francis, X, 81
The Founder, 433–4

30 AUGUST

A man named Martin took his oxen far from home to find pasture. The leg of one ox was accidentally broken so badly that Martin could think of no remedy. He was concerned about getting the hide, but since he had no knife, he returned home and left the ox in the care of Saint Francis, lest wolves devour it before his return. Early next morning he returned to the ox with his skinning knife, but found the ox grazing peacefully; its broken leg could not be distinguished from the other. He thanked the good shepherd who took such loving care of him, and procured the remedy.

Thomas of Celano, The Treatise on the Miracles of Saint Francis,
XVIII, 183
The Founder, 464

31 AUGUST

Let all the brothers, both the ministers and servants as well as the others, be careful not to be disturbed or angered at another's sin or evil because the devil wishes to destroy many because of another's fault. But let them spiritually help the one who has sinned as best they can, because those who are well do not need a physician, but the sick do.

Likewise, let all the brothers not have power or control in this instance, especially among themselves; for, as the Lord says in the Gospel: The rulers of the Gentiles lord it over them and the great ones make their authority over them felt; it shall not be so among the brothers. Let whoever wishes to be the greater among them be their minister and servant. Let whoever is the greater among them become the least [Mt 20:25–27].

Let no brother do or say anything evil to another; on the contrary, through the charity of the Spirit, let them serve and obey one another voluntarily. This is the true and holy obedience of our Lord Jesus Christ.

As often as they have turned away from the commands of the Lord and "wandered outside obedience," let all the brothers know, as the Prophet says, they are cursed outside obedience as long as they knowingly remain in such a sin. When they have persevered in the Lord's commands — as they have promised by the Holy Gospel and their life, let them know they have remained in true obedience and are blessed by the Lord.

The Earlier Rule (The Rule without a Papal Seal), V, 7–16
The Saint, 67–8

September

1 SEPTEMBER

Blessed is the servant who stores up in heaven the good things which the Lord shows to him and does not wish to reveal them to people under the guise of a reward, because the Most High Himself will reveal His deeds to whomever He wishes.

Blessed is the servant who safeguards the secrets of the Lord in his heart.

The Admonitions, XXVIII
The Saint, 137

2 SEPTEMBER

While the saint was secluded in a cell on Mount La Verna, one of his companions was yearning with great desire to have something encouraging from the words of our Lord, commented on briefly by Saint Francis and written with his own hand. He believed that by this means he would be set free from, or at least could bear more easily, a serious temptation which oppressed him, not in the flesh but in the spirit. Though growing weary with this desire, he feared to express it to the most holy father. But what man did not tell him, the Spirit revealed. One day Saint Francis called this brother and said: "Bring me paper and ink, because I want to write down the words of the Lord and his praises upon which I have meditated in my heart." What he had asked for was quickly brought to him. He then wrote down with his own hand the Praises of God and the words he wanted and, at the end, a blessing for that brother, saying: "Take this paper for yourself and keep it carefully to your dying day." The whole temptation disappeared immediately. The letter was preserved; and later it worked wonders.

Thomas of Celano, The Remembrance of the Desire of a Soul,
Second Book, XX, 49
The Founder, 280

3 SEPTEMBER

Leo of Assisi, who was with Francis on Mount La Verna at the end of 1224, wrote in red ink on one side of the piece of parchment containing The Praises of God (see 12 April): "Two years before his death, the blessed Francis spent forty days on Mount La Verna from the Feast of the Assumption of the holy Virgin Mary until the September Feast of Saint Michael, in honor of the Blessed Virgin Mary, the Mother of God, and the blessed Michael the Archangel. And the Lord's hand was upon him. After the vision and message of the Seraph and the impression of Christ's stigmata upon his body, he composed these praises written on the other side of this page and wrote them in his own hand, thanking God for the kindness bestowed on him."

On the other side of the same parchment Brother Leo wrote: "The blessed Francis wrote this blessing for me with his own hand."

May the Lord bless you and keep you.
May He show His face to you and be merciful to you.
May He turn His countenance to you and give you peace.

May the Lord bless you, Brother Leo.

Then Brother Leo wrote: "In a similar way he [blessed Francis] made with his own hand this sign TAU together with a skull."

A Blessing for Brother Leo
The Saint, 108–112

4 SEPTEMBER

Once he said that if an "eminent cleric" were to join the Order, he should in some way renounce even learning, so that having renounced even this possession, he might offer himself naked to the arms of the Crucified. "Learning," he would say, "makes many hard to teach, not allowing them to bend something rigid in them to humble disciplines. And so I wish an educated man would first offer me this prayer: "Look, Brother; I have lived for a long time in the world and have not really known my God.

Grant me, I pray you, a place removed from the noise of the world, where I may recall my years in sorrow and where I may gather the scattered bits of my heart and turn my spirit to better things." "What do you think will become," he asked, "of someone who begins in this way? He will emerge an unchained lion, strong enough for anything, and the blessed sap which he tapped in the beginning will grow in him through constant progress. To him at last the true ministry of the word will be given safely, for he will pour out what bubbles up in his heart."

What a holy teaching! What is more necessary, for someone returning from the land of unlikeness, than to scrape and wash away, by humble exercises, worldly feelings stamped and ground in for a long time? Whoever enters the school of perfection will soon reach perfection.

Thomas of Celano, The Remembrance of the Desire of a Soul,
Second Book, CXLVI, 194
The Founder, 371–2

5 SEPTEMBER

It grieved him when brothers sought learning while neglecting virtue, especially if they did not remain in that calling in which they were first called. He said: "Those brothers of mine who are led by curiosity for knowledge will find themselves empty-handed on the day of reckoning. I wish they would grow stronger in virtue, so that when the times of tribulation arrive they may have the Lord with them in their distress. For," he said, "a tribulation is approaching, when books, useful for nothing, shall be thrown into cupboards and into closets!" He did not say these things out of dislike for the study of the Scriptures, but to draw all of them back from excessive concern for learning, because he preferred that they be good through charity, than dilettantes through curiosity.

Besides, he could smell in the air that a time was coming, and not too far away, when he knew learning would be an occasion of ruin, while dedication to spiritual things would serve as a support to the spirit.

A lay brother who wanted to have a psalter asked him for permission: he offered him ashes instead of a psalter.

After his death he appeared in a vision to one of the companions who was once tending toward preaching, and he forbade it, commanding him to walk on the way of simplicity. As God is his witness, he felt such a sweetness after this vision that for many days it seemed the dew of the father's words was still dropping into his ears.

Thomas of Celano, The Remembrance of the Desire of a Soul, Second Book, CXLVII, 195
The Founder, 372

6 SEPTEMBER

When blessed Francis lay gravely ill in the palace of the bishop of Assisi, in the days after he returned from Bagnara, the people of Assisi, fearing that the saint would die during the night without them knowing about it, and that the brothers would secretly take his body away and place it in another city, placed a vigilant guard each night around the palace's walls.

Blessed Francis, although he was gravely ill, to comfort his soul and ward off discouragement in his severe and serious infirmities, often asked his companions during the day to sing the Praises of the Lord which he had composed a long time before in his illness. He likewise had the Praises sung during the night for the edification of their guards, who kept watch at night outside the palace because of him.

When Brother Elias reflected that blessed Francis was so comforting himself and rejoicing in the Lord in such illness, one day he said to him: "Dearest brother, I am greatly consoled and edified by all the joy which you show for yourself and your companions in such affliction and infirmity. Although the people of this city venerate you as a saint in life and in death, nevertheless, because they firmly believe that you are near death due to your serious and incurable sickness, upon hearing praises of this sort being sung, they can think and say to themselves:

'How can he show such joy when he is so near death? He should be thinking about death.'"

"Do you remember," blessed Francis said to him, "when you saw the vision at Foligno and told me that it told you that I would live for only two years? Before you saw that vision, through the grace of the Holy Spirit, who suggests every good in the heart, and places it on the lips of his faithful, I often considered day and night my end. But from the time you saw that vision, each day I have been even more zealous reflecting on the day of my death."

He continued with great intensity of spirit: "Allow me to rejoice in the Lord, Brother, and to sing His praises in my infirmities, because, by the grace of the Holy Spirit, I am so closely united and joined with my Lord, that, through His mercy, I can well rejoice in the Most High Himself."

The Assisi Compilation, 99
The Founder, 202–3

7 SEPTEMBER

Another time during those days, a doctor from the city of Arezzo, named Good John, who was known and familiar to blessed Francis, came to visit him in the bishop's palace. Blessed Francis asked about his sickness saying: "How does my illness of dropsy seem to you, Brother John?"

For blessed Francis did not want to address anyone called "Good" by their name, out of reverence for the Lord, who said: No one is good but God alone [Lk 18:19]. Likewise, he did not want to call anyone "father" or "master," nor write them in letters, out of reverence for the Lord, who said: Call no one on earth your father nor be called masters, etc. [Mt 23:9–10]

The doctor said to him: "Brother, by the grace of the Lord, it will be well with you." For he did not want to tell him that he would die in a little while.

Again blessed Francis said to him: "Tell me the truth. How does it look to you? Do not be afraid, for, by the grace of God, I am not a coward who fears death. With the Lord's help, by His mercy and grace, I am so united and joined with my Lord that I am equally as happy to die as I am to live."

The doctor then told him frankly: "According to our assessment, your illness is incurable and you will die either at the end of September or on the fourth day before the Nones of October." Blessed Francis, while he was lying on his bed sick, with the greatest devotion and reverence for the Lord stretched out his arms and hands with great joy of mind and body and said to his body and soul: "Welcome, my Sister Death!"

The Assisi Compilation, 100
The Founder, 203–4

8 SEPTEMBER

Brother Peter of Catanio, the saint's vicar, saw that great crowds of brothers from other places visited Saint Mary of the Portiuncula, and that the alms received were not sufficient to provide for their needs. He told Saint Francis: "Brother, I don't know what to do; I don't have enough to provide for all the crowds of brothers pouring in from all over. I beg you, please allow some of the goods of those entering as novices to be kept so that we can have recourse to these for expenses in due season." But the saint replied: "May that piety be elsewhere, my dear brother, which treats the Rule with impiety for the sake of anyone." "Then, what should I do?" asked Peter. "Strip the Virgin's altar and take its adornments when you can't care for the needy in any other way. Believe me, she would be happier to have her altar stripped and the Gospel of her Son kept than have her altar decorated and her Son despised. The Lord will send someone to return to his Mother what He has loaned to us."

Thomas of Celano, The Remembrance of the Desire of a Soul,
Second Book, XXXVII, 67
The Founder, 291–2

9 SEPTEMBER

While he was staying in Siena someone from the Order of Preachers happened to arrive; he was a spiritual man and a Doctor of Sacred Theology. He visited blessed Francis, and he and the holy man enjoyed a long and sweet conversation about the words of the Lord. This teacher asked him about the words of Ezekiel: If you do not warn the wicked man about his wickedness, I will hold you responsible for his soul [Ez 3:18–20; 33:7–9]. "I'm acquainted with many people, good Father, who live in mortal sin, as I'm aware. But I don't always warn them about their wickedness. Will I then be held responsible for their souls?" Blessed Francis then said that he was an unlettered man, and it would be better for him to be taught by the other rather than to answer a question about Scripture. But that humble teacher replied: "Brother, it's true I have heard these words explained by some wise men, still, I'd be glad to hear how you understand it." So blessed Francis said to him: "If that passage is supposed to be understood in a universal sense, then I understand it to mean that a servant of God should be burning with life and holiness so brightly, that by the light of example and the tongue of his conduct, he will rebuke all the wicked. In that way, I say, the brightness of his life and the fragrance of his reputation will proclaim their wickedness to all of them." That man went away greatly edified, and said to the companions of blessed Francis: "My brothers, the theology of this man, held aloft by purity and contemplation, is a soaring eagle, while our learning crawls on its belly on the ground."

Thomas of Celano, The Remembrance of the Desire of a Soul,
Second Book, LXIX, 103
The Founder, 315

10 SEPTEMBER

[H]ave the clerics say the Office with devotion before God not concentrating on the melody of the voice but on the harmony of the mind, that the voice may be in harmony with the mind, the mind truly in harmony with God. [Let them do this] that they may be able to please God by their purity of heart and not just charm the ears of people by their sweetness of voice.

For my part, I firmly promise to observe these things, as God shall give me the grace, and I pass them on to the brothers who are with me to be observed in the Office and the other prescriptions of the Rule.

I do not consider those brothers who do not wish to observe these things Catholics or my brothers; I do not even wish to see or speak with them until they have done penance. I even say this about all those who wander about, having put aside the discipline of the Rule, for our Lord Jesus Christ gave His life that He would not lose the obedience of His most holy Father.

A Letter to the Entire Order, 41–45
The Saint, 119–20

11 SEPTEMBER

Let all the brothers be careful not to slander or engage in disputes; let them strive, instead, to keep silence whenever God gives them the grace. Let them not quarrel among themselves or with others but strive to respond humbly, saying: I am a useless servant [Lk 17:10]. Let them not become angry because whoever is angry with his brother is liable to judgment; whoever says to his brother "fool" shall be answerable to the Council; whoever says "fool" will be liable to fiery Gehenna [Mt 5:22].

Let them love one another, as the Lord says: This is my commandment: love one another as I have loved you [Jn 15:12]. Let them express the love they have for one another by their deeds, as the Apostle says: Let us not love in word or speech, but in deed and truth [1 Jn 3:18].

Let them revile no one. Let them not grumble or detract from others, for it is written: Gossips and detractors are detestable to God [Rom 1:29–30]. Let them be modest by showing graciousness toward everyone. Let them not judge or condemn. As the Lord says, let them not consider the least sins of others [Mt 7:3; Lk 6:41]; instead, let them reflect more upon their own sins in the bitterness of their soul. Let them struggle to enter through the narrow gate, for the Lord says: The gate is narrow and the road that leads to life constricted; those who find it are few [Mt 7:14].

The Earlier Rule (The Rule without a Papal Seal), XI, 1–13
The Saint, 72

12 SEPTEMBER

Because of the disease of his eyes, blessed Francis at that time was staying in the church of San Fabiano near the same city, where there was a poor secular priest. At that time the Lord Pope Honorius and other cardinals were in the same city. Many of the cardinals and other great clerics, because of the reverence and devotion they had for the holy father, used to visit him almost every day.

That church had a small vineyard next to the house where blessed Francis was staying. There was one door to the house through which nearly all those who visited him passed into the vineyard, especially because the grapes were ripe at that time, and the place was pleasant for resting.

And it came about that for that reason almost the entire vineyard was ruined. For some picked the grapes and ate them there, while others picked them and carried them off, and still others trampled them underfoot.

The priest began to be offended and upset. "I lost my vintage for this year!" he said. "Even though it's small, I got enough wine from it to take care of my needs!"

When blessed Francis heard of this, he had him called and said to him: "Do not be disturbed or offended any longer. We can't do anything about it. But trust in the Lord, because for me, His little servant, He can restore your loss. But, tell me, how many measures of wine did you get when your vineyard was at its best?"

"Thirteen measures, father," the priest responded.

"Don't be sad over this anymore," blessed Francis told him, "and don't say anything offensive to anyone because of it, or argue with anyone about it. Trust the Lord and my words, and if you get less than twenty measures of wine, I will make it up to you."

The priest calmed down and kept quiet. And it happened by divine dispensation that he obtained twenty measures and no less, just as blessed Francis had told him. Those who heard about it, as well as the priest himself, were amazed. They considered it a great miracle due to the merits of blessed Francis, especially because not only was it devastated, but even if it had been full of grapes and no one had taken any, it still seemed impossible to the priest and the others to get twenty measures of wine from it.

We who were with him bear witness that whenever he used to say: "This is the way it is … or this is the way it will be …", it always happened as he said. We have seen many of these fulfilled not only while he was alive but also after his death.

The Assisi Compilation, 67
The Founder, 170–1

13 SEPTEMBER

Although he wanted his sons to keep peace with all, and to behave as little ones toward everyone, he taught them to be particularly humble toward clerics by his word and showed them by his example. He used to say: "We have been sent to help clerics for the salvation of souls so that we may make up whatever may be lacking in them. Each shall receive a reward, not on account of authority, but because of the work done. Know then, brothers, that the good of souls is what pleases God most, and this is more easily obtained through peace with the clergy than fighting with them. If they should stand in the way of the people's salvation, revenge is for God, and he will repay them in due time. So, be subject to prelates so that as much as possible on your part no jealousy arises. If you are children of peace, you will win over both clergy and people for the Lord, and the Lord will judge that more acceptable than only winning over the people while scandalizing the clergy. Cover up their failings, make up for their many defects, and when you have done this, be even more humble."

Thomas of Celano, The Remembrance of the Desire of a Soul,
Second Book, CVII, 146
The Founder, 341

14 SEPTEMBER

When Saint Francis came to Imola, a city of Romagna, he presented himself to the bishop of that region and asked him for permission to preach. But the bishop said: "Brother, I preach to my people and that is enough." Saint Francis bowed his head and humbly went outside, but less than an hour later he came back in. "What do you want now, brother?" the bishop asked. "What else do you want?" Blessed Francis replied: "My Lord, if a father throws his son out by one door, he should come back in by another!" The bishop, overcome by his humility, embraced him with a smile, saying: "From now on you and your brothers have my general permission to preach in my diocese. Holy humility earned it!"

Thomas of Celano, The Remembrance of the Desire of a Soul,
Second Book, CVIII, 147
The Founder, 342

15 SEPTEMBER

The saint taught those coming to the Order that, before giving to the world a bill of divorce they should first offer what was theirs outwardly and then offer themselves inwardly to God. He would admit to the Order only those who had given up everything and kept nothing, both because of the words of the holy Gospel and because they should not cause scandal by keeping a money bag.

It happened once in the March of Ancona after the saint had been preaching, that a man came to him humbly requesting to enter the Order. And the holy man said to him: "If you want to join God's poor, first distribute what you have to the poor of the world." When he heard this, the man went off and, led by the love of the flesh, distributed his goods to his relatives and not to the poor. When he came back and told the saint about his openhanded generosity, the father laughed at him: "Go on your way, Brother Fly," he said, "for you have not yet left your home and family. You gave what you had to your relatives and cheated the poor. You are not worthy of the holy poor. You began with flesh, and laid down a crumbling foundation for a spiritual building!" And so this carnal man returned to his own, and demanded back his goods: refusing to leave them to the poor; he soon left his proposal of virtue.

Today, this kind of stingy distribution fools many setting out on a blessed life with a worldly beginning. Nobody consecrates himself to God to make his relatives rich, but to acquire life by the fruit of good work, redeeming his sins by the price of piety.

He often taught that if the brothers were in want, it was better to have recourse to others than to those who were entering the Order, primarily for the sake of example and also to avoid any appearance of base interests.

Thomas of Celano, The Remembrance of the Desire of a Soul,
Second Book, XLIX, 80–1
The Founder, 299–300

16 SEPTEMBER

It was a custom for the angelic man Francis never to rest from the good, rather, like the heavenly spirits on Jacob's ladder, he either ascended into God or descended to his neighbor. For he had so prudently learned to divide the time given to him for merit, that he spent some of it working for his neighbor's benefit and dedicated the rest to the tranquil excesses of contemplation. Therefore, when he emptied himself according to the demand of times and places to gain the salvation of another, leaving the restlessness of the crowds, he would seek the secrets of solitude and a place of quiet, where freeing himself more freely for the Lord, he would shake off the dust that might have clung to him from the time spent with the crowds.

Therefore, two years before he returned his spirit to heaven, after a variety of many labors, he was led by divine providence to a high place apart called Mount La Verna. When according to his usual custom he had begun to fast there for forty days in honor of Saint Michael the Archangel, he experienced more abundantly than usual an overflow of the sweetness of heavenly contemplation, was on fire with an ever intense flame of heavenly desires, and began to be aware more fully of the gifts of heavenly entries. He was carried into the heights, not as a curious searcher of the supreme majesty crushed by its glory, but as a faithful and prudent servant, exploring God's good pleasure, to which, with the greatest ardor, he desires to conform himself in every way.

Through a divine sign from heaven he had learned that in opening the book of the Gospel, Christ would reveal to him what God considered most acceptable in him and from him. After completing his prayer with much devotion, he took the book of the sacred Gospels from the altar and had his companion, a holy man dedicated to God, open it three times in the name of the Holy Trinity. All three times, when the book was opened, the Lord's passion always met his eyes. The man filled with God understood that, just as he had imitated Christ in the actions of his life, so he should be conformed to him in the affliction and sorrow of his passion, before he would pass out of this world.

And although his body was already weakened by the great austerity of his past life and his continual carrying of the Lord's cross, he was in no way terrified, but was inspired even more vigorously to endure martyrdom. The unconquerable enkindling of love in him for the good Jesus had grown into lamps and flames of fire, that many waters could not quench so powerful a love.

Bonaventure, The Major Legend of Saint Francis, XIII, 1–2
The Founder, 630–1

17 SEPTEMBER

With the seraphic ardor of desires, therefore, he was being borne aloft into God; and by compassionate sweetness he was being transformed into Him Who chose to be crucified out of the excess of His love.

On a certain morning about the feast of the Exaltation of the Cross, while Francis was praying on the mountainside, he saw a Seraph having six wings, fiery as well as brilliant, descend from the grandeur of heaven. And when in swift flight, it had arrived at a spot in the air near the man of God, there appeared between the wings the likeness of a man crucified, with his hands and feet extended in the form of a cross and fastened to a cross. Two of the wings were raised above his head, two were extended for flight, and two covered his whole body. Seeing this, he was overwhelmed and his heart was flooded with a mixture of joy and sorrow. He rejoiced at the gracious way Christ looked upon him under the appearance of the Seraph, but the fact that He was fastened to a cross pierced his soul with a sword of compassionate sorrow.

He marveled exceedingly at the sight of so unfathomable a vision, knowing that the weakness of Christ's passion was in no way compatible with the immortality of the seraphic spirit. Eventually he understood from this, through the Lord revealing it, that Divine Providence had shown him a vision of this sort so that the friend of Christ might learn in advance that he was to be totally transformed into the likeness of Christ crucified, not by the martyrdom of his flesh, but by the enkindling of his soul. As the vision was disappearing, it left in his heart a marvelous fire and imprinted in his flesh a likeness of signs no less marvelous.

For immediately the marks of nails began to appear in his hands and feet just as he had seen a little before in the figure of the man crucified. His hands and feet seemed to be pierced through the center by nails, with the heads of the nails appearing on the inner side of the hands and the upper side of the feet and their points on the opposite sides. The heads of the nails in his hands and his feet were round and black; their points were oblong and bent as if driven back with a hammer, and they emerged from the flesh and stuck out beyond it. Also his right side, as if pierced with a lance, was marked with a red wound from which his sacred blood often flowed, moistening his tunic and underwear.

Bonaventure, The Major Legend of Saint Francis, XIII, 3
The Founder, 632–3

18 SEPTEMBER

As Christ's servant realized that he could not conceal from his intimate companions the stigmata that had been so visibly imprinted on his flesh, he feared to make public the Lord's sacrament and was thrown into an agony of doubt whether to tell what he had seen or to be silent about it. He called some of the brothers and, speaking in general terms, presented his doubt to them and sought their advice. One of the brothers, Illuminato, by name and by grace, understanding that Francis had seen something marvelous that made him seem completely dazed, said to the holy man: "Brother, you should realize that at times divine sacraments are revealed to you not for yourself alone but also for others. You have every reason to fear that if you hide what you have received for the profit of many, you will be blamed for burying that talent." Although the holy man used to say on other occasions: "My secret is for myself," he was moved by Illuminato's words. Then, with much fear, he recounted the vision in detail, adding that the one who had appeared to him had told him some things which he would never disclose to any person as long as he lived. We should believe, then, that those utterances of that sacred Seraph marvelously appearing to him on the cross were so secret that people are not permitted to speak of them.

After true love of Christ transformed the lover into His image, when the forty days were over that he spent in solitude as he had desired, and the feast of Saint Michael the Archangel had also arrived, the angelic man Francis came down from the mountain, bearing with him the likeness of the Crucified, depicted not on tablets of stone or on panels of wood carved by hand, but engraved on parts of his flesh by the finger of the living God. And because it is good to keep hidden the sacrament of the King, the man aware of the royal secret would then hide from men those sacred signs. Since it is for God to reveal what He does for his own great glory, the Lord himself, who had secretly imprinted those marks, openly revealed some miracles through them so that the hidden and marvelous power of the stigmata would display a brilliance of signs.

Bonaventure, The Major Legend of Saint Francis, XIII, 4–5
The Founder, 633–4

19 SEPTEMBER

As for the brothers who go, they can live spiritually among the Saracens and nonbelievers in two ways. One way is not to engage in arguments or disputes but to be subject to every human creature for God's sake and to acknowledge that they are Christians. The other way is to announce the Word of God, when they see it pleases the Lord, in order that [unbelievers] may believe in almighty God, the Father, the Son and the Holy Spirit, the Creator of all, the Son, the Redeemer and Savior, and be baptized and become Christians because no one can enter the kingdom of God without being reborn of water and the Holy Spirit.

They can say to them and the others these and other things which please God because the Lord says in the Gospel: Whoever acknowledges me before others I will acknowledge before my heavenly Father. Whoever is ashamed of me and of my words, the Son of Man will be ashamed of when he comes in his glory and in the glory of the Father [Lk 9:26].

The Earlier Rule (The Rule without a Papal Seal), XVI, 5–9
The Saint, 74

20 SEPTEMBER

Wherever they may be, let all my brothers remember that they have given themselves and abandoned their bodies to the Lord Jesus Christ. For love of Him, they must make themselves vulnerable to their enemies, both visible and invisible, because the Lord says: Whoever loses his life because of me will save it in eternal life [Lk 9:24; Mt 25:46]. Blessed are they who suffer persecution for the sake of justice, for theirs is the kingdom of heaven [Mt 5:10]. If they have persecuted me, they will also persecute you [Jn 15:20]. If they persecute you in one town, flee to another [Mt 10:23]. Blessed are you when people hate you, speak evil of you, persecute, expel, and abuse you, denounce your name as evil and utter every kind of slander against you because of me. Rejoice and be glad on that day because your reward is great in heaven [Mt 5:11–12; Lk 6:22–23].

I tell you, my friends, do not be afraid of them and do not fear those who kill the body and afterwards have nothing more to do

[Lk 12:4; Mt 10:28]. See that you are not alarmed [Mt 24:6]. For by your patience, you will possess your souls; whoever perseveres to the end will be saved [Lk 21:19; Mt 10:22; 24:13].

The Earlier Rule (The Rule without a Papal Seal), XVI, 10–21
The Saint, 14–5

ஒ

21 SEPTEMBER

Calling together the six brothers, Saint Francis, since he was full of the grace of the Holy Spirit, predicted to them what was about to happen. "Dearest brothers," he said, "let us consider our vocation, to which God has mercifully called us, not only for our own good, but for the salvation of many. We are to go throughout the world, encouraging everyone, more by deed than by word, to do penance for their sins and to recall the commandments of God. Do not be afraid that you seem few and uneducated. With confidence, simply proclaim penance, trusting in the Lord, who conquered the world. Because by his Spirit, He is speaking through and in you, encouraging everyone to be converted to him and to observe his commandments.

"You will find some faithful people, meek and kind, who will receive you and your words with joy. You will find many others, faithless, proud, and blasphemous, who will resist and reject you and what you say. Therefore, resolve in your hearts to bear these things with patience and humility."

When the brothers heard this, they began to be afraid. The saint told them: "Do not fear, because after not much time many learned and noble men will come to us, and will be with us preaching to kings and rulers and great crowds. Many people will be converted to the Lord, Who will multiply and increase His family throughout the entire world."

The Legend of the Three Companions, X, 36
The Founder, 89–90

ஒ

22 SEPTEMBER

And when he had said these things and blessed them, the men of God went on their way devoutly observing his warnings. Whenever they came upon a church or a cross, they bowed in prayer and said with devotion: "We adore you, Christ, and we bless you in all your churches throughout the whole world, because, by your holy cross, you have redeemed the world." For they believed they would find a place of God wherever they found a cross or a church.

Those who saw them, however, were greatly amazed that they differed from all others by their habit and life and seemed almost like wild men. In fact, whenever they entered especially a city, estate, town, or home, they announced peace, encouraging everyone to fear and love the Creator of heaven and earth and to observe the commandments.

Some people listened to them willingly; others, on the other hand, mocked them; and many tired them out with questions by saying to them: "Where do you come from?" Others wanted to know which was their Order. Although it was tiresome answering so many questions, they responded simply that they were penitents originally from the city of Assisi. At that time their religion was not yet called an order.

In fact, many judged them impostors or fools, and were unwilling to receive them into their homes lest, as thieves, they might slyly take their belongings. Therefore, in many places, after they had suffered a number of insults, they sought lodging in the porticos of churches and homes.

The Legend of the Three Companions, X, 37–8
The Founder, 90

23 SEPTEMBER

There was in him such harmony of flesh with spirit and such obedience that, as the spirit strove to reach all holiness, the flesh did not resist but even tried to run on ahead, according to the saying: For you my soul has thirsted; and my flesh in so many ways [Ps 63:2]! Repeated submission became spontaneous, as the flesh, yielding each day, reached a place of great virtue, for habit often becomes nature.

According to the laws of nature and the human condition day by day the body must decay though the inner being is renewed. So the precious vessel in which the heavenly treasure was hidden began to shatter all over and lose all its strength. Yet when a man has finished, then he will begin and when he has finished, then he will start to work. And so the spirit became willing in the flesh that was weak. He so desired the salvation of souls and longed to benefit his neighbors that, even though he could no longer walk on his own, he went through the towns riding on a little donkey.

The brothers often advised him, urging him to give some relief to his frail and weakened body through the help of doctors. But he absolutely refused to do this. His noble spirit was aimed at heaven and he only desired to be set free and to be with Christ. But he had not yet filled up in his flesh what is lacking in the sufferings of Christ, even though he bore the marks on his body. So God multiplied his mercy on him, and he contracted a serious disease of the eyes. Day after day the disease grew worse and seemed to be aggravated daily from lack of treatment. Brother Elias, the one he chose for the role of mother to himself and had made a father of the other brothers, finally forced him not to refuse medicine but to accept it in the name of the Son of God. Through Him it was created, as it is written: The Most High created medicine from the earth and the wise will not refuse it [Sir 38:4]. The holy father then gladly agreed with him and humbly accepted his direction.

Thomas of Celano, The Life of Saint Francis, Second Book, IV, 97–8
The Saint, 266–7

24 SEPTEMBER

In the sight of God and the people of this world the glorious father had been made perfect in grace. In all that he did he glowed brilliantly, yet he always kept thinking about how to undertake even more perfect deeds. Like a soldier, well-trained in the battle camps of God, challenging the enemy, he wanted to stir up fresh battles. With the Christ as leader, he resolved "to do great deeds," and with weakening limbs and dying body, he hoped for victory over the enemy in a new struggle. True bravery knows no real limits of time, for its hope of reward is eternal.

He burned with a great desire to return to his earliest steps toward humility; rejoicing in hope because of his boundless love, he planned to call his body back to its original servitude, although it had now reached its limit. He cut away completely the obstacle of all cares and silenced the noise of all concerns. When he had to relax this rigour because of illness, he used to say: "Let us begin, brothers, to serve the Lord God, for up until now we have done little or nothing." He did not consider that he had already attained his goal, but tireless in pursuit of holy newness, he constantly hoped to begin again.

He wanted to return to serving lepers and to be held in contempt, just as he used to be. He intended to flee human company and go off to the most remote places, so that, letting go of every care and putting aside anxiety about others, for the time being only the wall of the flesh would stand between him and God.

He saw many rushing for positions of authority. Despising their arrogance, he strove by his own example to call them back from such sickness. Indeed, he used to say that it was a good and acceptable thing in God's sight to take care of others. He held it was appropriate for some to take on the care of souls as long as in this they sought nothing of their own will, but in all things constantly obeyed God's will. Such people should consider in the first place their own salvation and aim for the growth of their subjects, not their applause. They should seek glory before God, not honor from people, never desiring but fearing the office of prelate. If given to them it would humble them, not exalt them; were it taken away, it would not leave them dejected, but uplifted.

He maintained it was dangerous to direct others and better to be directed, especially in these times when malice is growing so much and wickedness is increasing. It hurt him that some had abandoned their early deeds and, in the midst of new discoveries, had forgotten their original simplicity. That is why he grieved over those who now sank to the level of what was low and cheap, although they once had striven for higher things with all their desire. They had abandoned true joy and were running here and there, wandering through the fields of an empty freedom. So he prayed for God's mercy to set his sons free and fervently begged that they be preserved in the grace given to them.

Thomas of Celano, The Life of Saint Francis, Second Book, VI, 103–4
The Saint, 272–4

25 SEPTEMBER

Six months before the day of his death, he was staying in Siena for treatment of his eye disease. But then all the rest of his body started to show signs of serious illness. His stomach had been destroyed, and his liver was failing. He was vomiting a lot of blood, so much that he seemed close to death. On hearing of this in a place far away, brother Elias rushed to his side. At his arrival the holy father had recovered so much that they left that area and went together to Le Celle near Cortona. After reaching the place he stayed for a while, but then the swelling began in his abdomen, his legs, and his feet. His stomach became so weak that he could hardly eat any food at all. At that point, he asked brother Elias to have him carried to Assisi. The good son did what the kind father commanded and, when everything was ready, led him to the place he longed for. The city rejoiced at the arrival of the blessed father and all the people with one voice praised God, since the whole multitude of the people hoped that the holy one of God would die close to them, and this was the reason for such great rejoicing.

And so it was also the will of God that his holy soul, freed from the flesh, would pass over to the kingdom of heaven from that place where, while still living in the flesh, he had first been given the knowledge of higher things and had the oil of salvation poured out upon him. He knew that the kingdom of heaven was established in every corner of the earth and he believed that divine grace was given to God's chosen ones in every place. Yet he knew from his own experience that the place of the church of Saint Mary of the Portiuncula was especially full of grace and filled with visits of heavenly spirits. So he often told the brothers: "See to it, my sons, that you never abandon this place. If you are driven out from one side, go back in from the other, for this is truly a holy place and the dwelling place of God. Here the Most High increased our numbers when we were only a few; here He enlightened the hearts of his poor ones with the light of His wisdom; here He kindled our wills with the fire of His love; here all who pray wholeheartedly will receive what they ask, while offenders will be severely punished. Therefore, my sons, hold this place, God's dwelling, as worthy of all honor and here praise God in cries of joy and praise with your whole heart."

Thomas of Celano, The Life of Saint Francis, Second Book, VII, 105–6
The Saint, 274–5

26 SEPTEMBER

Now fixed with Christ to the cross, in both body and spirit, Francis not only burned with a seraphic love into God but also thirsted with Christ crucified for the multitude of those to be saved. Since he could not walk because of the nails protruding from his feet, he had his half-dead body carried through the towns and villages to arouse others to carry the cross of Christ. He used to say to the brothers: "Let us begin, brothers, to serve the Lord our God, for up to now we have done little." He burned with a great desire to return to the humility he practiced at the beginning; to nurse the lepers as he did at the outset and to treat like a slave once more his body that was already in a state of collapse from his work.

With the Christ as leader, he resolved "to do great deeds," and although his limbs were weakening, he hoped for victory over the enemy in a new struggle with a brave and burning spirit. For there is no room for apathy and laziness where the goad of love always urges to greater things. There was in him such harmony of flesh with spirit, such readiness of obedience, that, when he strove to attain all holiness, not only did the flesh not resist, it even tried to run ahead.

Bonaventure, The Major Legend of Saint Francis, XIV, 1
The Founder, 640–1

27 SEPTEMBER

In order that his merits might increase, for these are brought to perfection in patience, the man of God started to suffer from various illnesses, so seriously that scarcely the rest of his body remained without intense pain and suffering. Through varied, long-lasting, and continual illness he was brought to the point where his flesh was already all consumed, as if only skin clung to his bones. But when he was tortured by harsh bodily suffering, he called his tribulations not by the name of "pains" but of "Sisters."

Once when he was suffering more intensely than usual, a certain brother in his simplicity told him: "Brother, pray to the Lord that he treat you more mildly, for he seems to have laid his hand on you more heavily than he should." At these words, the holy man wailed and cried out: "If I did not know your simplicity and sincerity, then I would from now on shrink from your company because you dared to judge God's judgments upon me as reprehensible." Even though he was completely worn out by his prolonged and serious illness, he threw himself on the ground, bruising his weakened bones in the hard fall. Kissing the ground, he said: "I thank you, Lord God, for all these sufferings of mine; and I ask you, my Lord, if it pleases you, to increase them a hundredfold. Because it will be most acceptable to me, that you do not spare me, afflicting me with suffering, since the fulfillment of your will is an overflowing consolation for me."

So it seemed to the brothers, therefore, that they were almost seeing another Job, for whom, as the weariness of his flesh was increasing, so too was the vigor of his soul. He knew long in advance the time of his death, and as the day of his passing grew near, he told the brothers that laying aside the tent of his body was at hand, as it had been revealed to him by Christ.

For two years after the imprinting of the sacred stigmata that is, in the twentieth year of his conversion, under the many blows of agonizing illness, he was squared like a stone to be fitted into the construction of the heavenly Jerusalem, and like a work of malleable metal he was brought to perfection under the hammering blows of many tribulations.

Bonaventure, The Major Legend of Saint Francis, XIV, 2–3
The Founder, 641–2

28 SEPTEMBER

He asked to be taken to Saint Mary of the Portiuncula so that he might yield up the spirit of life where he had received the spirit of grace. When he had been brought there, he showed by the example of Truth that he had nothing in common with the world. In that grave illness that ended all suffering, he threw himself in fervor of spirit totally naked on the naked ground so that in that final hour, when the enemy could still rage, he might wrestle naked with the naked. Lying like this on the ground stripped of his sackcloth garment, he lifted up his face to heaven in his accustomed way, and wholly intent upon that glory, he covered with his left hand the wound in his right side, so that no one would see it. And he said to his brothers: "I have done what is mine; may Christ teach you yours."

Pierced with the spear of compassion, the companions of the saint wept streams of tears. One of them, whom the man of God used to call his guardian, knowing his wish through divine inspiration, quickly got up. He took the tunic with a cord and underwear, and offered them to the little poor man of Christ, saying: "I am lending these to you as to a poor man, and you are to accept them with the command of holy obedience." At this the holy man rejoiced and was delighted in the gladness of his heart, because he saw that he had kept faith until the end with Lady Poverty. Raising his hands to heaven, he magnified his Christ, that now set free from all things, he was going to him free. For he had done all of this out of zeal for poverty, not wanting to have even a habit unless it were borrowed from another.

In all things he wished without hesitation to be conformed to Christ crucified, who hung on the cross poor, suffering, and naked. Naked he lingered before the bishop at the beginning of his conversion; and, for this reason, at the end of his life, he wanted to leave this world naked.

And so he charged the brothers assisting him, under the obedience of love, that when they saw he was dead, they should allow him to lie naked on the ground for as long as it takes to walk a leisurely mile.

O truly the most Christian of men, who strove by perfect imitation to be conformed while living to Christ living, dying to Christ dying, and dead to Christ dead, and deserved to be adorned with an expressed likeness!

Bonaventure, The Major Legend of Saint Francis, XIV, 3–4
The Founder, 642–3

29 SEPTEMBER

He venerated the angels with the greatest affection, for they are with us in battle, and walk with us in the midst of the shadow of death. He said that such companions should be revered everywhere, and invoked as protectors. He taught that their gaze should not be offended, and no one should presume to do in their sight what he would not do in the sight of others. And since in choir one sings the psalms in the presence of the angels, he wanted all who were able to gather in the oratory and sing psalms wisely.

He often said that Blessed Michael should be especially honored because his duty is presenting souls to God. In honor of Saint Michael he would fast with great devotion for forty days between the Feast of the Assumption and Saint Michael's feast day. For he used to say: "Each person should offer God some special praise or gift in honor of such a great prince."

Thomas of Celano, The Remembrance of the Desire of a Soul,
Second Book, CXLIX, 197
The Founder, 373–4

30 SEPTEMBER

As his illness grew worse, he lost all bodily strength, and deprived of all his powers, he could not even move. One of the brothers asked him what he would prefer to endure: this long-lasting illness or suffering a martyr's cruel death at the hands of an executioner. "My son," he replied, "whatever is more pleasing to the Lord my God to do with me and in me has always been and still is dearer, sweeter, and more agreeable to me. I desire to be found always and completely in harmony with and obedient to God's will alone in everything. But to suffer this illness, even for three days, would be harder for me than any martyrdom. I am not speaking about its reward but only of the pain and suffering it causes."

O martyr, martyr laughing and rejoicing, who endured so gladly what was bitter and painful for others to see!

Not one of his members remained without great pain and suffering; his bodily warmth gradually diminished, and each day he drew closer to his end. The doctors were amazed and the brothers were astonished that the spirit could live in flesh so dead, since with his flesh all consumed only skin clung to his bones.

Thomas of Celano, The Life of Saint Francis, Second Book, VII, 107
The Saint, 275–6

October

1 OCTOBER

When he saw his final day drawing near, as shown to him two years earlier by divine revelation, he called to him the brothers he chose. He blessed each one as it was given to him from above, just as Jacob of old, the patriarch, blessed his sons. He was like another Moses about to ascend the mountain that the Lord had shown him, when imparting blessings on the children of Israel.

When brother Elias sat down on his left side with the other brothers around him, the blessed father crossed his arms and placed his right hand on Elias' head. He had lost the sight and use of his bodily eyes, so he asked: "Over whom am I holding my right hand?" "Over brother Elias," they replied. "And this is what I wish to do," he said, "I bless you, my son, in all and through all, and just as the most High has increased my brothers and sons in your hands, so too, upon you and in you, I bless them all. May the king of all bless you in heaven and on earth. I bless you as I can, and more than I can, and what I cannot do may the One who can do all things do in you. May God remember your work and labors, and may a place be reserved for you among the rewards of the just. May you receive every blessing you desire and may your every worthy request be fulfilled."

"Good-bye, all my sons. Live in the fear of God and remain in Him always, for a great test will come upon you and tribulation is drawing near! Happy are those who will persevere in what they have begun: many will be separated from them by the scandals that are to come. But now I am hurrying to the Lord and I am confident that I am going to my God whom I have served in my spirit."

He was staying then in the palace of the bishop of Assisi, and he asked the brothers to carry him quickly to the place of Saint Mary of the Portiuncula. For he wanted to give back his soul to God in that place where, as noted above, he first came to know perfectly the way of truth.

Thomas of Celano, The Life of Saint Francis, Second Book, VII, 108
The Saint, 276–7

2 OCTOBER

Twenty years had now passed since his conversion, and his time was ending just as it had been shown to him by God's will. For, once the blessed father and brother Elias were staying at Foligno, and one night while they were sleeping, a priest of venerable appearance and great age dressed in white clothing appeared to brother Elias. "Get up, brother," he said, "and tell brother Francis that eighteen years have passed since he renounced the world and clung to Christ. He will remain in this life only two more years; then he will go the way of all flesh when the Lord calls him to Himself." So it came to pass that, at the established time, the word of the Lord spoken long before now was fulfilled.

After he had rested a few days in that place he so longed for, knowing the time of his death was close at hand, he called to him two brothers, his special sons, and told them to sing The Praises of the Lord with a loud voice and joyful spirit, rejoicing at his approaching death, or rather at the life that was so near. He himself, as best he could, broke into that psalm of David: "With a loud voice I cried to the Lord; with a loud voice I beseeched the Lord."

There was a brother there whom the holy man loved with great affection. Seeing what was happening and realizing the saint was nearing the end, he grew very concerned about all the brothers and said: "Oh, kind father, your sons will now be without a father, and will be deprived of the true light of their eyes! Remember the orphans you are leaving behind; forgive all their faults, and gladden them all, whether present or absent, with your holy blessing." The holy man answered: "See, my son, I am being called by God. I forgive all my brothers, present and absent, all their faults and offences, and I absolve them insofar as I am able. When you give them this message, bless them all for me."

Then he ordered the book of the Gospels to be brought in. He asked that the Gospel according to John be read to him, starting with the passage that begins: Six days before the Passover, Jesus, knowing that the hour had come for him to pass from this world to the Father [Jn 12:1/13:1]. This was the very gospel his minister had planned to read, even before he was told to do so; that was the passage that met his eye as he first opened the book, although he had the complete Bible from which to read the gospel. Then he told them to cover him with sackcloth and to sprinkle him with ashes, as he was soon to become dust and ashes.

Many brothers gathered there, for whom he was both father and leader. They stood there reverently, all awaiting his blessed departure and happy end. And then that most holy soul was released from the flesh, and as it was absorbed into the abyss of light, his body fell asleep in the Lord.

One of his brothers and followers, a man of some fame, whose name I will conceal for now since he does not wish to glory in such fame while still living in the flesh, saw the soul of the most holy father rise straight to heaven over many waters. It was like a star but as big as the moon, with the brilliance of the sun, and carried up upon a small white cloud.

Let me cry out therefore: "O what a glorious saint he is! His disciple saw his soul ascending into heaven: beautiful as the moon, bright as the sun, glowing brilliantly as it ascended upon a white cloud! O true lamp of the world, shining more brilliantly than the sun in the Church of Christ! Now, you have withdrawn the rays of your light, as you withdraw into that luminous homeland. You have exchanged our poor company for that of the angels and saints! In your glorious goodness and great renown, do not put aside care for your sons, though you have put aside flesh like theirs. You know, you truly know, the danger in which you have left them; for it was your blessed presence alone that always mercifully relieved their countless labors and frequent troubles! O truly merciful and most holy father, you were always kind and ready to show mercy and forgive your sinful sons! We bless you therefore, worthy father, as you have been blessed by the Most High, Who is God over all things blessed forever. Amen."

Thomas of Celano, The Life of Saint Francis, Second Book, VIII, 109–11
The Saint, 277–9

3 OCTOBER

In truth, in very truth, the presence of our brother and father Francis was a light, not only for us who were near, but even to those who were far from us in calling and in life. He was a light shed by the true light to give light to those who were in darkness and sitting in the shadow of death, to guide our feet into the way of peace. He did this because the true Daystar from on high shone upon his heart and enkindled his will with the fire of His love. By preaching the kingdom of God and turning the hearts of fathers to their children and the rebellious to the wisdom of the just, he prepared for the Lord a new people in the world. His name reached distant coasts and all lands were in awe at his marvelous deeds.

For this reason, sons and brothers, do not mourn beyond measure. God, the father of orphans, will give us comfort by his holy consolation. And if you weep, brothers, weep for yourselves and not for him. For "in the midst of life, we are caught in death," while he has passed from death to life. Rejoice, for, like another Jacob, he blessed all his sons before he was taken from us and forgave them all the faults which any one of us might have committed, or even thought of committing, against him.

A Letter on the Passing of Saint Francis Attributed to Elias of Assisi,
Second Book, 3–4
The Founder, 489–90

4 OCTOBER

And now, after telling you these things, I announce to you a great joy and the news of a miracle. Such a sign that has never been heard of from the dawn of time except in the Son of God, who is Christ the Lord.

Not long before his death, our brother and father appeared crucified, bearing in his body the five wounds which are truly the marks of Christ. His hands and feet had, as it were, the openings of the nails and were pierced front and back revealing the scars and showing the nails' blackness. His side, moreover, seemed opened by a lance and often emitted blood.

As long as his spirit lived in the body, there was no beauty in him for his appearance was that of a man despised. No part of his body was without great suffering. By reason of the contraction of his sinews, his limbs were stiff, much like those of a dead man. But after his death, his appearance was one of great beauty gleaming with a dazzling whiteness and giving joy to all who looked upon him. His limbs, which had been rigid, became marvelously soft and pliable, so that they would be turned this way and that, like those of a young child.

Therefore, brothers, bless the God of heaven and praise Him before all, for He has shown His mercy to us. Hold fast the memory of our father and brother, Francis, to the praise and glory of Him Who made him so great among people and gave him glory in the sight of angels. Pray for him, as he begged us, and pray to him that God may make us share with him in his holy grace. Amen.

On the fourth day before the nones of October, the Lord's day, at the first hour of the preceding night, our father and brother went to Christ. I am sure, dearest brothers, that when this letter reaches you, you will follow the footprints of the people of Israel as they mourned the loss of their great leaders, Moses and Aaron. Let us, by all means, give way to tears for we are deprived of so great a father.

Indeed, it is in keeping with our love for him that we rejoice with Francis. Still, it is right to mourn him! It belongs to us to rejoice with Francis, for he has not died but gone to the fair in heaven, taking with him a bag of money and will not return until the full moon.

At the same time it is right for us to weep for Francis. He who came and went among us, as did Aaron, who brought forth from his storehouse both the new and the old and comforted us in all our afflictions, has been taken from our midst. Now we are like orphans without a father. Yet, because it is written, "the poor depend on you and you are the helper of orphans" all of you, dearest brothers, must earnestly pray that, though this earthen jar has been broken in the valley of Adam's children, the Most High Potter will deign to repair and restore another of similar honor, who will rule over the multitude of our race and go before us into battle like a true Maccabee.

A Letter on the Passing of Saint Francis Attributed to Elias of Assisi,
Second Book, 5–9
The Founder, 490–1

5 OCTOBER

At Francis's death, a whole crowd of people praising God came together and said: "You, our Lord and God, be praised and blessed, for you have given us unworthy ones so precious a remnant! Praise and glory to you, O ineffable Trinity!"

The whole city of Assisi rushed down as a group and the entire region hurried to see the wonderful works of God which the Lord of majesty gloriously displayed in his holy servant. Each person burst into a song of joy at the urging of a joyful heart, and all of them had their desire fulfilled and blessed the almighty Savior. Still his sons were mourning, bereft of so great a father, and showed the deep feeling of their hearts in groaning and tears.

Then incredible joy lightened their grief! A new miracle turned their minds to amazement. Their mourning turned into song, their weeping to jubilation. For they had never heard or read in Scripture about what their eyes could see: they could not have been persuaded to believe it if it were not demonstrated by such clear evidence. In fact, there appeared in him the form of the cross and passion of the spotless lamb who washed away the sins of the world. It seemed he had just been taken down from the cross, his hands and feet pierced by nails and his right side wounded by a lance.

They looked at his skin which was black before but now shining white in its beauty, promising the rewards of the blessed resurrection. They saw his face like the face of an angel, as if he were not dead, but alive. All his limbs had become as soft and moveable as in childhood innocence. His muscles were not taut, as they usually are in the dead, his skin was not hard, his limbs were not rigid but could be easily moved back and forth.

Thomas of Celano, The Life of Saint Francis, Second Book, IX, 112
The Saint, 279–80

6 OCTOBER

This is a unique gift, a sign of special love: to decorate the soldier with the same arms of glory that in their great dignity belong to the King alone! This is a miracle worthy of everlasting remembrance and a sacrament to be remembered with unceasing and wondering reverence. It presents to the eyes of faith that mystery in which the blood of the spotless lamb, flowing abundantly through the five wounds, washed away the sins of the world. O sublime splendor of the living cross, giving life to the dead! Its burden presses so lightly and hurts so sweetly that through it dead flesh lives and the weak spirit grows strong. You have made radiantly beautiful this man who loved You so much! Glory and blessing to God, who alone is wise, and gives new signs and works new wonders to console the weak with revelations and to raise their hearts to the love of things unseen through wonderful works that are seen. O wonderful and loving plan of God! To allay suspicion about the newness of this miracle, there first appeared mercifully in the One from heaven what later appeared wondrously in the one who lived on earth. The true Father of mercies wanted to show how worthy of reward is the one who strives to love Him with his whole heart; worthy to be placed closer to Himself in the highest order of supercelestial spirits.

Thomas of Celano, The Life of Saint Francis, Second Book, IX, 114
The Saint, 281–2

7 OCTOBER

We too will certainly be able to reach these heights if, like the Seraphim, we spread two wings over our heads: that is, following blessed Francis's example, in every good work we have a pure intention and upright conduct, and, directing these to God, we strive untiringly to please God alone in all things. These two wings must be joined for us to cover our heads because the Father of lights will not accept our activity as upright without a pure intention nor vice versa, since He says: If your eye is sound, your whole body will be full of light; but if your eye is evil, your whole body will be full of darkness [Mt 6:22–23]. That eye is not sound if it does not see what should be seen, because it does not know the truth, or if it looks at what should not be seen, because it does not have a pure intention. An open mind will judge neither as sound; the first is blind and the second evil.

The feathers of the wings are the love of the saving and merciful Father and the fear of the Lord, the terrible judge. These lift the souls of the chosen above things of earth while restraining evil thoughts and ordering chaste affections.

The other two wings are for flying: showing a double charity to our neighbor, refreshing the soul with the word of God and nourishing the body with material aid. These wings are rarely joined together, since one person could hardly do both. The feathers of these wings are varied works of counsel and help offered to our neighbor.

The last two wings are to cover the body that is bare of merits. This happens regularly as it is stripped naked whenever sin breaks in, but is then clothed again in innocence through contrition and confession. The feathers of these wings are the wide range of affections arising from hatred of sin and developing a longing for justice.

Our blessed father Francis fulfilled all these things completely: he had both the image and the form of the Seraph and, remaining on the cross, he merited to fly away to the highest order of spirits. He was always upon his cross, never shirking labor or pain, fulfilling to the utmost the Lord's will in and about himself.

The brothers who lived with him know that daily, constantly, talk of Jesus was always on his lips, sweet and pleasant conversations about Him, kind words full of love. Out of the fullness of the heart his mouth spoke. So the spring of radiant love that filled his heart within gushed forth. He was always with Jesus: Jesus in his heart, Jesus in his mouth, Jesus in his ears, Jesus in his eyes, Jesus in his hands, he bore Jesus always in his whole body. Often he sat down to dinner but on hearing or saying or even thinking "Jesus" he forgot bodily food, as we read about another saint: "Seeing, he did not see; hearing, he did not hear." Often as he walked along a road, thinking and singing of Jesus, he would forget his destination and start inviting all the elements to praise Jesus. With amazing love he bore in his heart and always held onto Christ Jesus and Him crucified. For this reason, he, above others, was stamped with Christ's brilliant seal as, in rapture of spirit, he contemplated in unspeakable and incomprehensible glory the One sitting "at the right hand of the Father," the Most

High Son of the Most High, Who, with the Father, "in the unity of the Holy Spirit, lives and reigns," conquers and commands, God eternally glorified throughout all the ages. Amen.

Thomas of Celano, The Life of Saint Francis, Second Book, IX, 114–5
The Saint, 282–4

8 OCTOBER

His brothers and sons had assembled with the whole multitude of people from the neighboring cities, rejoicing to take part in such solemn rites. They spent that entire night of the holy father's death in the praises of God. The sweet sound of jubilation and the brightness of the lights made it seem that angels were keeping vigil.

When day was breaking, the multitude of the city of Assisi gathered with all the clergy. They lifted his sacred body from the place where he had died and carried it with great honor to the city, singing hymns and praises with trumpets blaring. They all took branches of olive and other trees and solemnly followed the funeral procession, bringing even more candles as they sang songs of praise in loud voices.

With the sons carrying their father and the flock following the shepherd who was hastening to the Shepherd of them all, he arrived at the place where he first planted the religion and the Order of the consecrated virgins and Poor Ladies. They laid him out in the church of San Damiano, home to those daughters he gained for the Lord. The small window was opened, the one used by these servants of Christ at the appointed time to receive the sacrament of the Lord's body. The coffin was also opened: in it lay hidden the treasure of supercelestial powers; in it he who had carried many was now carried by a few.

The Lady Clare! Clearly a woman of true brilliance and holiness, the first mother of all the others, the first plant of that holy Order: she comes with her daughters to see the father who would never again speak to them or return to them, as he was quickly going away. They looked upon him, groaning and weeping with great anguish of heart.

"Father, O father, what shall we do?" they began to cry out. "Why are you abandoning us poor women? We are forsaken! To whom are you entrusting us? Why didn't you send us ahead of you in joy to the place you are going, instead of leaving us behind in sorrow? What would you have us do, enclosed in this cell, without your usual visits? All consolation ebbs away along with you, just as no solace remains for us who are buried to the world! Who will comfort us in so great a poverty, poverty of merit as much as of goods?

"O father of the poor! O lover of poverty! Who will help us in temptation? You, who experienced so many temptations! You, who were such a careful judge of temptations! Who will comfort us in the midst of distress? You, who were so often our help in times of distress! What bitter separation, what painful absence!

"O death, dreadful death! You are killing thousands of his sons and daughters by taking away their father! Our poor efforts bore fruit through him, and you rush to tear him far from us, beyond recall!"

The virgins' modesty overcame their tears. To grieve too much over him was unbecoming, for at his passing a host of angels rushed to greet him, and the citizens of heaven and members of God's household rejoiced. Thus, torn between sorrow and joy, they kissed his most splendid hands that glittered with rare jewels and shining pearls. Once he was taken away, the door that never again will suffer such pain, was closed on them. O how great was the grief of all at the misery of these women! How full was their mourning and the devotion of their outcry! Above all how great was the wailing of his grieving sons! The sadness of each was shared by all, since no one could keep from crying when even the angels of peace wept bitterly.

Thomas of Celano, The Life of Saint Francis, Second Book, X, 116–7
The Saint, 284–6

9 OCTOBER

Finally all reached the city and with great joy and gladness laid the most holy body in a sacred place about to become even more sacred. In the past he had brightened that place wonderfully with instruction by his holy preaching. There he now enlightens the world with a multitude of new miracles glorifying the Most High God Almighty. Thanks be to God. Amen.

Now look at what I have done, most holy and blessed father, I have seen you through to the end with fitting and worthy praises, inadequate though they be, and I have written down your deeds telling the story as well as I could. Please allow me, pitiful as I am, to follow you worthily in the present, that I may mercifully merit joining you in the future.

O loving one, bear in mind your poor sons for whom, without you, their one and only consolation, there is little comfort. Even though you, their primary and prized portion, have joined the choirs of angels, and are seated with the apostles on a throne of glory, they still lie in a muddy swamp, enclosed in a dark cell, tearfully crying out to you: "O father, place before Jesus Christ, son of the Most High Father, His sacred stigmata; and show Him the signs of the cross on your hands, feet, and side, that He may mercifully bare His own wounds to the Father, and because of this the Father will ever show us in our anguish His tenderness. Amen. So be it, so be it."

Thomas of Celano, The Life of Saint Francis, Second Book, X, 118
The Saint, 286–7

10 OCTOBER

He once said to his companion: "I wouldn't consider myself a Lesser Brother unless I had the attitude I will describe to you. Suppose, as a prelate of the brothers, I go to the chapter, preach and admonish the brothers, and, at the end, they speak against me: 'You are not suitable for us, because you are uneducated, inarticulate, unlettered, and simple!' So, in the end, I am thrown out in disgrace, looked down upon by everyone. I tell you, unless

I hear these words with the same expression on my face, with the same joy, and with the same resolution for holiness, I am in no sense a Lesser Brother!" And he added: "In a prelacy there is a fall, in praise a precipice, in the humility of a subject profit for the soul. Why, then, do we pay more attention to dangers than to profits, while we have time for profit?"

For this reason, Francis, the pattern of humility, wanted his brothers to be called Lesser and the prelates of his Order to be called ministers, that he might use the words of the Gospel he had promised to observe, and that his followers might learn from this very name that they had come to the school of the humble Christ to learn humility. The teacher of humility, Jesus Christ, to instruct his disciples in true humility, said: "Whoever wishes to become great among you, let him be your servant; and whoever wishes to be first among you will be your slave." [Mt 20:26–27]

Bonaventure, The Major Legend of Saint Francis, VI, 5
The Founder, 572

11 OCTOBER

Where there is charity and wisdom,
there is neither fear nor ignorance.

Where there is patience and humility,
there is neither anger nor disturbance.

Where there is poverty with joy,
there is neither greed nor avarice.

Where there is rest and meditation,
there is neither anxiety nor restlessness.

Where there is fear of the Lord to guard an entrance,
there the enemy cannot have a place to enter.

Where there is a heart full of mercy and discernment,
there is neither excess nor hardness of heart.

The Admonitions, XXVII
The Saint, 136–7

12 OCTOBER

At that time, as Blessed Francis was with his brothers whom he had then, he was of such purity that, from the hour the Lord revealed to him that he and his brothers should live according to the form of the holy Gospel, he desired and strove to observe it to the letter during his whole lifetime.

Therefore he told the brother who did the cooking for the brothers, that when he wanted the brothers to eat beans, he should not put them in warm water in the evening for the next day, as people usually do. This was so the brothers would observe the words of the holy Gospel: "Do not be concerned about tomorrow [Mt 6:34]." So that brother used to put them in water to soften after the brothers said matins.

Because of this, for a long time many brothers observed this in a great many places where they stayed on their own, especially in cities. They did not want to collect or receive more alms than were enough for them for one day.

The Assisi Compilation, 52
The Founder, 151–2

13 OCTOBER

For, at another time when the servant of God was suffering from a severe illness at the hermitage of Sant'Urbano, he was feeling the weakness of his nature, and requested a drink of wine. He was told that there was no wine that they could give him; so he ordered some water and when it was brought, he blessed it with the sign of the cross. At once what had been brought as pure water became excellent wine; and what the poverty of a deserted place could not provide, the purity of the holy man obtained.

At its taste, he immediately recovered with such ease, that the newness of taste and the renewal of health, supernaturally renewing the tasted and the taster, confirmed by a twofold witness, that he had perfectly stripped away the old man and put on the new.

Bonaventure, The Major Legend of Saint Francis, V, 10
The Founder, 567

14 OCTOBER

While living at this same place [Rieti], the father of the poor was dressed in an old tunic. One day he said to one of his companions, whom he had made his guardian: "Brother, if possible, I wish you would find me material for a tunic." On hearing this, the brother started turning over in his mind how he could get the necessary cloth so humbly requested. The next day at the break of dawn he went to the door, on his way to town for the cloth. There he found a man sitting on the doorstep and wishing to speak to him. This man said to the brother: "For the love of God, please accept this cloth, enough for six tunics; keep one for yourself and distribute the rest as you please for the good of my soul."

The brother was exhilarated, and returned to Brother Francis, announcing to him the gift sent from heaven. And our father said: "Accept the tunics, for this man was sent to care for my need in this way." And he added: "Thanks be to him who seems to be the only one concerned for us!"

Thomas of Celano, The Remembrance of the Desire of a Soul,
Second Book, XIV, 43
The Founder, 275

15 OCTOBER

Consider, O human being, in what great excellence the Lord God has placed you, for He created and formed you to the image of His beloved Son according to the body and to His likeness according to the Spirit.

And all creatures under heaven serve, know, and obey their Creator, each according to its own nature, better than you. And even the demons did not crucify Him, but you, together with them, have crucified Him and are still crucifying Him by delighting in vices and sins.

In what, then, can you boast? Even if you were so skilful and wise that you possessed all knowledge, knew how to interpret every kind of language, and to scrutinize heavenly matters with skill: you could not boast in these things. For, even though someone may have received from the Lord a special knowledge of the highest wisdom, one demon knew about heavenly matters and now knows more about those of earth than all human beings.

In the same way, even if you were more handsome and richer than everyone else, and even if you worked miracles so that you put demons to flight: all these things are contrary to you; nothing belongs to you; you can boast in none of these things.

But we can boast in our weaknesses and in carrying each day the holy cross of our Lord Jesus Christ.

The Admonitions, V
The Saint, 131

16 OCTOBER

Bartolomeo, a citizen of Gaeta, was very hard at work on the construction of the church of blessed Francis. A beam, in an unsteady position, crashed down, and he was severely crushed, pinned down by the neck. Sensing that his death was imminent, and being a faithful and pious man, he asked one of the brothers for Viaticum. The brother was not able to bring it that quickly, and thinking he would die at any moment, quoted to him the words of blessed Augustine, "Believe, and you have eaten." That night blessed Francis appeared to him with eleven brothers; he carried a little lamb between his breasts. He approached the bed, called him by name, and said, "Do not fear, Bartolomeo, because the enemy will not prevail against you. He wanted to keep you from my service. Here is the lamb you asked for: you have received it because of your good desire. What is more, by His power you will also obtain health in body and spirit." Then drawing his hand across the wounds, he told him to return to the work he had begun. The man got up very early the next morning, and the workers who had left him half-dead were shocked and amazed when he appeared, unharmed and happy, inspiring their spirits to love and respect for blessed Francis as much by his example as by the miracle of the Saint.

Bonaventure, The Major Legend of Saint Francis: the Miracles, III, 8
The Founder, 662

17 OCTOBER

When he returned from his private prayers, in which he was changed almost into a different man, he tried his best to resemble the others; lest, if he appeared glowing, the breeze of favor might cancel what he had gained.

Often he would say to those close to him: "When a servant of God is praying, and is visited by the Lord in some new consolation, he should lift his eyes up to heaven before he comes away from prayer, fold his hands and say to the Lord: "Lord, you have sent this sweetness and consolation from heaven to me, an unworthy sinner, and I send it back to you so you may save it for me, because I am a thief of your treasure." And also, "Lord, take away your gift from me in this world, and keep it for me in the next." This is the way it should be," he said. "When one comes away from prayer he should appear to others a poor sinner, who had not obtained any new grace." He also used to say: "It happens that one loses something priceless for the sake of a small reward, and may easily provoke the giver not to give again."

Finally, his custom was to be so secret and quiet in rising for prayer that none of his companions would notice his rising or praying. But in the evening he made a good loud noise in going to bed, so that everyone would hear him as he went to rest.

Thomas of Celano, The Remembrance of the Desire of a Soul,
Second Book, LXV, 99
The Founder, 312–3

18 OCTOBER

It would not be right to pass over in silence the memory of a spiritual building, much nobler than that earthly one, that the blessed father established in that place with the Holy Spirit leading for the increase of the heavenly city, after he had repaired the material church. We should not believe that for the sake of repairing a crumbling and perishable building, that Christ spoke to him from the wood of the Cross and in such an amazing way that it strikes fear and inflicts pain upon anyone who hears of it. But, as earlier foretold by the Holy Spirit, an Order of holy virgins was to be established there to be brought one day as a polished collection of living stones for the restoration of the heavenly house. The virgins of Christ had begun to gather in that place, assembled from diverse regions of the world, professing the greatest perfection in the observance of the highest poverty and the beauty of every virtue. Though the father gradually withdrew his bodily presence from them, he still offered in the Holy Spirit, his affection to care for them. The saint recognized that they were marked with many signs of the highest perfection, and that they were ready to bear any loss and undergo any labor for Christ and did not ever want to turn aside from the holy commandments. Therefore, he firmly promised them, and others who professed poverty in a similar way of life, that he and his brothers would perpetually offer them help and advice. And he carried this out carefully as long as he lived, and when he was close to death he commanded it to be carried out without fail always, saying that one and the same Spirit had led the brothers and those little Poor Ladies out of this world.

The brothers were sometimes surprised that he did not often visit such holy handmaids of Christ in his bodily presence, but he would say: "Don't imagine, dear brothers, that I don't love them fully. For if it were a crime to cherish them in Christ, wouldn't it be even worse to have joined them to Christ? Not calling them would not have been harmful, but not to care for them after calling them would be the height of cruelty. But I am giving you an example, that as I do, so should you also do. I don't want one volunteering to visit them, but rather command that those who are unwilling and very reluctant should be assigned to their service, as long as they are spiritual men tested by a longstanding, worthy way of life."

> Thomas of Celano, The Remembrance of the Desire of a Soul,
> Second Book, CLV, 204–5
> *The Founder,* 377–9

19 OCTOBER

While the holy father was staying at San Damiano, he was pestered by his vicar with repeated requests that he should present the word of God to his daughters, and he finally gave in to his insistence. The Ladies gathered as usual to hear the word of God, but no less to see their father, and he raised his eyes to heaven, where he always had his heart, and began to pray to Christ. Then he had ashes brought and made a circle with them round himself on the floor, and then put the rest on his own head.

As they waited, the blessed father remained in silence within the circle of ashes, and real amazement grew in their hearts. Suddenly he got up, and to their great surprise, recited the "Have mercy on me, God," instead of a sermon. As he finished it, he left quickly. The handmaids of God were so filled with contrition by the power of this mime that they were flowing with tears, and could hardly restrain their hands from punishing themselves. By his action he taught them to consider themselves ashes, and that nothing else was close to his heart except what was in keeping with that view.

This was his way of behaving with holy women; this was his way of visiting them rare and constrained, but very useful! This was his will for all the brothers, whom he wanted to serve for the sake of Christ, whom they serve: that they might always, like winged creatures, beware of the nets before them.

> Thomas of Celano, The Remembrance of the Desire of a Soul,
> Second Book, CLVII, 207
> *The Founder,* 379–80

20 OCTOBER

Brother James of Massa, to whom God opened the door of His secrets and gave perfect knowledge and understanding of Holy Scripture and future events, was a man of such holiness that Brother Giles of Assisi and Brother Marco of Montino and Brother Juniper and Brother Lucido said that they knew no one in the world greater before God than this Brother James.

I had a great desire to see him, because while I was asking Brother John, companion of that same Brother Giles, to explain to me certain things of the spirit, he said to me: "If you want to be well instructed in the spiritual life, try to talk to Brother James of Massa, because Brother Giles desired to be enlightened by him, and nothing can be added or subtracted from his words, since his spirit has passed through heavenly secrets, and his words are the words of the Holy Spirit, and there is no man on earth whom I so desire to see." This Brother James, at the beginning of the ministry of Brother John of Parma, was once rapt into God while praying and remained rapt in this ecstasy for three days, suspended from any bodily feeling, and he remained there so unaware that the brothers began to wonder if he was dead. And in this rapture God revealed to him what must happen concerning our religion, and when I heard this, my desire to hear him and speak with him increased.

And when it pleased God that I have the chance to talk with him, I asked him: "If what I heard said about you is true, I ask you not to hide it from me. I heard that when you remained as if dead for three days, God revealed to you, among other things, what is to happen in this Religion of ours, and this was said by Brother Matteo, Minister of the March, to whom you revealed it under obedience." Then Brother James, with great humility, admitted to him that what Brother Matteo said was true.

The Little Flowers of Saint Francis, 48
The Prophet, 646–7

21 OCTOBER

What he said, that is Brother Matteo, Minister of the March, was this: "I know this from Brother James, to whom God revealed everything that is to happen in our Religion, because Brother James of Massa confided in me and told me the following. After God revealed many things to him about the status of the Church Militant, he saw in a vision a beautiful and very large tree: its root was of gold; its fruit was men, and they were all Lesser Brothers. Its main branches were divided according to the number of the provinces of the Order, and each branch had as many brothers as there were in the province designated for that branch. And so he knew the number of all the brothers of the Order and of each province, and also their names, their ages, their conditions, their important duties, their dignities, and the graces of all, their merits and their faults. And he saw Brother John of Parma at the tip of the middle branch of this tree, and on the tips of the branches around this middle branch were the ministers of all the provinces. And after this he saw Christ sitting on a very large, dazzling white throne, and Christ called Saint Francis and gave him a chalice full of the spirit of life and ordered him: "Go and visit your brothers and give them to drink of this chalice of the spirit of life, because the spirit of Satan will rise up against them and strike them, and many of them will fall and will not rise up again." And Christ gave Saint Francis two angels to accompany him.

And so Saint Francis came to offer the chalice of life to his brothers and began to offer it to Brother John, who took it and quickly and devoutly drank it all, and immediately became all shining like the sun. And after him Saint Francis offered it to all the others, and there were few of them who would take it and drink it all with proper reverence and devotion. Those who took it devoutly and drank it all quickly became as bright as the sun; and those who poured it out and did not take it with devotion became black and dark and deformed and horrible to see. Those who drank some and poured out some, became part shining and part shadowy, more or less according to the amount they drank or poured out. But Brother John was resplendent beyond all the others, he who had most fully drunk the chalice of life, and so he contemplated most deeply that abyss of the infinite divine light, and in this he understood the adversity and the storm which was to arise against that tree, breaking and displacing its branches. Because of this that same Brother John left the top of the branch on which he was standing and, descending below all the branches he hid himself at the foot of the tree's trunk and stayed there, very pensive. And Brother Bonaventure, who had taken some from the chalice and had poured out some, went up onto that branch to the place from which Brother John had come down. And while he was standing in that place, his fingernails became fingernails of iron, sharp and cutting like razors; and at this he moved from the place to which he had climbed, and with force and fury tried to throw himself against that same Brother John to harm him. But Brother John, seeing this, cried out loudly and entrusted himself to Christ, who was sitting on the throne: and Christ, at his cry, called Saint Francis and gave him a sharp flint, and said to him: "Go with this flint and cut Brother Bonaventure's fingernails, with which he wants to scratch Brother John, so that he cannot harm him." Then Saint Francis went and did what Christ had commanded. When this was done, a windstorm arose and struck the tree so hard that the brothers fell from it to the ground, and the first to fall from it were those who poured out the whole chalice of the spirit of life, and they were carried off by the demons to dark and painful places. But that same Brother John, together with those who had drunk the whole chalice were transported by the angels to a place of life and eternal light and blessed splendor. And the aforesaid Brother James, who saw this vision, knew and discerned specifically and distinctly all that he was seeing, regarding the names, the conditions and the status of each with clarity. And that storm lasted long enough that the tree fell and was carried away by the wind. And then, as soon as the storm ended, from this tree's root, which was gold, another tree sprang up, all of gold, which produced golden leaves and fruit. About this tree, its growth, its depth, beauty and fragrance and virtues, at the present time it is better to keep silent than to speak.

The Little Flowers of Saint Francis, 48
The Prophet, 647–8

22 OCTOBER

They learned time and again by clear signs and their own experience that the hidden recesses of their hearts were not hidden from their most holy father.

How often he knew the deeds of absent brothers, not by human teaching but the revelation of the Holy Spirit! He opened up the hidden recesses of their hearts, and examined their consciences! How many he warned in their dreams, both ordering what they should do and forbidding what they should not! How many future evil deeds he foretold of those whose present deeds seemed so good in appearance! So too did he announce the future grace of salvation to many, since he foresaw the ending of their misdeeds. In fact, if someone in a spirit of purity and simplicity merited enlightenment, he would gain a singular consolation from a vision of him, something not experienced by others.

I shall report just one of the many stories that I have learned from the reports of reliable witnesses. At one time, brother John of Florence was appointed by Saint Francis as minister of the brothers in Provence. He celebrated a chapter of the brothers in that province, and the Lord God with his usual favor opened the door of eloquence for him and made all the brothers willing and attentive listeners. Among them was a certain brother priest named Monaldo, distinguished by a brilliant reputation and by an even more brilliant life. His virtue was grounded in humility, aided by frequent prayer, and preserved by the shield of patience.

Also at that chapter was brother Anthony whose mind the Lord had opened to understand the Scriptures and who poured forth among all the people sweet words about Jesus, sweeter than milk and honey. He was preaching to the brothers fervently and devoutly on the verse, "Jesus of Nazareth, king of the Jews." Brother Monaldo glanced at the door of the house in which the brothers were all gathered. He saw there with his bodily eyes blessed Francis lifted up in the air with his hands extended as if on a cross, blessing the brothers. All of them seemed filled with the consolation of the Holy Spirit and were so taken with the joy of salvation that they believed readily what they heard regarding the vision and the presence of the glorious father.

Thomas of Celano, The Life of Saint Francis, First Book, XVIII, 48
The Saint, 224–5

23 OCTOBER

[H]e knew the hidden recesses of troubled hearts, something that many often experienced.

There was a certain brother named Riccerio, noble by birth but more noble in character, a lover of God and despiser of himself. With a devout spirit he was led wholeheartedly to attain and possess the favor of the blessed father Francis. He was quite fearful that the holy man Francis would detest him for some secret reason and thus he would become a stranger to the gift of his love. That brother, since he was fearful, thought that any person the holy man Francis loved intimately was also worthy to merit divine favor. On the other hand, he judged that someone to whom he did not show himself kindly and pleasant would incur the wrath of the supreme Judge. This brother turned these matters over in his heart; he silently spoke of these matters to himself, but revealed to no one else his secret thoughts.

One day the blessed father was praying in his cell and that brother came to the place disturbed by his usual thoughts. The holy one of God knew both that the brother had come and understood what was twisting in his heart. So the blessed father immediately called him to himself. "Let no temptation disturb you, son," he said to him, "and do not be troubled by any thought. You are very dear to me and you should know that, among those dearest to me, you are worthy of my love and intimacy. Come to me confidently whenever you want, knowing you are welcome, and, in this intimacy, speak freely." That brother was amazed and from then on became even more reverent. The more that he grew in the holy father's grace, the more he began to enjoy God's mercy with confidence.

How bitterly they feel your absence, holy father, who completely despair of ever finding anyone like you on earth! We ask you, through your intercession, help those covered by the harmful stain of sin. Though you were already filled with the spirit of all the just, foreseeing the future and knowing the present, to avoid all boasting you always displayed the image of holy simplicity.

Thomas of Celano, *The Life of Saint Francis*, First Book, XVIII, 48
The Saint, 226–7

24 OCTOBER

Once Saint Francis was staying in the place of the Portiuncula with Brother Masseo of Marignano, a man of great holiness, discernment and grace in speaking of God, for which Saint Francis loved him very much. One day Saint Francis was returning from the woods and from prayer, and when he was at the edge of the woods, that same Brother Masseo, wanting to test how humble he was, went up to him and, as if joking, said, "Why after you, why after you, why after you?" Saint Francis responded, "What do you mean?" Brother Masseo said, "I'm saying why does the whole world come after you, and everyone seems to desire to see you and hear you? You aren't a handsome man in body, you aren't someone of great learning, you're not noble; so why does the whole world come after you?" Hearing this, Saint Francis was overjoyed in spirit and, turning his face to heaven, stood for a long time with his mind lifted up into God. Then returning to himself, he knelt down and gave praise and thanks to God. Then with great fervor of spirit he turned to Brother Masseo and said, "Do you want to know why after me? You want to know why after me? You want to know why the whole world comes after me? I have this from those eyes of the Most High God, which gaze in every place on the good and the guilty. Since those most holy eyes have not seen among sinners anyone more vile, nor more incompetent, nor a greater sinner than me; to perform that marvelous work, which he intends to do, He has not found a more vile creature on the earth, and therefore He has chosen me to confound the nobility and the greatness and the strength and beauty and wisdom of the world, so that it may be known that every virtue and every good is from Him, and not from the creature, and no person may boast in His sight. But whoever boasts must boast in the Lord, to whom is every honor and glory forever." Brother Masseo was shocked at such a humble response, said with such fervor, and knew certainly that Saint Francis was truly grounded in humility.

The Little Flowers of Saint Francis, 10
The Prophet, 583

25 OCTOBER

How Francis proved himself the bridegroom's friend, by striving to conform himself to Jesus through the favor of his charity and desire for the salvation of those to whom he was brother, is evinced by the fact that from the beginning of his conversion to the end he blazed continually like a fire with an ardent love for Jesus. Fanned by the breath of the Holy Spirit, he kept the furnace of his heart ever ignited, so that once he heard the love of God mentioned he was as excited, moved, and animated as the beloved spouse, calling out continuously, Sustain me with flowers, refresh me with apples; for I am sick with love [Sg 2:5]. All things created were a means by which he fired this love of his. Through looking on things of beauty he would contemplate the Beautiful; in frail creatures he could recognize the infirmities which Jesus in His goodness bore for our salvation. He made a ladder of every thing, by which he could reach the One he loved. Altogether special, however, was the love for Christ crucified which had such a recurrent transforming effect that he bore, not only in mental attitude but in bodily appearance, the likeness of the crucified Jesus. Our achievement of eternal happiness in the higher world was a passion that devoured him inwardly; he did not regard himself as Christ's friend unless he were all the time cherishing the souls He redeemed. Hence his exertions in prayer, his preaching labors, the lengths to which he went to give good example.

Ubertino di Casale, The Tree of the Crucified Life of Jesus,
V, III, 18,29
The Prophet, 173–4

26 OCTOBER

Francis would not forget to retreat to a place of solitude at frequent intervals; engaged though he might be with crowds, by day or by night he would try to leave them, to give himself to contemplation on his own. He was continually recommending to his brothers this form of leading the life of preaching. Hence he wanted their places to be close to where people lived, so that they could kindly comply with their needs. Not so close, though, as to have no leisure, through over-involvement, no rest for attending to contemplation and prayer. What he wanted was to be near people while maintaining a certain distance; the places ought to be located alongside people and yet beyond where they actually lived, in quiet areas suitable for solitude.

In this he was imitating his good Master Jesus, who showed His preachers of the evangelical life how to be at the disposal of others while maintaining the rightful demands of holy solitude.

Ubertino di Casale, The Tree of the Crucified Life of Jesus,
V, III, 44,56
The Prophet, 177

27 OCTOBER

In order to make a profit in every possible way, and melt down all the present time into merit, this very shrewd businessman chose to do everything under the harness of obedience and to submit himself to the rule of another. He not only resigned the office of general, but also, for the greater good of obedience, he asked for a special guardian to honor as his personal prelate. And so he said to Brother Peter of Catanio, to whom he had earlier promised obedience: "I beg you for God's sake to entrust me to one of my companions, to take your place in my regard and I will obey him as devoutly as you. I know the fruit of obedience, and that no time passes without profit for one who bends his neck to the yoke of another." His request was granted, and until death he remained a subject wherever he was, always submitting to his own guardian with reverence.

One time he said to his companions: "Among the many things which God's mercy has granted me, he has given me this grace, that I would readily obey a novice of one hour, if he were given to me as my guardian, as carefully as I would obey the oldest and most discerning. For a subject should not consider his prelate a human being, but rather the One for love of whom he is subject. And the more contemptibly he presides, the more pleasing is the humility of the one who obeys."

Thomas of Celano, The Remembrance of the Desire of a Soul,
Second Book, CXI, 152
The Founder, 344–5

28 OCTOBER

Another time, when he was sitting with his companions, blessed Francis let out a sigh: "There is hardly a single religious in the whole world who obeys his prelate perfectly!" His companions, disturbed, said to him: "Tell us, father, what is the perfect and highest obedience?" And he replied, describing someone truly obedient using the image of a dead body: "Take a lifeless corpse and place it wherever you want. You will see that it does not resist being moved, does not complain about the location, or protest if left. Sit it on a throne, and it will look down, not up; dress it in purple and it will look twice as pale. This," said he, "is someone who really obeys: he doesn't argue about why he's being moved; he doesn't care where he's placed; he doesn't pester you to transfer him. When he's raised to an office, he keeps his usual humility, and the more he's honored, the more he considers himself unworthy."

On another occasion, speaking about this same matter, he said that things granted because of a request were really "permissions," but things that are ordered and not requested he called "holy obediences." He said that both were good, but the latter was safer. But he believed that the best of all, in which flesh and blood had no part, was the one by which one goes "among the non-believers, by divine inspiration" either for the good of one's neighbor or from a desire for martyrdom. He considered this request very acceptable to God.

Thomas of Celano, The Remembrance of the Desire of a Soul,
Second Book, CXII, 152
The Founder, 345

29 OCTOBER

His opinion was that only rarely should something be commanded under obedience, for the weapon of last resort should not be the first one used. As he said, "The hand should not reach quickly for the sword." He who does not hurry to obey what is commanded under obedience neither fears God nor respects man. Nothing could be truer. For, what is command in a rash leader, but a sword in the hands of a mad man? And what could be more hopeless than a religious who despises obedience?

Thomas of Celano, The Remembrance of the Desire of a Soul, Second Book, CXIII, 152
The Founder, 345

30 OCTOBER

Many people as well, not only driven by devotion but also inflamed by a desire for the perfection of Christ, once they had condemned the emptiness of everything worldly, followed the footsteps of Francis. Their numbers increased daily and quickly reached even to the ends of the earth.

Holy poverty, which was all they had to meet their expenses, made them prompt for every obedience, robust for work, and free for travel. And since they had nothing earthly they loved nothing and feared losing nothing. They were safe wherever they went, held back by no fear, distracted by no cares; they lived with untroubled minds, and, without any anxiety, looked forward to the morrow and to finding a lodging for the night.

In different parts of the world many insults were hurled against them as persons unknown and looked down upon, but true love of the Gospel of Christ had made them so patient, that they sought to be where they would suffer physical persecution rather than where their holiness was recognized and where they could glory in worldly favor.

Their very poverty seemed to them overflowing abundance since, according to the advice of the Wise Man, a little pleased them instead of much.

When some of the brothers went to the lands of non-believers, a certain Saracen, moved by piety, once offered them money for the food they needed. When they refused to accept it, the man was amazed, seeing that they were without means. Realizing they did not want to possess money because they had become poor out of love of God, he felt so attracted to them that he offered to minister to all their needs as long as he had something to give.

O ineffable value of poverty, whose marvelous power moved the fierce heart of a barbarian to such sweet pity! What a horrible and unspeakable crime that a Christian should trample upon this noble pearl which a Saracen held in such veneration!

Bonaventure, The Major Legend of Saint Francis, IV, 7
The Founder, 554

31 OCTOBER

Holy Virgin Mary, among the women born into the world, there is no one like you. Daughter and servant of the most high and supreme King and of the Father in heaven, Mother of our most holy Lord Jesus Christ, Spouse of the Holy Spirit, pray for us with Saint Michael the Archangel, all the powers of heaven and all the saints, at the side of your most holy beloved Son, our Lord and Teacher. Glory to the Father, and to the Son, and to the Holy Spirit. As it was in the beginning, is now, and will be forever. Amen.

The Office of the Passion, Antiphon
The Saint, 141

November

1 NOVEMBER

This beloved one of God showed himself greatly devoted to divine worship and left nothing that is God's dishonored through carelessness.

When he was at Monte Casale in the province of Massa he commanded the brothers to move with all reverence the holy relics from an abandoned church to the place of the brothers. He felt very bad that they had been robbed of the devotion due them for a long time. When, for an urgent reason, he had to go somewhere else, his sons, forgetting the command of their Father, disregarded the merit of obedience. But one day the brothers wanted to celebrate, and when as usual they removed the cloth cover from the altar they discovered some beautiful and very fragrant bones. They were stunned at this, since they had never seen them there before. Shortly afterwards the holy one of God returned, and he took care to inquire if his orders about the relics had been carried out. The brothers humbly confessed their fault of neglecting obedience, and won pardon together with a penance. And the saint said: "Blessed be the Lord my God, who himself carried out what you were supposed to do!"

Consider carefully Francis's devotion, pay attention to God's good pleasure towards our dust; magnify the praise of holy obedience. For when humans did not heed his voice, God obeyed his prayers.

Thomas of Celano, The Remembrance of the Desire of a Soul,
Second Book, CLIII, 202
The Founder, 376–7

2 NOVEMBER

At a human's end, says the wise man, comes the disclosing of his works [Sir:27–28], and we see this gloriously fulfilled in this saint. Running eagerly on the road of God's commandments, he scaled the steps of all the virtues until he reached the very summit. Like a malleable metal, he was brought to perfection under the hammering blows of many tribulations, and saw the end of all perfection. Then his wonderful work shone all the brighter, and it flared out in the judgment of truth that everything he lived was divine. He trampled on the allure of mortal life and escaped free into the heights. For he considered it dishonor to live for the world, loved his own to the very end, and welcomed Death singing. When he approached his final days — when light eternal was replacing the limited light that had been removed — he showed by his example of virtue that he had nothing in common with the world.

As he was wasted by that grave illness which ended all his sufferings, he had himself placed naked on the naked ground, so that in that final hour, when the Enemy could still rage, he might wrestle naked with the naked. The fearless man awaited triumph and, with hands joined, held the crown of justice. Placed on the ground and stripped of his sackcloth garment, he lifted up his face to heaven as usual, and, totally intent upon that glory, he covered the wound on his right side with his left hand, so no one would see it. Then he said to his brothers: "I have done what is mine; may Christ teach you what is yours!"

Seeing this, his sons wept streams of tears, drawing sighs from deep within, overwhelmed by sorrow and compassion.

Meanwhile, as their sobs somewhat subsided, his guardian, who by divine inspiration better understood the saint's wish, quickly got up, took the tunic, underwear and sackcloth hood, and said to the father: "I command you under holy obedience to acknowledge that I am lending you this tunic, underwear and hood. And so that you know that they in no way belong to you, I take away all your authority to give them to anyone." The saint rejoiced, and his heart leaped for joy seeing that he had kept faith until the end with Lady Poverty. For he had done all of this out of zeal for poverty, not wanting to have at the end even a habit of his own, but one borrowed from another. He had been wearing a sackcloth cap on his head to cover the scars he had received in the treatment of his eyes; what was really needed for this was a smooth cap of the softest and most expensive wool.

After this the saint raised his hands to heaven and glorified his Christ; free now from all things, he was going to him free.

But in order to show himself in all things a true imitator of Christ, his God, he loved to the very end the brothers and sons he had loved from the beginning. He had them call to him all the brothers present there, and, comforting them about his death with words of consolation, he exhorted them to the love of God with fatherly affection. He spoke at length about patience, about preserving poverty, and about placing the Holy Gospel ahead of all other observances.

As all the brothers sat around him he stretched out his right hand over them and, beginning with his vicar, he placed it on each of their heads saying:

"Good bye, my sons, live in the fear of the Lord and remain in it always! A great trial and tribulation is at hand! Happy are they who will persevere in the things they have begun! I am hurrying to God, to whose grace I commend all of you!" He then blessed in those who were there, all the other brothers who were living anywhere in the world, and those who were to come after them unto the end of all ages.

Thomas of Celano, The Remembrance of the Desire of a Soul,
Second Book, CLXII, 214–16
The Founder, 385–7

3 NOVEMBER

At the very same hour that evening [of his death] the glorious father appeared to another brother of praiseworthy life, who was at that moment absorbed in prayer. He appeared to him clothed in a purple dalmatic and followed by an innumerable crowd of people. Several separated themselves from the crowd and said to that brother: "Is this not Christ, brother?" And he replied: "It is he." Others asked him again, saying: "Isn't this Saint Francis?" And the brother likewise replied that it was he. For it really seemed to that brother, and to the whole crowd, as if Christ and Saint Francis were one person.

And this will not seem at all like a rash statement to those who rightly understand it, for whoever clings to God, becomes one spirit with Him, and that God will be all in all.

Finally the blessed father and the crowd arrived at a very beautiful place, watered with the clearest waters, flourishing with the beauty of flowers and full of every delightful sort of tree. There, too, was a palace of amazing size and singular beauty. The new inhabitant of heaven entered it eagerly. He found inside many brothers sitting at a splendidly set table loaded with various delicacies and with them he delightfully began to feast.

Thomas of Celano, The Remembrance of the Desire of a Soul,
Second Book, CLXV, 219
The Founder, 389

4 NOVEMBER

For who, oh outstanding saint, could be able to bring into himself the burning ardor of your spirit or to impress it on others? Who would be able to conceive those inexpressible feelings which flowed uninterruptedly between you and God? ...

You who once were hungry, now feed upon the finest wheat; you who once were thirsty, now drink of the torrent of delight. But we do not believe that you are so far inebriated with the abundance of God's house, as to have forgotten your own children when he who is your very drink keeps us in mind.

Draw us, then, to yourself, that we may run after the fragrance of your perfumes, for, as you can see, we have become lukewarm in apathy, listless in laziness, half-dead in negligence! This little flock is stumbling along in your footprints; the weakness of our eyes cannot bear the shining rays of your perfection. Give us such days as we had of old, oh mirror and exemplar of the perfect! Do not allow that those who are like you by profession be unlike you in life.

At this point we lay down the prayer of our lowliness before the merciful kindness of the eternal Majesty for Christ's servant, our minister, the successor of your holy humility, and emulator of your true poverty, who, for the love of your Christ, shows diligent care for your sheep with gentle affection.

We ask you, oh holy one, so to encourage and embrace him that, by constantly adhering to your footprints, he may attain forever the praise and glory which you have achieved.

We also pray with all our heart's affection, oh kind father, for that son of yours who now and earlier has devoutly written your praises. He, together with us, offers and dedicates to you this little work which he put together, not in a manner worthy of your merit but at least devoutly, and as best he could.

From every evil mercifully preserve and deliver him. Increase holy merit in him, and, by your prayers, join him forever to the company of the saints.

Remember all your children, father. You, most holy one, know perfectly how, lost in a maze of mystifying perils, they follow your footprints from how great a distance. Give them strength, that they may resist. Purify them, that they may shine radiantly. Fill them with joy, that they may delight.

Pray that the spirit of grace and of prayer may inundate them that they may have the true humility you had; that they may cherish the poverty you embraced; that they may be filled with the love with which you always loved Christ crucified. Who with the Father and the Holy Spirit lives and reigns forever and ever. Amen.

Thomas of Celano, The Remembrance of the Desire of a Soul,
Second Book, CLXVII, 221–4
The Founder, 392–3

5 NOVEMBER

Not only was this man attacked by Satan with temptations, he even had to struggle with him hand to hand. On one occasion Lord Leo, the Cardinal of Santa Croce, invited him to stay with him for a little while in Rome. He chose to stay in a detached tower, which offered nine vaulted chambers like the little rooms of hermits. The first night, when he had poured out his prayer to God and wanted to go to sleep, demons came and fiercely attacked the holy one of God. They beat him long and hard, and finally left him half dead. When they left and he had caught his breath, the saint called his companion who was sleeping under another vault of the roof. When he came over he said to him: "Brother, I want you to stay by me, because I'm afraid to be alone. A moment ago demons were beating me." The saint was trembling and quaking in every limb, as if he had a high fever.

They spent a sleepless night, and Saint Francis said to his companion: "Demons are the police of our Lord, whom he assigns to punish excesses. It is a sign of special grace that he does not leave anything in his servant unpunished while he still lives in the world. I do not recall my offence which, through God's mercy, I have not washed away by reparation. For He has always acted toward me with such fatherly kindness, that in my prayer and meditation He shows me what pleases or displeases Him. But it could be that He allowed His police to burst in on me because my staying at the courts of the great doesn't offer good example to others. When my brothers who stay in poor little places hear that I'm staying with cardinals, they might suspect that I am living in luxury. And so, brother, I think that one who is set up as an example is better off avoiding courts, strengthening those who suffer want by putting up with the same things." So in the morning they went to the cardinal, told him the whole story, and said goodbye to him.

Let those in palaces be aware of this, and let them know that they are aborted, torn from their mother's womb. I do not condemn obedience; but ambition, idleness, and luxuries I denounce. Finally, I put Francis ahead of all obediences. We have to endure what displeases God, seeing that it pleases men.

Thomas of Celano, The Remembrance of the Desire of a Soul,
Second Book, LXXXIV, 119–20
The Founder, 326–7

6 NOVEMBER

He did not want the brothers to live in any place unless it had a definite owner who held the property rights. He always wanted the laws of pilgrims for his sons: to be sheltered under someone else's roof, to travel in peace, and to thirst for their homeland. Once at the hermitage of Sarteano, one brother asked another brother where he was coming from. "I'm coming from Brother Francis's cell," he answered. The saint heard this and replied: "Since you have put the name 'Francis' on the cell making it my property, go and look for someone else to live in it. From now on I will not stay there. When the Lord stayed in a cell where he prayed and fasted for forty days, he did not have a cell made for him or any kind of house, but stayed beneath a rock on the mountainside. We can follow him in the way prescribed: holding nothing as our own property, even though we cannot live without the use of houses."

Thomas of Celano, The Remembrance of the Desire of a Soul,
Second Book, XXIX, 59
The Founder, 286–7

7 NOVEMBER

He burned with great zeal for the common profession and Rule, and endowed those who were zealots about it with a special blessing.

He called it their Book of Life, the hope of salvation, the marrow of the Gospel, the way of perfection, the key of Paradise, the pact of an eternal covenant. He wanted all to have it, all to know it, in all places to let it speak to the inner man as encouragement in weariness and as a reminder of a sworn oath.

He taught them to keep it always before their eyes as a reminder of the life they should lead and, what is more, that they should die with it.

This teaching was not forgotten by a certain lay brother whom we believe should be venerated among the martyrs, since he gained the palm of glorious victory. When he was taken by the Saracens to his martyrdom, he held the Rule in his uplifted hands, and kneeling humbly, said to his companion: "Dear brother, I proclaim myself guilty before the eyes of Majesty of everything that I ever did against this holy Rule!" The stroke of the sword followed this short confession, and with this martyrdom he ended his life, and afterward shone with signs and wonders. This brother had entered the Order so young that he could hardly bear the Rule's fasting, yet even as a boy he wore a harness next to his skin. Oh happy child, who began happily, that he might finish more happily!

Thomas of Celano, The Remembrance of the Desire of a Soul,
Second Book, CLVIII, 208
The Founder, 380–1

8 NOVEMBER

The most holy Father once saw by heavenly revelation a vision concerning the Rule. It was at the time when there was discussion among the brothers about confirming the Rule, and the saint was extremely anxious about this matter. This is what was shown to him in a dream: It seemed to him that he was gathering tiny bread crumbs from the ground, which he had to distribute to a crowd of hungry brothers who stood all around him. He was afraid to give out such little crumbs, fearing that such minute particles might slip between his fingers, when a voice cried out to him from above: "Francis, make one host out of all the crumbs, and give it to those who want to eat." He did this, and whoever did not receive it devoutly, or showed contempt for the gift received, soon appeared obviously infected with leprosy.

In the morning the saint recounted all this to his companions, regretting that he did not understand the mystery of the vision. But shortly afterward, as he kept vigil in prayer, this voice came down to him from heaven: "Francis, the crumbs you saw last night are the words of the Gospel; the host is the Rule, and the leprosy is wickedness."

The brothers of those times did not consider this promise which they had sworn either hard or harsh; they were always more than ready to give more than required in all things. For there is no room for apathy or laziness where the goad of love is always urging to greater things.

Thomas of Celano, The Remembrance of the Desire of a Soul,
Second Book, CLIX, 209
The Founder, 381–2

9 NOVEMBER

Pope Gregory the Ninth, of happy memory (about whom this holy man had prophetically foretold that he would be raised up to the apostolic dignity) carried a certain scruple of doubt in his heart about whether he had really received a wound in his side. But one night — as that blessed pontiff himself used to tell with tears in his eyes — blessed Francis appeared to him in a dream with a certain show of sternness in his face. Reproving him for his inner uncertainty, blessed Francis raised up his right arm, uncovered the wound on his side, and asked him for a vial in which to gather the spurting blood that flowed from it. In the dream the Supreme Pontiff brought him the vial requested, and it seemed to be filled to the brim with the blood which flowed abundantly out of the side. From that day he began to feel such devotion towards this sacred miracle, and to burn with such a zeal for it, that he would not allow anyone to obscure these signs with arrogant presumption without striking him with a severe rebuke.

Bonaventure, The Major Legend of Saint Francis: the Miracles, I, 2
The Founder, 651

10 NOVEMBER

With the passing of time when the number of brothers had increased, the watchful shepherd began to summon them to a general chapter at Saint Mary of the Portiuncula to allot to each a portion of obedience in the land of their poverty, according to the measuring cord of divine distribution. Although there was a complete lack of all necessities and sometimes the number of the brothers was more than five thousand, nevertheless with the assistance of divine mercy, they had adequate food, enjoyed physical health and overflowed with spiritual joy.

Because he could not be physically present at the provincial chapters, he was present in spirit through his solicitous care for governing, fervor of prayer, and effectiveness of blessing, although, he did sometimes appear visibly by God's wonderful power.

For the outstanding preacher, who is now a glorious confessor of Christ, Anthony, was preaching to the brothers at the chapter of Arles on the inscription on the cross: Jesus of Nazareth, King of the Jews [Jn 19:19]. As he glanced at the door of the chapter, a brother of proven virtue, Monaldo by name, moved by a divine reminder, saw with his bodily eyes blessed Francis lifted up in the air with his arms extended as if on a cross, blessing the brothers. All the brothers felt themselves filled with a consolation of spirit, so great and so unusual, that it was certain to them that the Spirit was bearing witness to the true presence of the holy father among them. This was later confirmed not only by the evidence of signs, but also by the external testimony of the words of the holy father himself.

It must be clearly believed that the almighty power of God, which allowed the holy bishop Ambrose to attend the burial of the glorious Saint Martin and to honor that holy prelate with his holy presence, also allowed his servant Francis to be present at the preaching of his true herald Anthony, in order to attest to the truth of his words, especially those concerning Christ's cross, of which he was both a carrier and a minister.

Bonaventure, The Major Legend of Saint Francis, IV, 10
The Founder, 557

11 NOVEMBER

One day he met a poor, half-naked knight, and moved by piety, for love of Christ, he generously gave him the finely tailored clothes he was wearing. Did he do any less than the great Saint Martin? They did the same thing, with the same purpose, though in different ways.

Francis first gave away his clothes, then everything else; Martin gave away everything else and then gave away his clothes. Both lived poor and humble in this world and both entered heaven rich. Martin was poor, but a knight, and clothed a poor man with part of his clothes. Francis was rich, but not a knight, and he clothed a poor knight with all of his clothes. Both of them, having carried out Christ's command deserved to be visited by Christ in a vision. Martin was praised for his perfection and Francis was graciously invited to what was still missing.

A little later, he saw in a vision a beautiful palace, and there he saw various suits of armour and a lovely bride. In that same dream Francis was called by name and was attracted by the promise of all these things. He therefore tried to go to Apulia in order to gain knighthood, and richly outfitted, he hastened to achieve the honors of knightly rank. The spirit of the flesh prompted him to give an interpretation of the flesh to the vision. In fact, in the treasury of God's wisdom something even more magnificent was hidden there.

As he slept one night, someone spoke to him a second time in a vision and asked him with concern where he was going. He explained his plan and said he was going to Apulia to become a knight. The other questioned him anxiously "Who can do more for you, the servant or the lord?" "The lord!" said Francis. "Then why do you seek the servant instead of the lord?" Francis then asked: "Lord, what do you want me to do?" And the Lord said to him: "Go back to the land of your birth because I will fulfill your dream in a spiritual way."

He turned back without delay becoming even now a model of obedience. Giving up his own will he changed from Saul to Paul. Paul was thrown to the ground and his stinging lashes bore fruit in soothing words; while Francis turned his fleshly weapons into spiritual ones, and, instead of knightly glory, received a divine rank. To the many who marveled at his unusual joy, he said that he was going to become a great prince.

Thomas of Celano, The Remembrance of the Desire of a Soul,
First Book, II, 5–6
The Founder, 244–6

12 NOVEMBER

Once, when a poor man asked him for something, he had nothing at hand, so he unstitched the hem of his tunic and gave it to the poor man. More than once in the same situation he took off his trousers.

With such depths of piety he knew no bounds for the poor; with such depths of feeling he followed the footprints of the poor Christ.

The mother of two of the brothers once came to the saint, confidently asking for alms. Sharing her pain the holy father said to Brother Peter of Catanio: "Can we give some alms to our mother?" He used to call the mother of any brother his mother and the mother of all the brothers. Brother Peter replied: "There is nothing left in the house which we could give her." Then he added: "We do have one New Testament, for reading the lessons at matins, since we don't have a breviary." Blessed Francis said to him: "Give our mother the New Testament so she can sell it to care for her needs, for through it we are reminded to help the poor. I believe that God will be pleased more by the giving than by the reading." So the book was given to the woman, and the first Testament in the Order was given away though this sacred piety.

Thomas of Celano, The Remembrance of the Desire of a Soul,
Second Book, LVII–LVIII, 90–91
The Founder, 305–6

⁂

13 NOVEMBER

At the time when Saint Francis was staying at the palace of the bishop of Rieti to be treated for his eye disease, a poor woman from Machilone who had the same disease as the saint came to see the doctor.

Then the saint, speaking familiarly to his guardian, nudged him a bit: "Brother Guardian, we have to give back what belongs to someone else." And he answered: "Father, if there's such a thing with us, let it be returned." And he said: "Yes, there is this mantle, which we received as a loan from that poor woman; we should give it back to her, because she has nothing in her purse for her expenses." The guardian replied: "Brother, this mantle is mine, and nobody lent it to me! Use it as long as you like, and when you don't want to use it any longer, return it to me." In fact the guardian had recently bought it because Saint Francis needed it. The saint then said to him: "Brother Guardian, you have always been courteous to me; now, I beg you, show your courtesy." And the guardian answered him: "Do as you please, father, as the Spirit suggests to you!" The saint called a very devout layman and told him: "Take this mantle and twelve loaves of bread, and go say to that poor woman "The poor man to whom you lent this mantle thanks you for the loan, but now take what is yours!" "The man went and said what he was told, but the woman thought she was being mocked, and replied to him, all embarrassed: "Leave me in peace, you and your mantle! I don't know what you're talking about!" The man insisted, and put it all in her hands. She saw that this was in fact no deception, but fearing that such an easy gain would be taken away from her, she left the place by night and returned home with the mantle, not caring about caring for her eyes.

Thomas of Celano, The Remembrance of the Desire of a Soul,
Second Book, LIX, 92
The Founder, 306–7

14 NOVEMBER

Blessed Francis lay there [at San Damiano] for more than fifty days, and was unable to bear the light of the sun during the day or the light of a fire at night. He stayed in the dark in the house, inside that little cell. In addition, day and night he had great pains in his eyes so that at night he could scarcely rest or sleep. This was very harmful and was a serious aggravation for his eye disease and his other illnesses.

Sometimes he did want to rest and sleep, but there were many mice in the house and in the little cell made of mats where he was lying, in one part of the house. They were running around him, and even over him, and would not let him sleep. They even disturbed him greatly at the time of prayer. They bothered him not only at night, but also during the day, even climbing up on his table when he was eating, so much so that his companions, and he himself, considered it a temptation of the devil, which it was.

One night as blessed Francis was reflecting on all the troubles he was enduring, he was moved by piety for himself. "Lord," he said to himself, "make haste to help me in my illnesses, so that I may be able to bear them patiently." And suddenly he was told in spirit: "Tell me, brother, what if, in exchange for your illnesses and troubles, someone were to give you a treasure? And it would be so great and precious that, even if the whole earth were changed to pure gold, all stones to precious stones, and all water to balsam, you would still judge and hold all these things as nothing, as if they were earth, stones and water, in comparison to the great and precious treasure which was given you. Wouldn't you greatly rejoice?"

"Lord," blessed Francis answered, "this treasure would indeed be great, worth seeking, very precious, greatly lovable, and desirable."

"Then, brother," he was told, "be glad and rejoice in your illnesses and troubles, because as of now, you are as secure as if you were already in my kingdom."

The next morning on rising, he said to his companions: "If the emperor were to give a whole kingdom to one of his servants, shouldn't he greatly rejoice? But, what if it were the whole empire, wouldn't he rejoice even more?" And he said to them: "I must rejoice greatly in my illnesses and troubles and be consoled in the Lord, giving thanks always to God the Father, to His only Son, our Lord Jesus Christ, and to the Holy Spirit for such a great grace and blessing. In His mercy He has given me, His unworthy little servant still living in the flesh, the promise of His kingdom.

"Therefore for His praise, for our consolation and for the edification of our neighbor, I want to write a new Praise of the Lord for his creatures, which we use every day, and without which we cannot live. Through them the human race greatly offends the Creator, and every day we are ungrateful for such great graces, because we do not praise, as we should, our Creator and the Giver of all good."

Sitting down, he began to meditate and then said: "Most High, all-powerful, good Lord." He composed a melody for these words and taught it to his companions so they could repeat it.

The Assisi Compilation, 83
The Founder, 185–6

15 NOVEMBER

Most High, all-powerful, good Lord,
    Yours are the praises, the glory, and the honor,
        and all blessing,
To You alone, Most High, do they belong,
    and no human is worthy to mention Your name.
Praised be You, my Lord, with all Your creatures,
    especially Sir Brother Sun,
        Who is the day and through whom You give us
        light.
And he is beautiful and radiant with great splendor;
    and bears a likeness of You, Most High One.
Praised be You, my Lord, through Sister Moon
    and the stars,
        in heaven You formed them clear
        and precious and beautiful.
Praised be You, my Lord, through Brother Wind,
    and through the air, cloudy and serene,
        and every kind of weather,
    through whom You give sustenance to Your
    creatures.
Praised be You, my Lord, through Sister Water,
    who is very useful and humble and precious
    and chaste.
Praised be You, my Lord, through Brother Fire,
    through whom You light the night,
    and he is beautiful and playful and robust
    and strong.
Praised be You, my Lord, through our
  Sister Mother Earth,
    who sustains and governs us,
        and who produces various fruit with colored
        flowers and herbs.
Praised be You, my Lord, through those who give
  pardon for Your love,
    and bear infirmity and tribulation.

Blessed are those who endure in peace
> for by You, Most High, shall they be crowned.

Praised be You, my Lord, through our Sister Bodily Death,
> from whom no one living can escape.
> Woe to those who die in mortal sin.
> Blessed are those whom death will find in Your most holy will,
> for the second death shall do them no harm.

Praise and bless my Lord and give Him thanks
> and serve Him with great humility.

The Canticle of the Creatures
The Saint, 113–4

16 NOVEMBER

[H]is spirit was then in such sweetness and consolation, that he wanted to send for Brother Pacifico, who in the world was called "The King of Verses," and was a very courtly master of singers. He wanted to give him a few good and spiritual brothers to go through the world preaching and praising God

He said that he wanted one of them who knew how to preach, first to preach to the people. After the sermon, they were to sing the Praises of the Lord as minstrels of the Lord. After the praises, he wanted the preacher to tell the people: "We are minstrels of the Lord, and this is what we want as payment: that you live in true penance."

He used to say: "What are the servants of God if not His minstrels, who must move people's hearts and lift them up to spiritual joy?" And he said this especially to the Lesser Brothers, who had been given to the people for their salvation.

The Praises of the Lord that he composed, that is, "Most High, all-powerful, good Lord," he called "The Canticle of Brother Sun," who is more beautiful than all other creatures and can be most closely compared to God.

He used to say: "At dawn, when the sun rises, everyone should praise God, who created it, because through it the eyes are lighted by day. And in the evening, when it becomes night, everyone should praise God for another creature, Brother Fire, because through it the eyes are lighted at night."

He said: "For we are all like blind people, and the Lord lights up our eyes through these two creatures. Because of this, we must always praise the glorious Creator for these and for His other creatures which we use every day."

He did this and continued to do this gladly, whether he was healthy or sick. And he encouraged others to praise the Lord. Indeed, when his illness grew more serious, he himself began to say the Praises of the Lord, and afterwards had his companions sing it, so that in reflecting on the praise of the Lord, he could forget the sharpness of his pains and illnesses. He did this until the day of his death.

The Assisi Compilation, 83
The Founder, 186–7

17 NOVEMBER

At that same time when he lay sick, the bishop of the city of Assisi at the time excommunicated the podestà. In return, the man who was then podestà was enraged, and had this proclamation announced, loud and clear, throughout the city of Assisi: no one was to sell or buy anything from the bishop, or to draw up any legal document with him. And so they thoroughly hated each another.

Although very ill, blessed Francis was moved by piety for them, especially since there was no one, religious or secular, who was intervening for peace and harmony between them. He said to his companions: "It is a great shame for you, servants of God, that the bishop and the podestà hate one another in this way, and that there is no one intervening for peace and harmony between them."

And so, for that reason, he composed one verse for the Praises:

Praised be by You, my Lord, through those who give
    pardon for Your love,
  and bear infirmity and tribulation.

> Blessed are those who endure in peace for by You,
> Most High, they shall be crowned.

Afterwards he called one of his companions and told him: "Go to the podestà and, on my behalf, tell him to go to the bishop's residence together with the city's magistrates and bring with him as many others as he can."

And when the brother had gone, he said to two of his other companions: "Go and sing the Canticle of Brother Sun before the bishop, the podestà, and the others who are with them. I trust in the Lord that He will humble their hearts and they will make peace with each other and return to their earlier friendship and love."

When they had all gathered in the piazza inside the cloister of the bishop's residence, the two brothers rose and one of them said: "In his illness, blessed Francis wrote the Praises of the Lord for His creatures, for His praise and the edification of his neighbor. He asks you, then, to listen to them with great devotion." And so, they began to sing and recite to them. And immediately the podestà stood up and, folding his arms and hands with great devotion, he listened intently, even with tears, as if to the Gospel of the Lord. For he had a great faith and devotion toward blessed Francis.

When the Praises of the Lord were ended, the podestà said to everyone: "I tell you the truth, not only do I forgive the lord bishop, whom I must have as my lord, but I would even forgive one who killed my brother or my son." And so he cast himself at the lord bishop's feet, telling him: "Look, I am ready to make amends to you for everything, as it pleases you, for the love of our Lord Jesus Christ and of his servant, blessed Francis."

Taking him by the hands, the bishop stood up and said to him: "Because of my office humility is expected of me, but because I am naturally prone to anger, you must forgive me." And so, with great kindness and love they embraced and kissed each other.

And the brothers marveled greatly, considering the holiness of blessed Francis, that what he had foretold about peace and harmony between them had been fulfilled, to the letter. All the others who were present and heard it took it for a great miracle, crediting it to the merits of blessed Francis, that the Lord had so quickly visited them, and that without recalling anything that had been said, they returned to such harmony from such scandal.

The Assisi Compilation, 84
The Founder, 187-8

18 NOVEMBER

I did not come to be served, but to serve [Mt 20:28], says the Lord.

Let those who are placed over others boast about that position as much as they would if they were assigned the duty of washing the feet of their brothers. And if they are more upset at having their place over others taken away from them than at losing their position at their feet, the more they store up a money bag to the peril of their soul.

Let all of us, brothers, consider the Good Shepherd Who bore the suffering of the cross to save His sheep.

The Lord's sheep followed Him in tribulation and persecution, in shame and hunger, in weakness and temptation, and in other ways; and for these things they received eternal life from the Lord.

Therefore, it is a great shame for us, the servants of God, that the saints have accomplished great things and we want only to receive glory and honor by recounting them.

The Admonitions, IV, VI
The Saint, 130, 131

19 NOVEMBER

Saint Francis, the servant of Christ, late one evening reached the house of a great and powerful gentleman, who received him as a guest, him and a companion, like angels of God, with the greatest courtesy and devotion. For this reason Saint Francis had great love for him, considering how on entering the house he had embraced him and kissed him in a friendly way, and then had washed his feet and dried them and kissed them humbly, and lit a great fire and prepared the table with many good kinds of food, and while he was eating the man kept serving him constantly with a happy expression. So, when Saint Francis and the companion had eaten, this gentleman said: "Look, my father. I offer you myself and my things; whenever you have need of a tunic or mantle or anything at all, buy it and I will pay; and you see that I'm prepared to provide for all your needs since, by the grace of God, I can do so because I have an abundance of temporal goods, but for the love of God, who gave them to me, I gladly give them to His poor."

Saint Francis, seeing such courtesy and loving kindness in him and the generous offer, conceived such love for him that as he left with his companion he said: "Truly this gentleman would be good for our religion and company, he is so thankful and grateful to God and so loving and courteous to his neighbor and to the poor. Dear Brother, know that courtesy is one of the qualities of God, who gives His sun and his rain to the just and unjust out of courtesy; and courtesy is the sister of charity, extinguishing hatred and preserving love. And since I have recognized such divine virtue in this good man, I'd gladly have him as a companion; so I want us to return to him one day, if God should perhaps touch his heart to make him want to join us in the service of God; and in the meantime we'll pray to God that He put this desire in his heart and gives him the grace to put it into practice." Something amazing happened: a few days later, after Saint Francis had made his prayer, God put that desire in the heart of this gentleman; and Saint Francis said to the companion: "My brother, let's go to that courteous man, because I have firm hope in God that he who shows courtesy in temporal things will give his very self and will be our companion." And off they went.

The Little Flowers of Saint Francis, 37
The Prophet, 627–8

20 NOVEMBER

On reaching his house, Saint Francis said to the companion: "Wait for me a bit, because I first want to pray to God that He make our journey fruitful, that Christ, by virtue of His most holy passion, be pleased to give us poor and weak men this noble prey that we're planning to take from the world." Having said this, he placed himself in prayer in a place where that courteous man could see him. And it pleased God, as that man was looking here and there he saw Saint Francis devoutly at prayer before Christ, who had appeared to him during that prayer and was in front of him; and as the man stood there, he saw Saint Francis lifted up bodily from the earth. Because of this he was so touched by God and inspired to leave the world, that he suddenly came out from his palace and in fervor of spirit ran toward Saint Francis and coming up to him, as he was still in prayer, knelt down at his feet and with great urgency and devotion begged him to be pleased to receive him to do penance together with him. Then Saint Francis, seeing that his prayer had been heard by God, and that what he desired was what that gentleman was asking with great urgency, he got up in fervor and joy of spirit and embraced and kissed the man, devoutly thanking God, who had added to his company such a knight. And that gentleman said to Saint Francis: "What do you command me to do, my father? See, I am prepared at your command to give what I possess to the poor and with you to follow Christ, letting go of every temporal thing."

And he did just that, following the advice of Saint Francis: he distributed what he had to the poor and entered the Order, and he lived in great penance and holiness of life and worthy behavior.

The Little Flowers of Saint Francis, 37
The Prophet, 628–9

21 NOVEMBER

In the days when he was staying at Rieti for the treatment of his eyes, he called one of the companions, who in the world had been a lute player, and said to him: "Brother, the children of this world do not understand the divine sacraments. Human lust has turned musical instruments, once assigned to the divine praises, into enjoyment for their ears. But I would like you, brother, to borrow a lute secretly and bring it here and to play some decent song to give some consolation to Brother Body, which is filled with pain." But the brother answered: "I would be quite embarrassed to do this, father, for I fear people will suspect me of being tempted to my old levity." And the saint said to him: "Then, brother, let's let it go! It is good to let go of many things to avoid offending people's opinion."

The following night, as the holy man was keeping vigil and meditating on God, suddenly a lute was playing with wonderful harmony an extraordinarily sweet melody. He could see no one, but the changes in his hearing suggested that the lute player was moving back and forth from one place to another. At last, with his spirit turned to God, he enjoyed such delight in that sweet-sounding song that he thought he had exchanged this world for the other.

When he arose in the morning, the saint called the brother in question and told him everything from beginning to end, adding: "The Lord, who consoles the afflicted, has never left me without consolation. See, since I could not hear the lutes of humans, I have heard a more delightful lute."

Thomas of Celano, The Remembrance of the Desire of a Soul,
Second Book, LXXXIX, 126
The Founder, 330

22 NOVEMBER

Fear the Lord and give Him honor [Rv 14:7].
Worthy is the Lord to receive praise and honor [Rv 4:11].
All you who fear the Lord praise Him [Ps 21:23].
Hail Mary, full of grace, the Lord is with you [Lk 1:28].

Heaven and earth, praise Him [Ps 69:35].
All you rivers, praise the Lord [Dn 3:78].
All you children of God, praise the Lord [Dn 3:82].
This is the day the Lord has made, let us rejoice and be glad in it! [Ps 118:24]

>Alleluia, alleluia, alleluia! The King of Israel! [Ps 105:1; Jn 12:33]

Let every spirit praise the Lord [Ps 150:6].
Praise the Lord because He is good [Ps 147:1];
  all you who read this, bless the Lord [Ps 103:21].
All you creatures, bless the Lord [Ps 103:22].
All you birds of heaven, praise the Lord [Dn 3:30].
All you children, praise the Lord [Ps 113:1].
Young men and virgins, praise the Lord [Ps 148:12].
Worthy is the Lamb Who was slain to receive praise, glory, and honor [Rv 5:12].
Blessed be the Holy Trinity and Undivided Unity.
Saint Michael the Archangel, defend us in battle.

Exhortation to the Praise of God
The Saint, 138

23 NOVEMBER

Indeed, in this great and awesome mystery of the cross, the charisms of graces, the merits of virtue, and the treasures of wisdom and of knowledge are concealed in such profound depths as to be hidden from the wise and the prudent of this world. But it is revealed in such fullness to the little one of Christ, that in his whole life he followed nothing except the footsteps of the cross, he tasted nothing except the sweetness of the cross, and he preached nothing except the glory of the cross. In the beginning of his conversion he could truly say with the Apostle: Far be it from me to glory except in the cross of our Lord Jesus Christ [Gal 6:14]. In the course of his life he could more truly add: Whoever follows this rule, peace and mercy be upon them [Gal 6:16]. In the finishing of his life he could most truly conclude: I bear in my body the brand marks of the Lord Jesus [Gal 6:17]. As for us, our daily wish is to hear him say: May the grace of our Lord Jesus Christ be with your spirit, brothers. Amen.

Now, therefore, safely glory in the glory of the cross, glorious standard-bearer of Christ! For you began from the cross; you went forward according to the rule of the cross, and in the end you finished on the cross. By the evidence of the cross you make known to all believers how great is your glory in the heaven. Now too you may be safely followed by those who come forth from Egypt. With the sea parted by the staff of Christ's cross, they shall cross the desert; crossing the Jordan of mortality, they shall enter the promised land, the land of the living, by the wonderful power of the cross. May we be brought there by the true Leader and Savior of the people, Christ Jesus crucified, through the merits of His servant Francis, to the praise and glory of God, One and Three, who lives and reigns forever and ever. Amen.

Bonaventure, The Major Legend of Saint Francis: the Miracles, X, 8–9
The Founder, 681–3

24 NOVEMBER

While the Lord Bishop of Ostia, who later became the Supreme Pontiff Alexander, was preaching in the Church of Saint Francis at Assisi in the presence of the Roman curia, a large and heavy stone carelessly left above the raised stone pulpit was pushed out by the strong pressure, and fell onto a woman's head. Since the bystanders assumed that she was definitely dead, with her head completely crushed, they covered her with the mantle she was wearing, intending to take the pitiful corpse out of the church when the sermon ended. She, however, commended herself with faith to Saint Francis, before whose altar she lay. And behold, when the sermon was finished, the woman rose up in the sight of everyone, unharmed, not showing the least trace of a wound. And, what is even more amazing, she had for many years and up to that very hour suffered from almost uninterrupted headaches, but now was completely freed from them, as she herself later attested.

Bonaventure, The Major Legend of Saint Francis: the Miracles, III, 4
The Founder, 660–1

25 NOVEMBER

When blessed Francis was praised and called a saint, he would respond to such expressions by saying: "I'm still not sure that I won't have sons and daughters. If at any moment the Lord wanted to take back the treasure He has entrusted to me, what would be left except just body and soul, which even non-believers have? I must believe, rather, that if the Lord had granted a thief and even a non-believer as many gifts as He has given me, they would be more faithful to the Lord than I.

"For, as in a painting of the Lord and the Blessed Virgin on wood, it is the Lord and the Blessed Virgin who are honored, while the wood and the paint attribute nothing to themselves. In the same way, a servant of God is a painting of God, in whom God is honored because of His goodness. But he must not attribute anything to himself, because, in comparison with God, he is less than wood and paint. Indeed, he is nothing at all. Therefore, honor and glory should be given to God alone, and while he lives amid the miseries of the world he should attribute to himself only shame and trouble."

A Mirror of Perfection, III, 45
The Prophet, 291

26 NOVEMBER

In order to preserve the virtue of holy humility, a few years after his conversion, at a chapter, he resigned the office of prelate before all the brothers of the religion, saying: "From now on, I am dead to you. But here you have Brother Peter of Catanio; let us all, you and I, obey him." And bowing down immediately, he promised him "obedience and reverence." The brothers were weeping, and sorrow drew deep groans from them, as they saw themselves orphaned of such a father.

As blessed Francis got up, he joined his hands and, lifting his eyes to heaven, said: "Lord, I give back to you the family which until now you have entrusted to me. Now, sweetest Lord, because of my infirmities, which you know, I can no longer take care of them and I entrust them to the ministers. If any brother should perish because of their negligence, or example, or even harsh correction, let them be bound to render an account for it before You, Lord, on the Day of Judgment."

From that time on, he remained subject until his death, behaving more humbly than any of the others.

Thomas of Celano, The Remembrance of the Desire of a Soul,
Second Book, CIV, 143
The Founder, 340

27 NOVEMBER

The brothers of Nocera asked a man named Peter for a certain cart that they needed for a short time. He foolishly replied, "I would rather skin the two of you, and Saint Francis too, rather than loan you a cart." The man immediately regretted his blasphemous words, slapped his mouth, and asked forgiveness. He feared revenge, and it came soon after. At night he saw in a dream his home full of men and women dancing with loud jubilation. His son, named Gafaro, soon took sick and shortly afterwards gave up his spirit. The dances he had seen were turned into a funeral's mourning, and the jubilation to lament. He recalled the blasphemy he had uttered against Saint Francis.

His punishment showed how serious was his fault. He rolled about on the ground and called out to Saint Francis again and again, saying, "It is I who have sinned; you were right to punish me. Give me back, dear saint, the one you took from this wicked blasphemer, for now I have repented. I surrender myself to you; I promise you lasting service, and will always offer you all the first fruits." Amazing! At these words the boy arose, called for a halt to the wailing, and spoke about his experience of death. "When I had died," he said, "blessed Francis came and led me along a very dark and long road. Then he put me in a garden so beautiful and delightful that the whole world can't be compared to it. Then he led me back along the same road and said to me, 'Return to your mother and father; I do not want to keep you here any longer.' And, as he wished, I have returned."

Thomas of Celano, The Treatise on the Miracles of Saint Francis, VII, 43
The Founder, 421–2

28 NOVEMBER

Unflagging zeal for prayer with a continual exercise of virtue had led the man of God to such serenity of mind that, although he had no expertise in Sacred Scripture through learning, his intellect, nevertheless enlightened by the splendor of eternal light, probed the depths of Scripture with remarkable incisiveness. For his genius, pure and unstained, penetrated hidden mysteries, and where the knowledge of teachers stands outside, the passion of the lover entered. Whenever he read the Sacred Books, and something struck his mind he imprinted it tenaciously on his memory, because he did not grasp in vain what his attentive mind heard, for he would mull over it with affection and constant devotion.

Once, when the brothers asked him whether he was pleased that the learned men, who, by that time, had been received into the Order, were devoting themselves to the study of Sacred Scripture, he replied: "I am indeed pleased, as long as, after the example of Christ, of whom we read that he prayed more than he read, they do not neglect zeal for prayer; and, as long as they study, not to know what they should say, but to practise what they have heard and, once they have put it into practice, propose it to others. I want my brothers," he said, "to be Gospel disciples and so progress in knowledge of the truth that they increase in pure simplicity without separating the simplicity of the dove from the wisdom of the serpent which our eminent Teacher joined together in a statement from his own blessed lips."

Bonaventure, The Major Legend of Saint Francis, XI, 1
The Founder, 612–13

29 NOVEMBER

At Siena, a religious, who was a Doctor of Sacred Theology, once asked him about certain questions that were difficult to understand. He brought to light the secrets of divine wisdom with such clarity in teaching, that the learned man was absolutely dumbfounded. With admiration he responded: "Truly the theology of this holy father, borne aloft, as it were, on the wings of purity and contemplation, is a soaring eagle; while our learning crawls on its belly on the ground."

For although he was unskilled in word, nevertheless, full of knowledge, he often untangled the ambiguities of questions and brought the hidden into light. Nor is it inconsistent! If the holy man had received from God an understanding of the Scriptures, it is because, through his imitation of Christ he carried in his activity the perfect truth described in them and, through a full anointing of the Holy Spirit, held their Teacher in his heart.

Bonaventure, The Major Legend of Saint Francis, XI, 2
The Founder, 613

30 NOVEMBER

The man of God then gathered with his companions in an abandoned hut near the city of Assisi, where they kept themselves alive according to the pattern of holy poverty in much labor and want, drawing their nourishment more from the bread of tears than of delights.

They spent their time there praying incessantly, directing their effort mentally rather than vocally to devoted prayers, because they did not yet have liturgical books from which to chant the canonical hours. In place of these they had the book of Christ's cross which they studied continually day and night, taught by the example and words of their father who spoke to them constantly about the cross of Christ.

When the brothers asked him to teach them to pray, he said: "When you pray, say 'Our Father ... ' and 'We adore you, O Christ, in all your churches throughout the whole world, and we bless you, for by your holy cross you have redeemed the world.'" He also taught them to praise God in all and with all creatures, to honor priests with a special reverence, and to believe with certainty and to confess with simplicity the truth of the faith, as the holy Roman Church holds and teaches. They observed the holy father's teaching in every detail, and prostrated themselves humbly before every church and crucifix which they were able to see from a distance, praying the formula he had taught them.

Bonaventure, The Major Legend of Saint Francis, IV, 3
The Founder, 551

December

1 DECEMBER

The most Blessed Father, having in a certain way transformed the brothers into saints by the ardor of his love and the fervent zeal which he had for their perfection, often used to ponder within himself about the qualities and virtues which should abound in a good Lesser Brother.

And, he used to say that a good Lesser Brother is one who would possess the life and qualities of the following holy brothers: namely, the faith and love of poverty which Brother Bernard most perfectly had; the simplicity and purity of Brother Leo who was truly a man of most holy purity; the courtly bearing of Brother Angelo who was the first soldier to enter the Order and was endowed with every courtesy and kindness; the friendly manner and common sense of Brother Masseo, together with his attractive and gracious eloquence; the mind raised in contemplation which Brother Giles had even to the highest perfection; the virtuous and constant prayer of Brother Rufino who, whatever he was doing, even sleeping, always prayed without ceasing and whose mind was always intent on the Lord; the patience of Brother Juniper, who achieved the perfect state of patience because he always kept in mind the perfect truth of his low estate and the ardent desire to imitate Christ through the way of the cross; the bodily and spiritual strength of Brother John of Lauds, who at that time in his robust body surpassed everyone; the charity of Brother Roger whose life and conduct were spent in ardent love; the solicitude of Brother Lucidus who had the greatest care and concern and did not want to remain in any place for a month, and when he enjoyed staying some place, would immediately leave, saying: "We do not have a dwelling here on earth, but in heaven."

A Mirror of Perfection, V, 85
The Prophet, 333

2 DECEMBER

At another time, after his return from overseas, he went to Celano to preach; and a certain knight invited him very insistently, with humble devotion, to dine with him. So he came to the knight's home and the whole family delighted at the arrival of the poor guests. Before they took any food, the man offered prayers and praise to God as was his custom, standing with his eyes raised to heaven. When he finished his prayer, he called his kind host aside and confidentially told him: "Look, brother host, overcome by your prayers, I have entered your home to eat. Now heed my warnings quickly because you shall not eat here but elsewhere. Confess your sins right now, contrite with the sorrow of true repentance; and leave nothing in you unconfessed that you do not reveal in a true confession. The Lord will reward you today for receiving His poor with such devotion." The man agreed to the saint's words without delay; and telling all of his sins in confession to his companion, he put his house in order and did everything in his power to prepare for death. Then they went to the table; and while the others began to eat, suddenly their host breathed forth his spirit, carried away by sudden death according to the words of the man of God.

In recompense for the kindness of his hospitality, it happened according to the word of Truth that because he had received a prophet, he received a prophet's reward. Through the prophetic warning of the holy man, that devout knight prepared himself for a sudden death so that, protected by the armour of repentance, he escaped perpetual damnation and entered into the eternal dwellings.

Bonaventure, The Major Legend of Saint Francis, XI, 4
The Founder, 614–15

3 DECEMBER

A young man, very noble and refined, came to the Order of Saint Francis. After a few days, at the instigation of the demon, he began to feel such disgust for the habit which he was wearing that it seemed to him that he was wearing a filthy rag. He loathed the sleeves and hated the capuche; and he thought its length and roughness were an unbearable burden. His distaste for the Religion also increased and he finally decided to give up the habit and return to the world.

He had already taken up the custom, as his master had taught him, that whenever he passed in front of the altar of the convent, in which the Body of Christ was reserved, to kneel with great reverence, pull back his capuche, and to bow with his arms crossed. It happened that on the night when he was to depart and leave the Order he had to pass in front of the altar of the friary. As he passed, according to his custom, he knelt down and made his reverence. Immediately he was caught up in spirit, and a marvelous vision was shown to him by God. For he saw in front of him, an almost infinite multitude as in a procession, two by two, clothed in very beautiful robes of precious cloth. Their faces and hands shone like the sun, and they walked along with the singing and music of angels. Among those saints there were two more nobly dressed and adorned than all the others, and there were surrounded by such brightness that they caused great wonder to those who saw them. Almost at the end of the procession he saw one adorned with such glory that he seemed like a new knight, more honored than the others. When the young man saw this, he was amazed and did not know what that procession meant. He did not dare to ask about it, and he remained dumbstruck with sweetness. Nevertheless, when the whole procession had passed by, he decided to dare and ran toward the ones at the end and, with great fear, asked them: "Dear friends, I beg you, please tell me who are these marvelous people forming this venerable procession?" They replied: "Son, realize that we are all Lesser Brothers who have now come from the glory of paradise." Then he asked: "Who are those two who shine more brightly than the others?" They responded: "Those are Saint Francis and Saint Anthony, and that last one you saw so greatly honored is a holy brother who just died. Because he fought valiantly against temptations and persevered to the end, we are leading him with triumph to the glory of Paradise. These robes of beautiful cloth which we wear were given to us by God in exchange for the harsh tunics which we patiently wore in the Religion. The glorious brightness which you see in us was given to us by God for the humility and patience, holy poverty and obedience and chastity which we observed to the end. Therefore, dear son, do not let the wearing of such a fruitful thing as the tunic of the Religion be hard for you, because if, with the tunic of Saint Francis, for the love of Christ you despise the world and mortify the flesh and fight courageously against the demon, you will have, together with us, a similar robe and the brightness of glory." When these words ended, the youth returned to himself and, comforted by this vision, he drove away from himself every temptation. He acknowledged his fault before the Guardian and the brothers, and from then on he longed for the harshness of penance and of clothing, and he finished his life within the Order in great holiness.

The Little Flowers of Saint Francis, 20
The Prophet, 600-1

4 DECEMBER

Saint Francis .... had a horrible loathing for slanderers, more than any other kind of vicious people, and used to say that they had poison in their tongues, with which they infect others. And so he avoided rumor mongers like biting fleas, and when they spoke he turned away his ears — as we ourselves have seen — so they would not be contaminated by hearing them.

One time, when he heard one brother blackening the reputation of another, he turned to brother Peter of Catanio, his vicar, and threw out these terrifying words: "Danger threatens religion if it doesn't stop slanderers. Unless the mouths of stinking men are closed, soon enough the sweet smell of many will stink. Get up! Get up! Search thoroughly; and if you find the accused brother innocent, make the accuser known publicly by a severe punishment. If you can't punish him yourself, throw him to the Florentine boxer!" (Brother John of Florence was a man of great height and tremendous strength, and so he used to call him "the boxer.") "I want you and all the ministers," he said, "to take extreme care that this foul disease does not spread."

More than once he decided that a brother should be stripped of his tunic if he had stripped his brother of his good reputation, and that he could not raise his eyes up to God until he had given back what he had stolen. Because of this the brothers of those days had a special abhorrence for this vice, and set up a firm rule among themselves carefully to avoid anything that might take away the honor of another. That was right and good! For what is a slanderer? If not the bile of humanity, the yeast of wickedness, the shame of the earth! What is a backbiter? If not the scandal of the Order, the poison of the cloister, a breaker of unity! Ah, the surface of the earth is crawling with these poisonous animals, and it is impossible for the righteous to avoid the fangs of the envious! Rewards are offered to informers, and after innocence is undermined, the palm of victory often enough goes to falsehood. Where a man cannot make a living by reputable means, he can always earn his food and clothing by devastating the reputation of others.

Thomas of Celano, The Remembrance of the Desire of a Soul,
Second Book, CXXXVIII, 182
The Founder, 363–4

5 DECEMBER

About this Saint Francis often used to say: "These are the words of the slanderer: 'My life is far from perfect, and I don't have at my disposal any supply of learning or special grace, and so I cannot find a position with God or men. I know what I will do: let me put a stain on the chosen, and so I'll win the favor of the great. I know my prelate is human; he sometimes uses my same method: cut down the cedars so only the buckthorn can be seen in the forest.'

"You wretch! Go ahead and feed on human flesh; since you can't survive otherwise, gnaw at your brothers' entrails! That type strives to appear good, not to become good; they point out vices; they do not give up vices. They only praise people whose authority they want for protection. Their praises go silent if they think they will not be reported to the person they praised. They sell for the price of pernicious praise the pallor of their fasting faces, that they may appear to be spiritual men who can judge all, and may be judged by none. They rejoice in the reputation, not the works of holiness, in the name, not in the virtue of 'angels.'"

Thomas of Celano, The Remembrance of the Desire of a Soul,
Second Book, CXXXVIII, 183
The Founder, 364

6 DECEMBER

The Lord teaches in the Gospel: Watch, beware of all malice and greed [Lk12:15]. Guard yourselves against the anxieties of this world and the cares of this life [Lk 21:34; Mt:13:22].

Let none of the brothers, therefore, wherever he may be or go, carry, receive, or have received in any way coin or money, whether for clothing, books, or payment for some work — indeed, not for any reason, unless for an evident need of the sick brothers; because we should not think of coin or money having any greater usefulness than stones. The devil wants to blind those who desire or consider it better than stones. May we who have left all things, then, be careful of not losing the kingdom of heaven for so little.

If we find coins anywhere, let us pay no more attention to them than to the dust we trample underfoot, for vanity of vanities and all is vanity [Eccl 1:2]. If by chance, which God forbid, it happens that some brother is collecting or holding coin or money, unless it is only for the aforesaid needs of the sick, let all the brothers consider him a deceptive brother, an apostate, a thief, a robber, and as the one who held the money bag, unless he has sincerely repented.

The Earlier Rule (The Rule without a Papal Seal), VIII, 1–7
The Saint, 69–70

7 DECEMBER

People then saw that the brothers rejoiced in their tribulations, persisted in prayer with eagerness and devotion, neither accepted nor carried money, and possessed a great love for one another; and through this they were known to be really the Lord's disciples. Many came to them with heartfelt sorrow, asking pardon for the offences they had committed against them. They forgave them from their hearts, saying: "May the Lord forgive you," and encouraged them soundly about their eternal salvation.

Some asked those brothers to receive them into their company. And because of the small number of the brothers — all six of them possessed authority from blessed Francis to receive others into the Order — they accepted some of them into their company. After they were received, they all returned at a predetermined time to Saint Mary of the Portiuncula.

When they saw one another again, however, they were filled with such delight and joy, as if they didn't remember anything of what they had endured at the hands of the wicked.

Each day they were conscientious in prayer and working with their hands to avoid all idleness, the enemy of the soul. They rose conscientiously in the middle of the night, and prayed most devoutly with copious tears and sighs. They loved each other deeply, served one another, and took care of each other as a mother for an only and beloved child. Charity burned so ardently in them that it seemed easy for them to give their bodies to death, not only for the love of Christ, but also for the salvation of the soul or the body of their confrères.

One day, when two of the brothers were walking along, they came across a simpleton who began to throw rocks at them. One of them, noticing that stones were being thrown at the other, ran directly in front of him, preferring that the stones strike him rather than his brother. Because of the mutual charity with which they burned, they were prepared to lay down their life in this way, one for the other.

They were so rooted and grounded in humility and love, that one respected the other as father and master, while those who excelled by way of the office of prelate or some grace, seemed humble and more self-effacing than the others. They all dedicated themselves wholeheartedly to obedience, ever prepared for the will of the one giving orders. They did not distinguish between a just and an unjust command because they considered whatever they were ordered to be the Lord's will. Fulfilling commands, therefore, was pleasant and easy for them. They abstained from carnal desires, judging themselves carefully and taking care that in no way would one offend the other.

The Legend of the Three Companions, XI, 41–2
The Founder, 92–3

8 DECEMBER

Hail, O Lady,
Holy Queen,
Mary, holy Mother of God,
Who are the Virgin made Church,
chosen by the most Holy Father in heaven
whom he consecrated with His most holy beloved Son
and with the Holy Spirit the Paraclete,
in whom there was and is
all fullness of grace and every good.

Hail His Palace!
Hail His Tabernacle!
Hail His Dwelling!
Hail His Robe!
Hail His Servant!
Hail His Mother!

And hail all You holy virtues
which are poured into the hearts of the faithful
through the grace and enlightenment of the
   Holy Spirit,
that from being unbelievers,
You may make them faithful to God.

A Salutation of the Blessed Virgin Mary
The Saint, 163

9 DECEMBER

This account, however, is the one the holy brother Leo gave and the one he wrote, when he was fasting with the blessed Francis on the mountain they had gone to for the writing of the Rule.... Then Jesus who is all goodness, sympathizing with the Saint's difficulties and wishing to give full assurance to a future generation, cried from heaven, so loudly and clearly that his words were heard and understood throughout the valley and the mountain: "Francis, I am Jesus and I am speaking to you from heaven. The Rule is my doing, and you have put nothing of your own in it. I am willing to give the help which I recognize is needed, as I recognize human frailty too. And taking these into consideration, I know that the Rule can very well be kept, and therefore I want it to be observed exactly as it is written, without any gloss. Those who are not happy with it, let them be gone, for I have no wish to make any changes in it."

On hearing the thunder of Christ's voice, the holy man exulted in spirit and said to the brothers who were standing down in the valley: "My brothers, you have just heard the blessed Jesus; do you want me to have him repeat his words to you? You can now see clearly that it is our divine Jesus Christ's Rule, not mine, and that it was He who put into it whatever it contains." A trembling came upon the brothers, who beat their breasts and with bowed heads asked for pardon; and when they had received a blessing they went back to their own places.

It is the holy brother Leo who testifies to this; he was there for it all and heard the Lord Jesus Christ speaking.

So, is there anyone left who is still unconvinced? If not, then let us no longer harden our hearts to the Rule's observance. Through those he spoke to from heaven Jesus was speaking to all, and bearing witness to a Rule that is holy and apostolic. He signified that it was apostolic by dividing it into twelve chapters, as if they were twelve apostolic foundation stones and twelve gates leading into the gospel life. It is like the new Jerusalem that comes down from God out of heaven, on whose gates are written the names of the twelve Apostles of the Lamb [Rv 21:10–14].

Ubertino di Casale, The Tree of the Crucified Life of Jesus, V, V, 31, 445b2, 23, 32
The Prophet, 199–201

10 DECEMBER

Francis, the herald of God, put his footprints on the ways of Christ through innumerable labors and serious diseases, and he did not retreat until he had more perfectly completed what he had perfectly begun. When he was exhausted and his whole body completely shattered, he never stopped on the race of his perfection and never allowed relaxing the rigor of discipline. For even when his body was already exhausted he could not grant it even slight relief without some grumbling of conscience.

So, when even against his will it was necessary to smear medical remedies on his body, which exceeded his strength, he spoke kindly one day with a brother whom he knew was ready to give him advice: "What do you think of this, dear son? My conscience often grumbles about the care of the body. It fears I am indulging it too much in this illness, and that I'm eager for fine lotions to help it. Actually, none of this gives it any pleasure, since it is worn out by long sickness, and the urge for any savoring is gone."

The son replied attentively to his father, realizing that the words of his answer were given to him by the Lord. "Tell me, father, if you please, how attentively did your body obey your commands while it was able?" And he said:

"I will bear witness to it, my son, for it was obedient in all things. It did not spare itself in anything, but almost rushed headlong to carry out every order. It evaded no labor, it turned down no discomfort, if only it could carry out commands. In this it and I were in complete agreement: that we should serve the Lord Christ without any objection."

The brother said: "Well, then, my father, where is your generosity? Where is your piety and your great discernment? Is this a repayment worthy of faithful friends: to accept favors gladly but then not give anything in return in time of need? To this day, what service could you offer to Christ your Lord without the help of your body? Haven't you admitted that it exposed itself to every danger for this reason?"

"I admit, son," said the father, "this is nothing but the truth."

And the son replied: "Well, is it reasonable that you should desert a faithful friend in great need, who risked himself and all that he had for you, even to the point of death? Far be it from you, father, you who are the help and support of the afflicted; far be it from you to sin against the Lord in such a way!" "Blessed are you also, son," he said, "you have wisely given me a drink of healing medicine for my disquiet!" And he began to say jokingly to his body: "Cheer up Brother Body, and forgive me, for I will now gladly do as you please, and gladly hurry to relieve your complaints!"

But, what could delight this little body already so ruined? What could uphold it, already broken in every way? Francis was already dead to the world, but Christ lived in him. The delights of the world were a cross to him, since he carried the cross of Christ rooted in his heart. And that is why the stigmata shone outwardly in his flesh, because inwardly that root was growing deep in his spirit.

Thomas of Celano, The Remembrance of the Desire of a Soul,
Second Book, CLX, 210–11
The Founder, 382–3

11 DECEMBER

Worn out with sufferings on all sides, it was amazing that his strength could bear it. But in fact he did not call these tribulations by the name of "pains," but rather "Sisters." There is no question that they came from many causes. Truly, in order that he might become more famous through victories, the Most High not only entrusted to him difficult tasks during his early training but also gave him occasions for triumph while he was a veteran.

In this too the followers have him for an example, for he never slowed down because of age or became more self-indulgent because of his illness. And there was a reason that his purgation was complete in this vale of tears: so he might repay up to the last penny, if there was anything to burn left in him, so at the end completely cleansed he could fly quickly to heaven. But I believe the principal reason for his sufferings was, as he affirmed about others, that in bearing them there is great reward.

One night, when he was more worn out than usual because of various serious discomforts from his illnesses, he began to feel sorry for himself in the depths of his heart. But, lest his willing spirit should give in to the flesh in a fleshly way even for a moment, unmoving he held the shield of patience by praying to Christ.

And as he prayed in this struggle, he received a promise of eternal life through this comparison: "If the whole mass of the earth and fabric of the universe were made of the most precious gold, and you with all pain gone were given as the reward for the hard suffering you're bearing a treasure of such glory that all this gold would be as nothing in comparison to it, — not even worth mentioning — wouldn't you rejoice, and gladly bear what you're bearing at the moment?" "I'd be happy to," said the saint, "I'd be immeasurably happy."

"Rejoice, then," the Lord said to him, "for your illness is the pledge of my Kingdom; by merit of your patience you can be firm and secure in expecting the inheritance of this Kingdom."

Can you imagine the joy felt by one blessed with such a happy promise? Can you believe the great patience, and even the charity, he showed in embracing bodily discomforts? He now knows it perfectly, but then it was impossible for him to express it. However, as he could, he told a little to his companions. It was then that he composed the Praises about Creatures, rousing them in any way to praise of the Creator.

Thomas of Celano, The Remembrance of the Desire of a Soul,
Second Book, CLXI, 212–13
The Founder, 383–4

12 DECEMBER

Let all the brothers strive to follow the humility and poverty of our Lord Jesus Christ and let them remember that we should have nothing else in the whole world except, as the Apostle says: having food and clothing, we are content with these [1 Tm 6:8].

They must rejoice when they live among people considered of little value and looked down upon, among the poor and the powerless, the sick and the lepers, and the beggars by the wayside.

When it is necessary, they may go for alms. Let them not be ashamed and remember, moreover, that our Lord Jesus Christ, the Son of the all powerful living God, set His face like flint and was not ashamed. He was poor and a stranger and lived on alms — He, the Blessed Virgin, and His disciples. When people revile them and refuse to give them alms, let them thank God for this because they will receive great honor before the tribunal of our Lord Jesus Christ for such insults. Let them realize that a reproach is imputed not to those who suffer it but to those who caused it. Alms are a legacy and a justice due to the poor that our Lord Jesus Christ acquired for us. The brothers who work at acquiring them will receive a great reward and enable those who give them to gain and acquire one; for all that people leave behind in the world will perish, but they will have a reward from the Lord for the charity and almsgiving they have done.

The Earlier Rule (The Rule without a Papal Seal), IX, 1–9
The Saint, 70–1

13 DECEMBER

At another time when the man of God and a companion were walking on the banks of the Po while on a journey of preaching between Lombardy and the Marches of Treviso, they were overtaken by the darkness of night. The road was exposed to many great dangers because of the darkness, the river and some swamps. His companion said to the holy man: "Pray, father, that we may be saved from these threatening dangers!" Full of confidence, the man of God answered him: "God is powerful, if it pleases him in his sweetness, to disperse this darkness and give us the benefit of light." Scarcely had he finished speaking when, behold, such a great light began to shine around them with a heavenly radiance that they could see in clear light not only the road, but also many other things all around, although the night remained dark elsewhere. By the guidance of this light they were led physically and comforted spiritually; singing hymns of praise to God they arrived safely at their lodging, which was a long way off.

Consider that, at his nod, that man of admirable purity and great virtue tempered the heat of fire, changed the taste of water, brought comfort with angelic melody and was led by divine light, so that, in this way, it might be proved that the entire fabric of the universe came to the service of the sanctified senses of the holy man.

Bonaventure, The Major Legend of Saint Francis, V, 12
The Founder, 568

14 DECEMBER

In the city of Rome a certain matron of upright life and noble family chose Saint Francis for her advocate, and kept his image in the secluded chamber, where she prayed to the Father in secret. One day as she gave herself to prayer, she noticed that the Saint's image did not show the sacred marks of the stigmata. She was very sad and surprised. No wonder they were not in the painting: the painter left them out! For several days she wondered anxiously about the reason for this lack, when suddenly, one day those wonderful signs appeared in the picture, just as they are usually painted in other images of the Saint. The woman, shaken, quickly called her daughter, who was devoted to God, inquiring whether the image before then had been without the stigmata. The daughter affirmed and swore that before it had been without the stigmata, but now truly appeared with the stigmata. But, since the human mind sometimes stumbles over itself, and calls the truth into doubt, harmful doubts again entered the woman's heart: perhaps the image had those marks from the beginning. So the power of God added a second, so that the first would not be denied. Suddenly the marks disappeared, and the image remained denuded of those privileged signs. Thus the second sign became proof of the first.

Bonaventure, The Major Legend of Saint Francis: the Miracles, I, 4
The Founder, 652

15 DECEMBER

With all that is in me and more I beg you that, when it is fitting and you judge it expedient, you humbly beg the clergy to revere above all else the most holy Body and Blood of our Lord Jesus Christ and His holy names and the written words that sanctify His Body. They should hold as precious the chalices, corporals, appointments of the altar, and everything that pertains to the sacrifice. If the most holy Body of the Lord is very poorly reserved in any place, let It be placed and locked up in a precious place according to the command of the Church. Let It be carried about with great reverence and administered to others with discernment. Let the names and written words of the Lord, whenever they are found in dirty places, be also gathered up and kept in a becoming place.

In every sermon you give, remind people about penance and that no one can be saved unless he receives the most holy Body and Blood of the Lord. When It is sacrificed on the altar by a priest and carried anywhere, let all peoples praise, glorify and honor on bended knee the Lord God living and true. May you announce and preach His praise to all nations in such a way that praise and thanks may always be given to the all-powerful God by all people throughout the world at every hour and whenever bells are rung.

The First Letter to the Custodians, 2–8
The Saint, 56–7

16 DECEMBER

Clothed with power from on high, this man was warmed more by divine fire on the inside than by what covered his body on the outside.

He detested those in the Order who dressed in three layers of clothing or who wore soft clothes without necessity. As for "necessity" not based on reason but on pleasure, he declared that it was a sign of a spirit that was extinguished.

"When the spirit is lukewarm," he said, "and gradually growing cold as it moves from grace, flesh and blood inevitably seek their own interests. When the soul finds no delight, what is left except for the flesh to look for some? Then the base instinct covers itself with the excuse of necessity, and the mind of the flesh forms the conscience." And he added: "Let's say one of my brothers encounters a real necessity: he is affected by some need. If he rushes to satisfy it, what reward will he get? He found an occasion for merit, but clearly showed that he did not like it." With these and similar words he pierced those who would not tolerate necessity. He taught that not bearing patiently with need is the same as returning to Egypt.

He did not want the brothers to have more than two tunics under any circumstances, and these he allowed to be mended with patches sewn on them. He ordered the brothers to shun fine fabrics, and those who acted to the contrary he rebuked publicly with biting words. To confound them by his example he sewed sackcloth on his own rough tunic and at his death he asked that the tunic for his funeral be covered in cheap sackcloth.

But he allowed brothers pressed by illness or other necessity to wear a soft tunic next to the skin, as long as rough and cheap clothing was kept on the outside. For, he said: "A time will come when strictness will be relaxed, and lukewarmness will hold such sway, that sons of a poor father will not be the least ashamed to wear even velvet cloth, just changing the color."

Father! We are children who are strangers and, it is not you whom we deceive, but our own iniquity deceives itself! This is obvious, clear as day, and increases day by day.

Thomas of Celano, The Remembrance of the Desire of a Soul,
Second Book, XXXIX, 69
The Founder, 293–4

17 DECEMBER

Saint Francis wanted to make Brother Masseo humble, so that he would not lift himself up in vainglory because of the many gifts and graces God gave him, but by virtue of humility with these to grow from virtue to virtue. One time when he was staying in a solitary place with those truly holy first companions of his, among whom was the same Brother Masseo, he said one day to Brother Masseo, in front of all the companions: "O Brother Masseo, all these companions of yours have the grace of contemplation and prayer; but you have the gift of preaching the word of God to content the people. So I want you to have charge of the door and alms and cooking, so that these brothers may pursue contemplation. And when the other brothers eat, you will eat outside the door of the place, so that those who come to the place, before they start knocking, can be satisfied by some good words of God from you, so there will be no need then for anyone besides you to go outside. And do this in merit of holy obedience." Brother Masseo pulled back his capuche and bowed his head and humbly accepted and carried out this obedience for many days, taking charge of the door, alms and cooking.

The companions, as men enlightened by God, began to feel great remorse in their hearts over this, considering that Brother Masseo was a man of great perfection like them and even more, and the whole burden of the place was placed on him and not on them. For this reason all of them, moved by one will, went to ask the holy father that he be pleased to distribute those duties among them, since their consciences could not bear that Brother Masseo carry so many burdens. Hearing this, Saint Francis accepted their advice and agreed with their will. He called Brother Masseo and said to him, "Brother Masseo, your companions want to do part of the jobs I gave to you, so I want these jobs to be divided." Brother Masseo said, with great humility and patience, "Father, whatever you assign me, all or part, I'll consider it all God's doing." Then Saint Francis, seeing the humility of Brother Masseo and the charity of the others, preached to them a wonderful and great sermon about most holy humility, teaching them that the greater the gifts and graces God gives us, the more we must be humble, because without humility no virtue is acceptable to God. When he finished preaching he distributed the jobs with very great charity.

The Little Flowers of Saint Francis, 12
The Prophet, 585-6

18 DECEMBER

In wintertime because of his physical weakness and the rough roads, he was once riding on a donkey belonging to a poor man. It happened that he spent the night at the base of an overhanging cliff to try to avoid the inconveniences of a snowfall and the darkness of night that prevented him from reaching his place of lodging. When, however, the saint heard his helper tossing and turning, grumbling and groaning, since, as he had only thin clothing, the biting cold would not let him sleep; burning with the fire of divine love, he stretched out his hand and touched him. A marvelous thing happened! At the touch of his sacred hand, which bore the burning coal of the Seraph, the cold fled altogether and the man felt great heat within and without, as if he had been hit by a fiery blast from the vent of a furnace. Comforted in mind and body, he slept until morning more soundly among the rocks and snow than he ever had in his own bed, as he later used to say.

Bonaventure, The Major Legend of Saint Francis, XIII, 7
The Founder, 635

19 DECEMBER

Let the brothers not make anything their own, neither house, nor place, nor anything at all. As pilgrims and strangers in this world, serving the Lord in poverty and humility, let them go seeking alms with confidence, and they should not be ashamed because, for our sakes, our Lord made Himself poor in this world. This is that sublime height of most exalted poverty which has made you, my most beloved brothers, heirs and kings of the Kingdom of Heaven, poor in temporal things but exalted in virtue. Let this be your portion which leads into the land of the living. Giving yourselves totally to this, beloved brothers, never seek anything else under heaven for the name of our Lord Jesus Christ.

Wherever the brothers may be and meet one another, let them show that they are members of the same family. Let each one confidently make known his need to the other, for if a mother loves and cares for her son according to the flesh, how much more diligently must someone love and care for his brother according to the Spirit! When any brother falls sick, the other brothers must serve him as they would wish to be served themselves.

The Later Rule (With Papal Approval), VI
The Saint, 103

20 DECEMBER

Holy Simplicity, the daughter of grace, the sister of wisdom, the mother of justice, with careful attention he showed in himself and loved in others. It was not just any kind of simplicity that he approved, but only that which, content with her God scorns everything else. This is she who glories in the fear of God, who does not know how to do evil or speak it. This is she who examines herself and condemns no one by her judgment; who grants due authority to her betters and seeks no authority for herself. This is she who does not consider the best glories of the Greeks and would rather do, than teach or learn. This is she who, when dealing with all the divine laws, leaves all wordy wanderings, fanciful decorations, shiny trappings, showy displays and odd curiosities, who seeks not the rind but the marrow, not the shell but the kernel, not the many, but the much, supreme and enduring good.

She was what the most holy father demanded in the brothers, learned and lay; not believing she was the contrary of wisdom but rather, her true sister, though easier to acquire for those poor in knowledge and more quickly to put into use. Therefore, in the Praises of the Virtues which he composed, he says: "Hail, Queen Wisdom! May the Lord protect you, with Your Sister holy pure Simplicity!"

Thomas of Celano, The Remembrance of the Desire of a Soul,
Second Book, CXLII, 189
The Founder, 367–8

21 DECEMBER

More than all creatures lacking reason, he most affectionately loved the sun and fire. For he used to say: "At dawn, when the sun rises, everyone should praise God, who created it for our use, because through it our eyes are lighted by day. And in the evening, when it becomes night, everyone should praise God for another creature, Brother Fire through whom the eyes are lighted at night. For we are all almost blind, and the Lord lights up our eyes through these two brothers of ours. And, therefore, we should always give special praise to the glorious Creator for these and for His other creatures which we use every day."

He always did this until the day of his death. Indeed, when his illness grew more serious, he himself began to sing the Praises of the Lord that he had composed about creatures, and afterwards had his companions sing it, so that in reflecting on the praise of the Lord, he could forget the sharpness of his pains and illnesses.

And because he considered and said that the sun is more beautiful than other creatures, and could more easily be compared to God, especially since, in Scripture, the Lord Himself is called the sun of justice [Mal 3:20]; he therefore called those Praises he composed for creatures when the Lord had assured him of His kingdom the "Canticle of Brother Sun."

A Mirror of Perfection, XI, 119
The Prophet, 367

22 DECEMBER

Once Saint Clare was seriously ill, so that she could not go to say the Office in church with the other nuns. When the solemnity of the Nativity of Christ arrived, all the others went to matins, and she remained in bed, unhappy that she could not go together with the others to have that spiritual consolation. But Jesus Christ, her spouse, not wishing to leave her this way without consolation, had her miraculously carried to the Church of Saint Francis to be present for the whole Office of matins and the night Mass, and besides this, to receive Holy Communion, and then had her carried back to her bed.

When the Office in San Damiano was finished and the nuns returned to Saint Clare, they said to her: "O Sister Clare, our Mother, what great consolation we've had on this Holy Nativity! If only it pleased God that you could have been with us!" And Saint Clare replied: "My sisters and dearest daughters, I give thanks and praise to Our Blessed Lord Jesus Christ, because I have been present at all the solemnities of this holy night, and at greater ones than you have been, with much consolation to my soul, for by the intercession of my father Saint Francis and by the grace of Our Lord Jesus Christ, with the ears of my body and spirit I heard the whole Office and the music of the organ there and in that very place I received Holy Communion. Therefore, rejoice and thank God for such grace shown to me."

The Little Flowers of Saint Francis, 35
The Prophet, 626

23 DECEMBER

His highest aim, foremost desire, and greatest intention was to pay heed to the holy gospel in all things and through all things, to follow the teaching of our Lord Jesus Christ and to retrace His footsteps completely with all vigilance and all zeal, all the desire of his soul and all the fervor of his heart.

Francis used to recall with regular meditation the words of Christ and recollect His deeds with most attentive perception. Indeed, so thoroughly did the humility of the Incarnation and the charity of the Passion occupy his memory that he scarcely wanted to think of anything else.

We should note then, as matter worthy of memory and something to be recalled with reverence, what he did, three years prior to his death, at the town of Greccio, on the birthday of our Lord Jesus Christ. There was a certain man in that area named John who had a good reputation but an even better manner of life. Blessed Francis loved him with special affection, since, despite being a noble in the land and very honored in human society, he had trampled the nobility of the flesh under his feet and pursued instead the nobility of the spirit. As usual, blessed Francis had

John summoned to him some fifteen days prior to the birthday of the Lord. "If you desire to celebrate the coming feast of the Lord together at Greccio," he said to him, "hurry before me and carefully make ready the things I tell you. For I wish to enact the memory of that babe who was born in Bethlehem: to see as much as is possible with my own bodily eyes the discomfort of his infant needs, how he lay in a manger, and how, with an ox and an ass standing by, he rested on hay." Once the good and faithful man had heard Francis's words, he ran quickly and prepared in that place all the things that the holy man had requested.

Thomas of Celano, The Life of Saint Francis, First Book, XXX, 84
The Saint, 254–5

24 DECEMBER

Finally, the day of joy has drawn near, the time of exultation has come. From many different places the brethren have been called. As they could, the men and women of that land with exultant hearts prepare candles and torches to light up that night whose shining star has enlightened every day and year. Finally, the holy man of God comes and, finding all things prepared, he saw them and was glad. Indeed, the manger is prepared, the hay is carried in, and the ox and the ass are led to the spot. There simplicity is given a place of honor, poverty is exalted, humility is commended, and out of Greccio is made a new Bethlehem.

The night is lit up like day, delighting both man and beast. The people arrive, ecstatic at this new mystery of new joy. The forest amplifies the cries and the boulders echo back the joyful crowd. The brothers sing, giving God due praise, and the whole night abounds with jubilation. The holy man of God stands before the manger, filled with heartfelt sighs, contrite in his piety, and overcome with wondrous joy. Over the manger the solemnities of the Mass are celebrated and the priest enjoys a new consolation.

The holy man of God is dressed in the vestments of the Levites, since he was a Levite, and with full voice sings the holy gospel. Here is his voice: a powerful voice, a pleasant voice, a clear voice, a musical voice, inviting all to the highest of gifts. Then he preaches to the people standing around him and pours forth sweet honey about the birth of the poor King and the poor city of Bethlehem. Moreover, burning with excessive love, he often calls Christ the "babe from Bethlehem" whenever he means to call Him Jesus. Saying the word "Bethlehem" in the manner of a bleating sheep, he fills his whole mouth with sound but even more with sweet affection. He seems to lick his lips whenever he uses the expressions "Jesus" or "babe from Bethlehem," tasting the word on his happy palate and savoring the sweetness of the word. The gifts of the Almighty are multiplied there and a virtuous man sees a wondrous vision. For the man saw a little child lying lifeless in the manger and he saw the holy man of God approach the child and waken him from a deep sleep. Nor is this vision unfitting, since in the hearts of many the child Jesus has been given over to oblivion. Now he is awakened and impressed on their loving memory by His own grace through His holy servant Francis. At length, the night's solemnities draw to a close and everyone went home with joy.

The hay placed in the manger there was preserved afterwards so that, through it, the Lord might restore to health the pack animals and the other animals there, as He multiplied his holy mercy. It came to pass in the surrounding area that many of the animals, suffering from various diseases, were freed from their illnesses when they ate some of this hay. What is more, women who had been suffering with long and hard labor had an easy delivery after they placed some of this hay upon themselves. Finally, an entire group of people of both sexes obtained much-desired relief from an assortment of afflictions. At last, the site of the manger was consecrated as a temple to the Lord. In honor of the most blessed father Francis, an altar was constructed over the manger, and a church was dedicated.

This was done so that where animals once ate the fodder of the hay, there humans henceforth for healing of body and soul would eat the flesh of the immaculate and spotless lamb, our Lord Jesus Christ, who gave Himself for us with supreme and indescribable love, who lives and rules with the Father and the Holy Spirit as God, eternally glorious forever and ever. Amen.

Thomas of Celano, The Life of Saint Francis, First Book, XXX, 85–7
The Saint, 254–5

25 DECEMBER

He used to observe the Nativity of the Child Jesus with an immense eagerness above all other solemnities, affirming it was the Feast of Feasts, when God was made a little child and hung on human breasts. He would kiss the images of the baby's limbs thinking of hunger, and the melting compassion of his heart toward the child also made him stammer sweet words as babies do. This name was to him like honey and honeycomb in his mouth.

When there was discussion about not eating meat, because it was on Friday, he replied to Brother Morico: "You sin, brother, when you call "Friday" the day when unto us a Child is born. I want even the walls to eat meat on that day, and if they cannot, at least on the outside they be rubbed with grease!"

He wanted the poor and hungry to be filled by the rich, and oxen and asses to be spoiled with extra feed and hay. "If ever I speak with the Emperor," he would say, "I will beg him to issue a general decree that all who can should throw wheat and grain along the roads, so that on the day of such a great solemnity the birds may have an abundance, especially our sisters the larks."

He could not recall without tears the great want surrounding the little, poor Virgin on that day. One day when he was sitting down to dinner a brother mentioned the poverty of the blessed Virgin, and reflected on the want of Christ her Son. No sooner had he heard this than he got up from the table, groaning with sobs of pain, and bathed in tears ate the rest of his bread on the naked ground. He used to say this must be a royal virtue, since it shone so remarkably in a King and Queen.

When the brothers were debating in a gathering about which of the virtues made one a greater friend to Christ, he replied, as if opening the secret of his heart: "My sons, know that poverty is the special way to salvation; its fruits are many, and known only to a few."

Thomas of Celano, The Remembrance of the Desire of a Soul,
Second Book, CLI, 199–200
The Founder, 374–5

26 DECEMBER

We, who were with blessed Francis, and who wrote these things about him, bear witness that we often heard him say: "If I ever speak to the emperor, I will beg and persuade him, for the love of God and of me, to enact a special law forbidding anyone to catch or kill our sister larks or do them any harm. Likewise, all mayors of cities and lords of castles and villages should be bound to oblige people each year on the day of the Nativity of the Lord to scatter wheat and other grain along the roads outside towns and villages, so that our sister larks and other birds may have something to eat on such a solemn feast.

"Also, out of reverence for the Son of God whom the most blessed Virgin Mary on that night laid in a manger between an ox and ass, I would add that whoever has an ox and an ass be bound on that night to provide them a generous portion of the best fodder. Likewise, on that day, all the poor should be fed good food by the rich."

For blessed Francis held the Nativity of the Lord in greater reverence than any other of the Lord's solemnities, saying: "After the Lord was born to us, it was certain that we would be saved." On that day, he wanted every Christian to rejoice in the Lord, and, for love of Him Who gave Himself to us, wished everyone to provide generously not only to the poor but also to the animals and birds.

A Mirror of Perfection, XI, 114
The Prophet, 363

27 DECEMBER

Once at the hermitage of Poggio about the time of the Lord's nativity a large crowd assembled for the sermon, which he began with this opening: "You all believe me to be a holy man, and that is why you came to me with great devotion. But I declare to you that this whole Lent I have eaten food flavored with lard." In this way he often blamed pleasure for what was, in fact, a concession to illness.

With the same fervor, whenever his spirit was moved to vanity, he displayed it naked before everyone with a confession. Once as he was going through the city of Assisi, an old woman met him and asked him for something. As he had nothing except his mantle, he offered it with quick generosity. But then he felt an impulse of empty congratulations, and at once he confessed before everyone that he felt vainglory.

> Thomas of Celano, The Remembrance of the Desire of a Soul,
> Second Book, XCIV–XCV, 131-2
> *The Founder,* 333

28 DECEMBER

Saint Francis once visited Pope Gregory of venerable memory, at that time holding a lesser office. When it was time for dinner, he went out for alms, and on his return he placed some crusts of black bread on the bishop's table. When the bishop saw this he was rather embarrassed, especially since there were dinner guests he had invited for the first time. The father, however, with a smile on his face, distributed the alms he had received to the knights and chaplains who were his table companions, and they all accepted them with remarkable devotion. Some ate the crusts, while others saved them out of reverence.

When the meal was over the bishop got up from the table and, taking the man of God aside to a private place, lifting up his arms he embraced him "My brother," he said, "why did you shame me in a house, which is yours and your brothers', by going out for alms?" The saint replied: "I showed you honor instead, while I honored a greater Lord. For the Lord is pleased by poverty, and especially when one freely chooses to go begging. As for me, I consider it a royal dignity and an outstanding nobility to follow that Lord who, though he was rich, became poor for our sake." And he added: "I get greater delight from a poor table, set with some little alms, than from a great table with so many dishes that they can hardly be numbered."

The bishop, greatly edified, said to the saint: "Son, do what seems good in your eyes, for the Lord is with you."

> Thomas of Celano, The Remembrance of the Desire of a Soul,
> Second Book, XLIII, 73
> *The Founder,* 296

29 DECEMBER

Once when he was asked how he could protect himself against the bite of the winter's frost with such thin clothing, he answered with a burning spirit: "If we were touched within by the flame of desire for our heavenly home, we would easily endure that exterior cold." In the matter of clothes, he had a horror for softness and loved coarseness, claiming that John the Baptist had been praised by the Lord for this. If he felt the softness of a tunic that had been given to him, he used to sew pieces of cord on the inside because he used to say, according to the word of Truth itself, that we should look for soft clothes not in the huts of the poor but in the palaces of princes. For his own certain experience had taught him that demons were terrified by harshness, but were inspired to tempt one more strongly by what is pleasant and soft.

Bonaventure, The Major Legend of Saint Francis, V, 2
The Founder, 561

30 DECEMBER

From the time in which this man gave up transitory things and began to cling to the Lord, he allowed hardly a second of time to be wasted. Although he had brought into the treasury of the Lord a great abundance of merits he remained always new, always ready for spiritual exercise. He thought it a grave offence not to be doing something good, and he considered not going forward going backward.

Once, when he was staying in a cell near Siena, he called his companions one night while they were sleeping and said to them: "Brothers, I prayed to the Lord that he might deign to show me when I am his servant and when I am not, for I want to be nothing except his servant. And now the gracious Lord himself in his mercy is giving me this answer: "Know that you are in truth my servant when you think, speak, or do things that are holy." And so I have called you brothers, because I want to be shamed in front of you if ever I am not doing any of those three."

Thomas of Celano, The Remembrance of the Desire of a Soul,
Second Book, CXVII, 159
The Founder, 350

31 DECEMBER

Whenever it pleases them, all my brothers can announce this or similar exhortation and praise among all peoples with the blessing of God:

> Fear and honor,
> praise and bless,
> give thanks and adore
> the Lord God Almighty in Trinity and in Unity,
> Father, Son, and Holy Spirit,
> the Creator of all.
> Do penance,
> performing worthy fruits of penance
> because we shall soon die.
> Give and it will be given to you [Lk 6:38].
> Forgive and you shall be forgiven [Mt 6:4]].
> If you do not forgive people their sins,
> the Lord will not forgive you yours [Mk11:25].
> Confess all your sins [Jas 5:16].
> Blessed are those who die in penance,
> for they shall be in the kingdom of heaven.
> Woe to those who do not die in penance,
> for they shall be children of the devil
> whose works they do
> and they shall go into everlasting fire.
> Beware of and abstain from every evil
> and persevere in good till the end.

The Earlier Rule (The Rule without a Papal Seal), XXI, 1–9
The Saint, 78